LIVING WITH A SERIAL KILLER

LIVING WITH A SERIAL KILLER

DELIA BALMER

EBURY
PRESS

*Although this book is based on real people and real events,
some names, places and identifying features have been
changed in order to preserve their privacy.*

1 3 5 7 9 10 8 6 4 2

Ebury Press, an imprint of Ebury Publishing
20 Vauxhall Bridge Road
London SW1V 2SA

Ebury Press is part of the Penguin Random House group
of companies whose addresses can be found
at global.penguinrandomhouse.com

Penguin
Random House
UK

First published by Ebury Press in 2017

www.penguin.co.uk

A CIP catalogue record for this book is available
from the British Library

ISBN 9781785036248

Typeset in 9.93/12.25 pt Palatino LT Std by Jouve (UK), Milton Keynes

Printed and bound in Great Britain by Clays Ltd, St Ives PLC

'The court is like a palace of marble; it's composed of people very hard and very polished.'
— Jean de la Bruyère

Prologue

Nurses' home, North Middlesex Hospital, late 1970s

It was the scream that ripped me from my sleep.

In the still of the night, I woke to hear myself making a shrill, eerie wail that seemed to echo throughout the room. It sounded as if it came right from my very soul. It startled me awake.

Yet I recalled nothing that had caused me to cry out.

Many years later, I remembered that eerie wail; the wail that seemed to come from nowhere – not any dream, or nightmare.

I wondered: had it been a premonition of everything to come?

1

Kentish Town, London, Spring 1991

The key wouldn't turn. I struggled with it for several minutes, my fingers squeezing the metal tightly as I tried to twist it in the lock of the main front door. At last I succeeded, hesitantly opened the door, and stepped into a small dingy corridor. The walls were in need of fresh paint and a stained grey carpet lay upon the floor.

So this is where I have ended up.

Directly ahead was a short flight of stairs with a window at the top; at their apex, the stairs turned in the opposite direction before climbing further upwards in another flight. This four-storey building on Leighton Grove had been converted into four flats, one on each level; mine was to be on the ground floor, above the basement apartment. My front door was to the left: I opened it and walked quietly in.

As I crossed the threshold, a strange feeling settled over me. *Something is wrong,* I thought. *It's wrong for me to be here.* Immediately, I felt guilty for feeling like that – this was a council flat, and I knew I was lucky to have a roof over my head – but my apprehension remained. I sensed a bad aura around me; a sensation that I did not belong.

The door opened into the back room of the flat, which

had another door within it leading to the front room. I walked fully into the apartment and closed the main door behind me, realising as I did so that concealed behind it when open was a small corridor leading to the yellow-tiled kitchen, as well as the bathroom beyond that. *What an odd set-up*, I thought. In a way, it added to my feeling of something being wrong, for anyone could wait in that kitchen and you'd have no idea they were there, not until the moment you closed the door.

But that did not matter to me: for a long time now, I had been on my own. I had always been a loner, though not necessarily by choice. When I was little I'd moved around a lot: I was born in Australia, and had lived in Scotland, Canada and America by the time I was thirteen. I reached my teenage years in Detroit, USA; I was already very quiet and shy when we moved there and I did not fit in well. My Scottish parents took their cultural habits with them: my younger brothers – Gerard and Stewart – and I were brought up in a more reserved British style, rather than as Americans. Gerard brought this observation to my attention, many years later. It added to my feeling of not belonging: I was not forward and outgoing like the American kids, instead I became increasingly shy and introverted.

Much later, after I left home, I came to believe that my parents' British-style upbringing – with a trace of Victorian values, or at least more conventional, reserved ways – had, without my realising, possibly left me yearning for affection; something that perhaps proved to be my downfall, though I did not consider that until much later. There was a minimum amount of physical expression of affection from or between Mum and Dad. Kissing and cuddling within the family was uncommon. We even seemed embarrassed by it, and avoided physical contact. Although Mum sometimes used to ask for a kiss, it was a request, rather than it being spontaneous between

2

us. And so this longing, be it so, led me into all kinds of trouble.

My parents, still living in the States, had been disappointed when I told them I had moved into a council flat; *she'll never come back now* . . . I also had reservations: I was losing my freedom to travel, and had been forever questioning whether I should return home to my parents. When I moved into Leighton Grove I was almost forty-one years old, and wondered if this meant the point of no return, or freedom to do so.

The council flat provided a safety net just when I needed it most. I had broken up with someone with whom I had spent four years, and still had not got over it. I had planned to go to Australia, but he persuaded me to stay, that if I went he would never see me again. Reluctantly, but for him, I gave up my dream. When I left him, I had nowhere to go.

I managed to find a live-in job as an agency nurse. Then, three years later, Margaret Thatcher came into power, and the hospital became a Trust. As a result, I lost my job, and I had to leave the room in the nurses' home. Non-permanent staff were no longer needed, hence, the necessity for this council flat I so desperately required.

It was only a short while after that first visit to Leighton Grove that I moved in properly. I arrived with only two suitcases and a single cardboard box of possessions, as I had never settled permanently anywhere, and had not collected more than I needed. I valued my freedom. Standing by the brick wall at the front of the house, I stared up at the narrow terraced building, then slowly made my way up the seven concrete steps that led to the front door. Once again, I struggled with the badly fitting key, unable to make it turn. I felt a grim sense of foreboding.

Is this a sign that I don't really belong here?

*

For six weeks I cleaned and painted the ceilings and walls of my flat. I hoped the makeover would make me feel more comfortable and dispel the uncertain feelings I had about being there. I painted the back room white with a hint of rose, as I wished, but the front room turned out beige: a disappointment.

I slept on the floor in the back room, chosen as the bedroom, on my sleeping bag, covered over with colourful blankets from Mexico and Guatemala; for a curtain in the bedroom, I cut in half a blue cotton sari printed with small purple and yellow petals and hung it in the window. My only furnishings were the ornaments and pictures gathered on my travels.

Travelling was what I lived for. After qualifying as a registered nurse, I worked in a permanent position for more than a year, after which I began my first big trip, lasting one year. I had not intended that I should then continue working as an agency nurse, but this was the path I took. The non-permanent position gave me freedom and subsidised my travels, and allowed me to visit my parents for longer as well. I'd travelled on short trips to Europe, mostly Greece. On my first year-long trip, I lived for three months in Israel, as a volunteer on a kibbutz, before travelling around India and spending six weeks in Nepal. Later, in my thirties, I went to Mexico and Central America. The items I unpacked from my explorations made my life feel more enriched: shawls bought from Mexican Indians, an incense holder from a holy Hindu town near the Ganges River, two small soap-stone pots, a soapstone *Om* sign, a small ebony box from Bombay, shells from Mexico. I hung two framed pictures painted on banyan leaves on the wall, as well as a black-and-white Victorian photograph of my Scottish granny. Still, though, I did not consider myself at home; far from that, I remained unsettled.

Living in the nurses' home had given me a sense of

belonging: although a loner, I was not alone there because others were always around whom I could talk to if I wanted. In the nurses' home I had always left my door open, feeling closed in otherwise. But in Leighton Grove my door was always shut, and the only communication I had was when I went to the store to buy food.

Worry and anxiety filled me at not having stable work, losing experience, and my confidence so low. At a loss and alone, and with my confidence dwindling further, my anxiety increased. I felt unable to continue with whatever work I could find. I successfully applied for a therapeutic massage course, but it wasn't due to start until September. I knew no one nearby, had no one to speak to. Perhaps I would find acquaintances during the course.

One day, at the very end of April 1991, I went to Camden Lock Market and bought a purple rag rug for my bedroom. Back at the flat, I laid it over the plastic sheet I had placed upon the bare floorboards. I looked around me at everything in the flat, and felt a desperate sense of emptiness.

It's as clean as I can make this old place, I thought, *and everything is where I want it.*

Yet that in itself was the problem.

I almost wish it wasn't quite like this, I thought drearily. *I wish things were slightly out of place, so I would know someone else was here.*

Be careful what you wish for . . .

2

The first spring bank holiday Monday of 1991, I was alone – as usual – and at a loss what to do with myself. I walked down to Camden to wander around the market. I no longer went to the Caernarvon Castle pub around the corner, where I had once danced to live bands; the atmosphere had changed. Soon after moving into the flat, I began frequenting the Hawley Arms, which was ahead. Only on a Sunday did I usually spend the day there.

I don't know what else to do, I thought, *so I'll just go in for one drink.*

The Hawley had the best jukebox in town, everyone agreed. It had a vibrant atmosphere, the walls covered with old postcards and a bookshelf at one end filled with frayed, dusty books that no one seemed to read. The antiquated cash machine looked like something out of a museum.

I always sat at one end of the long bar with a half-pint of real ale and lost myself in the music; people-watching took the place of my dancing. But on that bank holiday Monday, the pub was almost empty, the jukebox playing less. I sipped my beer and hoped to find something of interest.

The people working behind the bar added to the colour with their attire, somewhat hippie in character, and dancing while they served drinks. The girl had long blonde hair, a colourful scarf thinly wrapped around her head; her midriff was visible under a short sleeveless top and she wore black leather jeans. Sometimes she wore a sarong with a purple Indian scarf tied around her waist, tassels dangling from the end, while I wore the red-and-purple brimmed pillbox hat I had bought in Manali over my shoulder-length blonde hair, along with my colourful Indian scarves, pink denim jacket and pink jeans.

At the far end of the room, on the wall, was a little lit-up mechanical man perched on a shelf: a cap on his head, a jovial laughing face, red cheeks and nose, a beer belly, and a beer glass in his hand – which he raised perpetually, up and down, to and from his mouth.

At the far table, situated below the little man, sat a guy drinking his pint. He was gazing intently at me. A reddish-brown bushy beard covered his face, his brown hair tied back in a small ponytail at the nape of his neck – though the top of his head was balding. With an elongated face and a prominent forehead, he had noticeably arched eyebrows, which framed his large eyes in such a distinctive way it was almost as if they had been painted on. The whites of his eyes showed noticeably beneath his green irises like horizontal half-moons.

Averting my gaze, I did my best to avoid eye contact. I didn't want to get mixed up with anyone; I didn't want any more disasters. Yet he kept on gazing intently at me.

In a short while, he left the pub and I forgot about him – but he returned soon after. He came over to my side of the bar and stood right next to me to order a drink. He was over six foot tall and very slim. Even perched on my stool, I was aware of the difference in our stature; I am only five foot one. He wore denim jeans and an embroidered waistcoat of yellow and green threads over a T-shirt – a marijuana-leaf brooch pinned to it – and a gold ring was pierced through his left earlobe. Despite his proximity, I gave no indication that I was aware of his presence.

Nor did he say a word to me. Taking his pint, he retreated to a table near the door. Yet still I could sense his constant gaze. His eyes never left me, not even when he stood and walked to the public telephone hanging on the wall, which was very close to me. While he talked on the phone, he faced in my direction. His eyes never left me.

Again he sat down and finished his pint, then stood closely on my right side once more, and ordered his beer. But this time curiosity got the better of me: I looked up at him.

Immediately, his eyes met mine.

'Would you like to have a drink with me?' he asked, his voice deep and seasoned with a strong Liverpudlian accent.

A nervous flutter ran through me. But I thought, *Oh, I suppose it wouldn't do any harm to have one drink with him, just to have someone to talk to for a little while. I don't have to get mixed up with him.*

We sat with our beers where he had been watching me.

'My name is John,' he told me. 'I'm a carpenter. I work on building sites here in London, and also travel to Germany to work on sites there as well.'

My interest heightened. *He works in other countries*, I thought with a hint of excitement. *He must be a travelling type – just the kind of person I would like to meet.* I found it attractive: that suggestion of bohemianism and freedom; his ability to come and go without anything tying him down.

'I love travelling too,' I told him. 'I've been to Nepal, several times to India, and to Mexico and Central America.'

Over our beers, we talked. John seemed quiet and humble; his occasional stutter suggesting he was nervous.

He must be very shy, I reasoned, *maybe that's why he's stumbling over his words*. He smoked roll-ups and carried his tobacco in an unusual handmade wooden box. Octagonal in shape, it was made entirely of matchsticks, with a skeleton's head and crossed long bones under it upon the lid.

We finished our drinks, but I found I still wanted to talk to him. My life had become so monotonous lately that I was desperate for something to change. Now, there was John. I felt a sensation of anticipation.

'Would you like to come back to my flat?' I asked hesitantly. 'You could have a cup of tea if you like?'

I was surprised when he accepted; I thought he would have better things to do. Together, we left the Hawley and made our way to Leighton Grove.

'It's not long since I moved in,' I explained when we reached the flat, 'so there's no furniture.'

As the layout demanded, we entered into the back room: my bedroom. I gestured towards the floor.

'You can sit here on my purple rug.'

While John made himself comfortable, his long legs bending to the floor, I made tea in the yellow kitchen, before returning with the ornate Chinese teapot and the Japanese teacups that I'd recently bought. Each cup had a different design, with birds and trees painted upon them; some of the details etched in gold leaf. The maroon teapot was an elegant oblong shape with Chinese symbols and a blue border at the bottom. I brewed the tea and poured a cup each for us, before sitting down across from him on my sleeping bag.

I spotted my green suitcase nearby, and eagerly opened it to show him the ethnic souvenirs gathered in my travels: shawls from Mexican Indians sitting outside in the square in a small colonial town; sarongs from India; and my Hardwar incense holder.

John rolled himself a joint.

'Yeah, you've got a few things there,' was all he said.

He had little to say, struggling to keep his eyelids open over bleary, bloodshot eyes. Even as I watched, his head dropped forward onto his chest and he dozed off. Although he soon woke with a start, his body giving a sudden jolt, it wasn't long before he slouched over again.

Why does he keep falling asleep? I wondered, fed up. My voice drifted off as he slouched over yet again. I'd thought we were going to have so much to say – I was longing for someone to talk with.

He lifted his head; his green eyes opened.

'I was at a rock concert in Brixton last night,' he explained. 'The whole night long. I didn't have any sleep; I came straight to the pub from there.'

I was surprised that he would go to the pub to drink after being up all night. *He seems so quiet in a way, but so reckless as well.*

I wished that I could have been there, but I wouldn't have wanted to go alone. John's talk of all-night rock concerts seemed so exciting and free. I didn't want him to know how boring my life was; I thought he might not want to talk to me then.

Not that he was talking to me now. He dozed off again, this time knocking over his cup. The tea spilled all over the rug.

'Oh no!' I cried out in dismay. 'You've spilled tea over my new rug and I wanted to keep it nice.'

He stuttered an apology. 'I think I'd better go now,' he added. 'Get some sleep.'

He seemed awkward and curled into himself. I held back my anger, not wanting to feel worse.

Before he stood up, he asked, 'Would you come out with me soon? I'd like to see you again.'

I was surprised. Given he'd spent his entire visit falling asleep I'd rather assumed that he'd only been passing time with me for something to do. I decided it wasn't a good idea to see him again. The spilled tea had left a noticeable stain on the rug: this was a sign that I should not have much to do with him, nor ask him back again.

'No, I can't,' I said, almost apologetically. 'I've got lots of things to do, and I won't have time.'

John did not push it. 'OK. Maybe I'll see you around.'

Alone again, with no one to talk to, I felt disappointed, and my new purple rug had a large tea stain on it.

It undeniably showed that John Sweeney had been there: he had left his mark, and neither the rug, nor I, would ever be the same again.

3

A month or two passed. I acquired a new neighbour in the downstairs flat: Tyler, a Nigerian. I introduced myself and told him I lived above him; he was friendly, and made it known to me that he had schizophrenia. I responded in an open, non-judgemental manner and thought he seemed harmless enough.

But Tyler's presence resulted in one of a series of events, in this house, that was to cause me much distress and fear, and increase my vulnerability. He started playing loud music on two stations simultaneously from 10pm until 3 in the morning, with his television blaring at the same time. His heavy footsteps could be heard throughout the flat, while he banged each door as he went through it. Though I went to the council offices several times to formally complain, I always received a lame excuse and was never taken seriously or given any help.

In time, Tyler's behaviour became more shocking and personal. Living below me, he had become aware of where and at what time I slept by listening to my movements. Like a predator, he observed and noted my habits so that he could choose when to make *his* move. Every night now when I was lying on my sleeping bag, covered with the colourful blankets, he made sure he was directly below me in his own flat, laughing and saying: 'Delia . . .

Delia . . . I want to fuck you. I love you, Delia, I want to fuck you.'

I felt threatened. His seeming awareness of my everyday actions left me tense; I felt naked, and as if I was being watched. With no one stepping in to help me, I felt more alone than ever that summer.

I called it 'The Year of the Rain': every day brought a constant downpour. Every day, I wore my purple plastic raincoat. I'd bought some lilac-coloured canvas shoes that year that I'd wanted to wear for summer days; I put them on despite the weather.

I was strolling down Kentish Town High Street in the latest downpour when I saw John Sweeney approaching. I'd thought I might never see him again, since that first day we met or, at least, that he might not speak to me again. Yet he greeted me warmly.

'It's so rainy, isn't it?' he remarked. 'It's like it's never going to stop.'

He looked down at my feet, and spotted my inappropriate footwear.

'Look,' he exclaimed, 'your shoes are getting all wet!'

He prodded lightly at the toe of my shoe with his heavy workman's boot.

'Oh, don't put your foot on them,' I cried. 'They'll get all dirty too.'

At my request, however, he immediately removed his foot.

Then he asked: 'Would you like to come out with me sometime for a drink?'

He was being so nice to me; it seemed as if he was really interested. I therefore felt guilty when I replied mournfully, 'I can't, I have other things to do.'

As before, it did not seem to bother him when I turned him down. 'Oh well, if you change your mind and you see me, just let me know.'

'OK,' I agreed. There was nothing else to say except: 'Bye.'

However, having turned him down once again, I now began to worry. Although he had spilled tea on my rug and kept falling asleep, he had been really quite nice, and I felt guilty in case I had hurt his feelings. For days and weeks I kept on worrying and wondering what to do. *Will he be feeling bad because I put him off? Does he think I'm awful? He seemed so nice – am I missing out in having said no to him? Or should I leave it and forget all about it?*

I continued to worry. *I can't bring myself to go and speak to him. He might laugh at me if I told him how badly I felt, or angrily walk away from me. I would feel embarrassed and stupid either way.*

I'll write him a letter, I decided in the end. Writing came easily to me, and giving him a letter would mean I'd be able to keep a distance from him and not look as though I was trying to get involved. I scribbled down the words I wanted to say, most of which escape my memory now, but I think I might have written that I felt bad for turning him down.

It seemed like weeks that I carried that letter with me. Every Sunday, when I went to the Hawley Arms, I took it with me and kept an eye out for John. I wanted to get it over and done with, and then forget it. As always, I sat at the bar, watching for him in the crowd. As the weeks went by with no sign of him, I thought I might never see him again.

Then he walked in the door. Though it was the moment I'd been waiting for, I felt apprehensive. Wondering what the hell I was doing, I hurried towards him, squeezing through the throng; the short distance that seemed to take forever.

Afterwards, nothing would be the same.

Without saying a word, I handed him the letter and disappeared into the mass of drinkers, heading back to my barstool. Then I worried about having given it to him, wondering what might happen now. I had managed, it seemed, to lose his interest – which deep down seemed the right thing for me to do – and now I might have started something. So I waited and worried.

The next Sunday, he wasn't there; nor the one after that. I began to think he was avoiding the pub so as not to see me. *Oh dear, he probably thinks I'm stupid*, I thought. *Why did I give him that letter? Why do I cause myself so much bother? What is wrong with me?*

It was mid-August before I saw him again. One Sunday, he turned up in the Hawley. I felt flustered and embarrassed when his green eyes settled on mine as he approached.

'When you gave me that letter I wondered what was going to be in it; I wondered what it was going to say,' he laughed. 'I was afraid to open it!' He chuckled again, a hint of relief on his face.

While he stood next to me, he explained his absence: 'In the last few weeks, I went to Germany to work; I can make good money there, working as a carpenter. I've just got back.'

My feelings swelled. *He is able to travel back and forward to Germany and with the complete freedom and ease to do so; it's really great; he's so interesting.*

Slowly and subtly, our friendship began.

4

John started visiting me at my flat after he finished work. I made tea; we sat and talked. He told me he lived in a squat with six other guys from Liverpool on the Peckwater housing estate. It was on the other side of Leighton Road, barely five minutes' walk from my flat. *Such a coincidence*, I thought, *it's like it's meant to be.*

He was only a year younger than me, he informed me, so that wasn't *too* bad. I had always had a problem about age. It seemed like all you did when you grew up was worry, and be bored. When I became a teenager, it was a shock when I realised I had to grow up. And then came the body changes – then the red-purple pustular spots on my face and on my chest, plaguing me – and it seemed you had to behave in a certain way. For a long time, if a guy I liked was even a year younger than me, I didn't want to know because it would make me feel old in comparison. With John, I let it go. It felt like this was my last chance to be with somebody who looked young, so I wouldn't feel old.

The second time he came to see me that August, I mentioned a problem I was having with the front bay window. He inspected the fault and with no hesitation offered to repair it for me; something I had not anticipated. In my life, if something went wrong I had no help. It was a pleasant change to have someone willing to assist me.

'After I finish work tomorrow,' John told me, 'I'll come straight here with my tools and fix your window for you. It won't take long.'

The following evening, he arrived with the necessary carpentry tools. I was surprised that he actually kept his word. He put his bag down beside my window and extracted what he needed for the job, removing his denim shirt before beginning work.

While he climbed my small ladder, I watched. His body was lean; *too* lean, giving an impression of boyishness. He moved with agility and adeptly repaired the window. I was impressed.

Soon, John was coming over nearly every evening. It made me feel special; it seemed as if he was really interested in me. I had not had so much attention from a guy before; not quite like this, anyway. I told him about the trouble I was having with Tyler.

One night, he invited me to the squat to have dinner. He was making roast chicken for us. I suppose I was flattered, and not just because he had offered to cook for me. It was rare for a female to enter the flat occupied by six or so other guys, or so John told me, and I felt important. My ego had taken over, and all insight had been dismissed.

The squat was a place of total unruliness, where anything could go, completely barbaric. I looked in awe as much as shock at the refrigerator. Its door was gaping wide open because of a huge block of ice sticking out of it; it had never been defrosted and the door was now impossible to close. Food items were jammed inside in whatever precarious fashion could be found. It was something I had never seen before; I found this total abandon stupefying.

Then there was the toilet. Already warned by John, who had joked about the state of the refrigerator, I prepared myself to see the toilet, expecting to witness absolute disgust. I was not disappointed. Never having been cleaned in the months that these squatters had occupied this flat, but continually used, it was caked with excrement. An occasional bottle of bleach was poured down to clean it somewhat, according to John.

Although very particular about cleanliness, I turned a blind eye; I was in so much need of someone to talk to. I wanted to feel wanted, to gain some relief from my mundane existence. So I put all sense of disgust and revolt to the back of my mind, difficult as it was for me, because my emotional needs were so strong.

The living room had an old couch and a chair, as well as a mattress on the floor where one of the six squatters slept; more mattresses were shoved in next to one another in the bedroom. No one took care of anything in the flat: they just lived in it and used things as and when it suited them. Somehow, this total abandon seemed exciting; it had a wildness to it, thrilling to me. I had never been in a place where there were no rules, where you could do anything you liked and no one would say anything about it. And they all seemed so laid-back as well, that nothing mattered; there seemed to be no sense of stress amongst them, which very much appealed to me.

As we ate John's chicken, the two of us shared a bottle of blood-red wine. We spent time in the company of the others in the flat; one of them played guitar. Not all of the six were there that evening: 'Dad', as they called him, was working nights as a doorman at a Soho sex club. Short and plump, he wore a peaked woollen cap over a head of sparse hair. Though not much older than the rest of them, his mannerisms made him appear so. Normally, he and John shared their bedroom with another squatter called Tony, but he was also absent, away in Bangkok.

'We have the room to ourselves,' John told me.

After eating, drinking wine and spending time with the other squatters, I felt at ease. Together, John and I entered the bedroom, which had three bare mattresses laid out wall-to-wall. John's was in the centre. I lay down beside him on the mattress.

That night, instead of him appearing as the shy, humble person I thought I'd correctly envisaged him to be, he seemed to develop an air of sophistication, with a mysteriousness and worldliness about him. I saw this in his body language, in the way he talked and in the tone of his voice: deep, quiet, meaningful. Increasingly curious, I wanted to know more. A sense of intrigue had developed in me.

In the dark, as we lay side by side, John began holding what seemed an intense and reflective conversation: 'Over the years I have had certain ways of thinking and my own ideas, but as time has gone by, I see things differently and my values have changed.'

He sounds so serious, and as though he really has given much thought to such things, and that he has such a great deal of insight. He seems so worldly and knowing, I thought. Somehow, he makes me feel privileged to be in his company.

Whereas before I had seemed to empathise with his timidity, I now found him awesome.

It attracted me to him even more.

5

Throughout that month of August 1991, in the dying days of summer, John and I spent a lot of time together. He often brought me flowers or boxes of chocolates. Though previous boyfriends had occasionally given me flowers, I had never had so much attention before. When I showed him three striped colourful cloths I had bought in a Guatemalan market, he made me a low, square table to fit their exact dimensions.

We spent our weekends drinking at the Hawley Arms, or outside the Stag, which was on the other side of the small park. I had never been there before but there, too, they had good music, with Irish bands playing live. Inside the pub, one or two people found room to dance near the musicians in a small, confined space. I would have liked to dance too, but somehow I never did, as I would normally have done without any hesitation.

The rain had finally stopped, the sun was shining and it was warm. The two of us always sat at the picnic tables in the fresh air, usually near to the pub door. John rolled joints continuously, concealing them under the table if the manager or bar staff happened to come out.

I entered the pub for toilet purposes only, and always looked longingly at the few people dancing. But I convinced myself I wanted to avoid being covered with the smell of smoke. It had never bothered me before when I danced – but John was waiting outside, anyway.

Our backs always faced the wall. We could see the park opposite, and everyone who passed. John's squatter friends usually sat with us, as well as several guys who worked on building sites. They became my only acquaintances. John would joke about with them; the guys talked, and I would listen, occasionally making a remark. Once, when John went inside to buy beer, one of them observed: 'He's such a nice guy, so considerate.' The others agreed.

During the day, after drinking outside the Stag, we sat in the park until it opened again in late afternoon. There was a small group of us; the others all seemed to know each other. They had that hippie look about them that I imagined to be so adventurous. We sat and smoked joints, which I considered daring. Usually, I was alone: now, I felt like I belonged to something, and was actually accepted.

One night, after the pub closed, we crossed over to the park. Several people were sitting on the grass, one playing guitar and another improvising drums. This impromptu small gathering, and the semblance of music, encouraged me to rise from my sitting position on the grass and begin to dance.

It had been my ambition to become a ballet dancer, ever since my mum had first taken me to see it performed live when I was ten or eleven. As the ballerinas graced the stage in their tulle tutus and pink pointed pumps, it looked like something from another world, a technicolour land, and I'd thought, *That's what I want to do*. But I received insufficient training and was unable to pursue my dream.

Dance and travel were what I lived for. The rhythms and beats from certain music excited me to dance.

As a person, I still tend to be shy occasionally, and to

keep myself to myself. At times, if I am with a group of people who are conversing, my voice is not always heard. But, as a dancer, people *notice* me. Once when I was travelling, taking a boat from Athens to Israel, a band was playing on the dining-room stage and I got up to dance to the traditional Greek music. There were about a hundred people in that room and they all clapped for me. I had been noticed, and it felt good.

That night in the park, I began to move, but before anyone could take too much notice, John had his eyes on me.

'Sit down, Delia,' he requested gently.

Disappointed, I obeyed him, like a little girl who might get too excited if she over-exerted herself. It took me a long time to realise that I had been looking for a father figure; and even at this stage, when I was aware of this, I still succumbed to my desire. I believe I missed my dad, and was trying to fill a gap.

Nevertheless, I felt irritated and taken aback too. *Why do I have to sit down?* I wondered. *Why can't I dance?* I had thought he'd like me to, that he'd like to see me do it.

He continued smoking and chatting. I wondered why he did not want me to dance – but I did not ask him.

We spent the last half of August together. As the month drew to a close, John came to call on me one Thursday night after work, as was now usual. I'd bought two large patterned cushions from Camden Lock Market and we sat on them in the centre of the room before the low table he had made for me, facing the fixed bay window and drinking tea.

On this particular evening, John seemed serious: he had some news to break.

'I'm going away for two or three months, until December, to work in Germany,' he said. 'I can make a lot more money working there than I can here in London.'

He sounded choked, I thought. It seemed as though he was finding it hard to leave me.

'I'm leaving tomorrow night,' he revealed. 'It's for the best: the money is good, and then when I come back, we can both have a good time.'

I felt flattered, hearing his words. Though we'd barely been going out with each other for a month, he was going there to make more money, and was thinking about me having a good time with him when he returned, whatever that might be. He was doing this for me; the intensity of his speech told me so. *John is showing so much thought and consideration for me, even though he is clearly finding it very hard to go.*

Then and there, an idea entered my head, with no forethought, no rationale, and no perception of the possible consequences. Although my inner self was trying to tell me I was taking a serious step, I ignored it. My justification was that he had been so comforting to me, was there for me, and cared about me. Whereas before I had no one to turn to, now I had him, and felt less insecure. I had someone to talk to; and he was protecting me, or so I thought.

I wanted to give him something back.

Somewhat holding my breath, I took the fateful step that would lead me into an extreme experience that can only be imagined, and is often only read about, or seen in a certain type of movie; something I could never anticipate.

'John,' I murmured, 'when you come back from Germany, would you like to come here and stay with me?'

A moment's hesitation and silence followed.

Instinctively, I felt as foolish as I always did, as the seconds ticked by without a response. I had not planned to ask him, and it seemed John had not expected me to ask. He had never made any suggestion about coming to stay with me, nor given any indication that he wished to do so. Now he appeared completely surprised that I had made such a proposal.

From his hesitation, my thoughts led me to believe I was imposing on him. *I should not have made such an offer. I feel stupid, and awkward. Maybe he* doesn't *like me as much as I'd thought.*

Yet it seemed his silence was only more evidence of his deep-thinking mind. He had clearly been using the time to consider the idea. For the words now tumbled from his mouth: 'Yes, I would like to come and stay with you. And don't worry, I'll be no trouble, I promise you. I won't give you any bother. I'll be working during the day, and I will be able to help you out if you need it.'

He sounded so warm, so grateful, and answered with such passion. He accepted my offer with such enthusiasm that I felt relief flooding through me. *I have* done the right thing, I thought, reassured. *He really* does *care about me.*

John came to see me before he went away. He had his large green canvas sack with him, packed with his belongings and his carpenter's tools, which he transported on a sturdy red workman's trolley. He would be leaving from Victoria, travelling to Germany by the coach and ferry route.

He left his belongings by the door and faced me.

'Will you be all right while I'm gone?' he asked. His voice was quiet and serious, laced with passion. 'I will be worried about you.

'I'll phone you twice a week while I'm over there,' he promised. 'Next Tuesday night, I'll phone you at 8pm and I'll let you know then when I'll phone again.'

Before he left, he put his arms around me and held me tight. He made me feel so protected. His gestures seemed so sincere, I had no doubts – no doubts at all – about his affection for me.

6

My downstairs neighbour, Tyler, began to attract all the unruly kids in the neighbourhood, who shouted, swore and drank cans of beer outside the house, and inside his basement flat.

Once when I returned home, the leader of the gang had closed the gate just when I was about to enter. This was my first encounter with them, but they had now become aware of my presence and I was marked a target for their vociferous behaviour.

I shoved the gate open.

'Shut that gate!' their leader ordered aggressively.

'I *live* here,' I exclaimed.

They swore, shouted and gave me orders. I stormed into the house and then my flat, glad to escape the threatening horde, but my heart was pounding. More unnerving scenes were yet to come.

After cycling home, an even unrulier crowd of kids confronted me; some of them resembling urchins out of a Charles Dickens novel. I was called a slut and similar names as I tried to battle my way to the front door. Despite my objections, they continued to exert control over me. They shoved me inside the door, along with my gold-coloured Claud Butler touring bicycle, then proceeded to bang and kick the door from outside, attempting to break it down.

When I called the police, they were never any assistance; if and when they did come, it was usually when the 'party' was over. The council, as usual, did nothing. Only John seemed to pay any attention. At the time, I never questioned his motives for doing so. Just as he had promised, he phoned regularly, always sounding so pleased to hear my voice.

'Is everything all right?' he would ask me in concern. 'Are you having much trouble with your neighbour downstairs?'

John knew I was having trouble with Tyler, but had seen none of it.

He grew serious when I explained the situation. 'Don't worry,' he said tightly. 'I'll see to him when I get back. I'll see that he stops bothering you.'

I had no idea how he intended to do that yet I found his words reassuring. Now I was no longer on my own, I had someone who was prepared to help if something was troubling me. If anything, I was merely curious to know what he might do.

One afternoon, a big party was in full swing. Kids were swarming in and out of Tyler's flat like flies, beer cans in hand, shouting, swearing and banging. I remained in my flat, afraid to go out, and wondering what damage was being done downstairs. The noise was so bad that I felt as though I was living above a demolition site or bomb site. How many holes were being made in the walls, I wondered.

I cowered in my bedroom. Sometimes I crawled through to the bay windows in the front room on my hands and knees, head low, trying to spy on what was happening, yet avoid being seen. The sound of destruction and smashing glass continued all afternoon. A prisoner in my own flat, I used the time to write a letter to the council.

When the mob had all departed, I left the house, and saw Tyler's smashed front window, a big hole in it as proof of damage done. I rushed to the council office just before it closed, put my envelope marked *'Urgent'* through the letterbox, and hoped that it would be noticed that same day, and that something would be done.

In the morning, I heard voices. I peered out the window to see Tyler being led away by two men.

No longer would I need to ponder about what John may have had in mind for him.

During the following days workmen, wearing white overalls, came to the downstairs flat, carrying large containers of bleach and other cleaning materials and tools.

I wondered what condition the flat was in. 'How many holes in the walls are there?' I asked.

'Walls, what walls?' one of the men replied. 'There are no walls.'

He laughed.

While John was away, he phoned on a Monday and Thursday night, as promised. There always seemed to be an air of excitement on the phone between us. He told me all about the German village where he was working, and described his hotel and the good food he was eating.

'You would love it here,' he enthused. 'It's the kind of place you would like: nice scenery and old-fashioned buildings.'

He said how much he was missing me, and that he couldn't wait to get back to see me. Always he was asking how I was, if everything was OK. I felt so important.

As he wished, I made sure I was always there to receive his calls. It seemed really critical for him to hear and speak to me.

'It's because I like you so much,' he informed me. He added: 'You have to be there when I phone, or else I will get angry with you.'

I felt so important.

One Thursday in October, only a few weeks after John

had gone away, I was surprised when he told me he was coming back to London the following night. I found his sudden return peculiar; he had seemed so determined to work there until December. He said, however, that the work was unsatisfactory for some reason and he'd had enough.

He said he couldn't wait to get back; I was looking forward to seeing him too. This would be the start of us really being together, I would no longer be alone.

On Friday, I anticipated his arrival at 8 or 9pm. I carefully prepared our dinner: a Chinese meal with the vegetables cut exactly to proportion, as they should be, and a sauce to serve with them. I had a fine set of kitchen knives with long silver blades as big as my hand and light-coloured wooden handles. That evening, I used them to slice up the vegetables, carefully cutting them into stick-sized shapes.

John phoned at 6pm to tell me he had arrived at Dover and would be getting the train. I made sure our meal was timed to perfection and would still be fresh for his arrival. Perhaps I wanted to impress him with my cooking; and I wanted to enjoy eating with someone instead of always eating alone.

The time passed, and I waited . . . and waited . . . and waited. I glanced at the clock as it grew later and later. *I can't understand it; he was so keen to get back to see me. What's happened to him?* I was puzzled.

The hours ticked by until the clock read 11.30pm. By then, I was tired of waiting and felt let down. I'd wanted us to eat my Chinese food together, so I had consumed none of it. I felt silly that I had gone to such bother to make something special.

Disappointed, I eventually gave up waiting and went to bed. Perhaps he wasn't coming after all.

However, not long after I lay down on my sleeping bag, the doorbell rang. It was more with uncertainty than enthusiasm that I answered the front door, unsure how to greet him. But I did not smile, or show any pleasure in seeing him. In fact, I felt annoyed.

John strode into the flat with his big green canvas sack. Nonchalantly, he told me that he had stopped for a drink with one of the other workers, Alex, who had also come back. I felt perturbed. I'd been under the impression that he'd been anxious to see me; now, it didn't seem to matter so much after all. Yet I held back my annoyance and irritation as best I could. But I still felt puzzled.

He was uninterested when offered the Chinese food. I felt hurt.

'Yes, that is what it is like. You go to the pub, get drunk, buy a Chinese takeaway, and then throw it away because you are too drunk, and it is too late to eat it. This might as well be the takeaway. It's no good now anyway. It was fresh, before, when I made it for you,' I told him.

I picked it up and threw it away, never having had the pleasure myself of eating what I had taken such great care to make. I still felt hurt, and stupid, and was unable to fathom it.

As he undressed to sleep, I was taken aback to see that his underpants were in tatters. *There are more holes in them than pants,* I thought. *Why is he wearing them? He may as well wear none at all.*

John was not at all bothered by the unusual way he'd dressed. As if he had every right to be there, he picked up the corner of the colourful blankets and lay down next to me.

I have someone in my flat I have invited to stay, I thought. *Here he is. I have brought him here, and this is how he presents himself.*

Dismay and uncertainly lay heavy in my mind. The impression something might be wrong niggled me. It was too much to confront so I kept quiet; I said nothing. I pushed the nagging doubts away and blocked them from my senses.

7

I handed over a set of house keys to John. Ordinary keys: one for the flat, and one for the front door, looped onto a metal ring. Such an everyday gesture – but one that would lead me to live a life less ordinary in more ways than I could ever have known.

We settled into living together. John suggested that I pay the rent and the bills, while he bought the food and drink. Sometimes he would cook for me, using my sharp kitchen knives to chop and slice and carve. I had no furniture, therefore it was obvious he would keep his few belongings within the big green bag, but he did remove a sturdy black frying pan that had 'Made in Austria' printed on its underside; I did not notice or register what was written on it at the time.

The second Sunday after he moved in, as we were getting ready to go to the pub, he laughed in a piss-taking sort of way and remarked, 'These jeans are my Sunday best. I wear them for special occasions.'

His jeans had various patches of different colours and sizes sewn onto them, which provided a framework for jeans that in reality were no longer there. I found it strangely amusing, but thought how much my parents would have disapproved had they seen me with someone dressed like that.

I noticed that John never seemed to buy any new

clothes, but simply sewed his old ones when they needed repairing. It seemed a part of his unusual behaviour, not caring about anything or anybody.

We went to the pub together. It was nice to have a boyfriend to go out with, someone to sit and have a drink with. I felt less alone, and blinded my eyes to that night when John had returned from Germany.

One morning, while John was at work, the doorbell rang. I answered to a pastor wearing his long black cloak and white collar. I was unaccustomed to such a visitor; was not a practising Catholic. Lightheartedly, I invited him inside, just for the fun of it in a way, to see what he would say. Having few acquaintances, it was someone to talk to for a little while.

'I came to visit, as you are new to the parish. Do you live alone?'

'No, my boyfriend is with me.' I smiled.

He stood next to the low table in the middle of the floor and looked around the room. An expression of alarm arose on his face. He appeared unsettled. *As though he was in a place of danger and evil?*

Hastily, he excused himself, said goodbye, and made his departure.

At first it was a bit of a laugh. Now, I felt disappointed, left on a hinge.

What was it that he saw? I wondered. *What bothered him? What did he see that I can't?*

It was not long before John made more furniture for the flat. He built a small, narrow wooden table that was only big enough for placing two plates upon. At mealtimes we sat opposite each other at either end, seated on the two wooden stools he had also made. His was higher than mine. On the lower, smaller stool, my legs felt cramped, but I felt I couldn't say anything or find fault – he was doing so much for me. I wondered: maybe the difference in height was to make me feel he was important, or did it symbolise his protection of me? Or was there a hidden meaning, consciously or unconsciously? Or did he just simply think that I was small, so should have a smaller stool?

A few weeks after John moved in, he asked if he could bring his pet tarantula to the flat, which he'd left in the squat when he went to Germany. I didn't mind, so he built a shelf for its aquarium above the radiator in the living room.

I thought we would have so much to say to each other once John had moved in, but instead he sat at the table for hours, constantly requesting pots of tea, which I made for him in my reddish-pink Chinese teapot. He remained quiet, sitting and drinking tea from the Chinese mug with the bamboo pattern, smoking joints, and staring incessantly at his tarantula. The locusts he fed it, which he bought from a pet shop on Parkway, crawled around, sometimes over its back.

'The tarantula keeps still for a long time,' he explained to me, engrossed, as though he were trying to enter its being. 'When its prey have forgotten it is there, and are no longer wary, *that's* when it strikes. It's like the police – they sit still, wait, and see what they want to get, don't move, and then suddenly pounce.

'Or,' he continued, his green eyes fixed on the big black spider, as she waited patiently to kill the crawling creatures, 'if you want to do something, you keep quiet, don't cause any trouble, then, when the police relax – you pounce.'

Is this just some kind of game he is thinking up? I was bewildered.

Though conversation was sparse, I do recall some of our exchanges. I remember one time he was reading the local paper and found some news he thought was hilarious: a pastor from a nearby church had strung himself up and was found hanging dead. His arms and legs were strapped to the ceiling in some sort of weird contraption, face downwards: some sort of sexual deviation that went too far. It seemed to fit in with John's unusual sense of humour.

Another time, I asked him what he would have done about Tyler.

He answered wryly: 'If you don't want to do it yourself, you get someone else to do it for you. If you want revenge, and you don't feel like doing it, you find someone else and pay them for it.'

His unexpected explanation flustered me. I'd wanted Tyler to stop bothering me, but what had John had in mind to deal with him?

Not long after the tarantula arrived, John remarked that it was getting cold, sleeping on the floor.

'I'll make us a bed,' he declared.

Influenced by my travels to India, and my constant desire to be in exotic places, I preferred any furniture I did have to be at a low height. 'Could you make a futon?' I requested. He obliged.

Each night after work, he arrived home carrying a few planks of wood – thick pale-oak planks that were clearly expensive. He was taking them from the building site he was working on.

'Won't you get in trouble?' I wondered.

'They won't miss it,' he said easily. Normal rules just didn't apply to John; he did whatever he liked. 'There's plenty. I take it at the end of the day when they are gone.'

He constructed a double-bed frame, and then lay the planks inside it like floorboards, leaving slight gaps between the boards. As the wood was so sturdy, it made the futon too heavy to fold into a sitting position once complete, but it served well as a flat base. John told me he would collect a mattress for it from a futon shop near the Hawley Arms and left with his workman's trolley to bring it home.

He returned in a foul mood, swearing and scowling. This was the first time I had witnessed such intimidating behaviour from him. I was taken aback.

'They told me to collect the mattress from their shop on Finchley Road!' he raged. 'It's so far away and in another direction!'

I stayed silent; I wanted no share of his wrath for part of me thought that, if I spoke up, he might blame *me*. I felt I had made a nuisance of myself, and that it was somehow my fault. Instinctively, I did not want his rage to blast in my direction.

8

My friend, Anne, phoned from Carlisle, where she lived and worked as a schoolteacher. She was coming down to London on a rare visit. John had already told me that some work had come up in Germany and he would be away the same weekend she mentioned, so I immediately invited her to stay and she delightedly accepted. The timing was perfect and I was really excited – at last, a friend was visiting. I broke the good news to John.

'Guess what?' I said happily. 'My friend Anne is coming to stay for the weekend. It fits in fine because you are going to Germany and she can sleep on the bed next to me.'

Anne liked her comforts as much as I did.

John said nothing in response to my excitement. Friday morning rolled around, the day Anne was due to arrive, and he made a sudden announcement: 'I'm not going to Germany now.'

He said it as if it didn't matter. I thought it strange. He regularly went back and forth for work, and all the other times he'd said he was going, he had gone. Why not this time, of all times?

'But you said you were going!' I protested.

John stared back at me. 'No,' he simply said.

'What about Anne?' I asked, upset. 'Where's she going to sleep?'

'The big cushions should be comfortable enough,' he said, offhand, untroubled by the chaos he had caused.

As scheduled, Anne arrived that afternoon, carrying a small suitcase. A short, slim lady with long black hair, she wore bright-red lipstick. She gave John a puzzled look as she entered the front room, having not expected to meet him. I tried to hide my awkwardness.

'This is my boyfriend, John,' I said tactfully. 'I know I told you he was going to Germany, but he's just told me today that he's not. I still want you to stay with me, though – but you'll have to sleep on the large cushions. John thinks they are comfortable enough.'

Worried she might leave, I waited for her reaction. I felt like I had played a dirty trick on her.

Anne paused and looked at the cushions, a hint of displeasure on her face. Would she go to her sister's instead?

'Oh well, all right,' she said at last.

I was glad she seemed OK about it, but I still felt funny.

Soon after her arrival, John suggested we all go out for a drink and pulled on his green coat. Anne exclaimed in recognition: 'Oh, I have a Barbour jacket as well! I wear it for my walks in the country, they are really good for keeping out the rain and wind.'

Over the course of the weekend, John bought Anne several drinks down the pub and they got on well. I was happy; everything seemed to be fine.

'He is really nice,' she enthused to me before she left. 'I would like to have someone like him.'

As I had little trust in my own judgements and was always unsure of myself, I felt reassured. Anne did not always warm to people, so I took that as a good sign. When I was little, I remembered my dad calling me 'Dizzy Delia' – I was delighted and turned in circles, laughing – but in truth I was still dizzy now, only not in a good way, following whichever whim took me without thinking of the consequences. Anne's endorsement was therefore much needed and I seized upon it thankfully.

As time passed, John settled into my flat. He began to show me some of his few possessions and every now and again revealed snippets about himself. Often, they simply showcased how little I really knew.

He showed me some photos of himself. In a recent snapshot he looked artistic and was without his bushy beard; he looked quite different. Another showed him as a schoolboy. Neat in his blazer and knee-length trousers, he appeared innocent and well turned out. Yet he said: 'I got expelled from a few different schools for getting in trouble.'

He didn't say why. The memory appeared to amuse him. I noticed the smart-looking schoolboy; nothing in the photograph would have led me to believe that this kid was troublesome.

John was amused about lots of odd things, including his own name. He joked about it frequently, laughing in that cackling way he had.

'My full name is John Patrick Sweeney,' he would say. 'They called me *Patrick* after Saint Patrick. Huh! I never *use* that name.'

I noted a certain scorn in his voice. The more he spoke about it, the more irritated he became.

The recent picture John had showed me of himself, where he looked artistic, turned out to be much more representative of him than the misleading schoolboy photograph. Though I had never seen him drawing, he confided that he was an artist – and that I was to be granted the privilege of seeing his drawings. I felt special; it was something to look forward to. The fact he was artistic was also appealing.

Yet it wasn't just drawings that John created.

'See my tobacco box,' he said one day, showing me

the unusual octagonal box he always kept on his person. 'I made it, entirely from matchsticks, but I had the time to do it. It is a coffin.'

Too impressed by his handiwork, I didn't focus on the macabre inspiration. 'Oh, it's really good,' I enthused. 'When did you make it?'

'When I was in Austria, in prison,' he replied.

How am I with someone who has been in prison? I thought in alarm.

'What were you in prison for?' I asked hesitantly, afraid to hear the answer.

'It was for drugs, that's all,' he said dismissively. 'Nothing serious.'

He appeared casual, and gave no further detail. *What kind of drugs?* I wondered. *What* exactly *had he done?* However, as I had seen him with nothing stronger than a joint, I thought to myself that it was probably just a conviction for marijuana. In which case, it wasn't *too* awful. *I don't need to worry too much about this person I am with,* I told myself, trying to convince myself.

Just as he had promised, John soon showed me his artwork; he also wrote poems but I read very few of those. Was it because I showed little interest; did they disturb me, or did he keep them secret? I am unsure now.

His artwork he shared openly, however. I believe some of the pictures he showed me that day may have included a sketch of a coffin, with a lady lying inside it. 'Rest in Peace, Anne' was written on the gravestone. Other paintings were self-portraits: one showed John holding a fishing rod over a goldfish bowl, while inside it a miniature long-haired nude female swam around; in another, he was lying in bed with horns like those of the Devil on his head, as a good-looking girl stood naked before him. Another drawing was of John eating a plate of spaghetti, the top of his head cut off: the spaghetti was his brain, steadily falling onto the plate.

Though he was clearly talented, I found the pictures very bizarre. Naked females often featured; some were almost pornographic. One striking artwork showed a nude girl lying on the ground tied up by rope. All over her were little men climbing ladders to stand on her. They crawled across her body, chipping away at her, using saws, bull-dozers and other building-site tools to work on her. Another picture depicted the police being blasted into the air, batons and helmets, and dismembered arms and legs, flew all around them.

Yet another picture caught my attention for its normal-ity, and raised a question. It was a colourful drawing, showing John with his arm around the shoulders of an attractive blonde. Wearing a bright-blue coat and a scarlet scarf, she was beaming, looking so happy that her eyes were closed in joy, her face pressed up close to his as he kissed her cheek and pulled her to him in a tight, loving embrace. The two of them were set against a red background that bled to the very edges of the paper.

'Who is she?' I asked curiously.

John stared impassively at the picture. 'She was my American girlfriend, Melissa,' he said. 'We travelled a lot together. She was a model and a photographer.'

A model . . . I thought it strange they were not still together. 'Why did you leave her?' I asked. He'd never spoken of her before.

'We split up . . .' was his hazy reply.

He seemed cut up about it.

So I spoke to him of my feelings about someone I had left – 'I can't stop bleeding inside,' I said – and he responded about his experience in similar words.

He told me just a little about their relationship: 'Melissa was in England illegally when I met her. We lived for a while in Stoke Newington, then in other areas of London.' He suddenly laughed, amused by a memory: 'I had my beard, and I would walk down the street in a black brimmed hat. I grew long ringlets down the sides of my face, and wore dark glasses. Orthodox Jews, with their hats and long coats, gave me funny looks when they passed.'

Melissa was deported from England because she had overstayed her visa, he added; they had left London and travelled together to mainland Europe. They went to Milan, Italy, where she worked as a model, and apparently John worked as a make-up artist, but it was low paid. Then they went to Vienna, Austria, where Melissa worked on photography. John mentioned again his time spent in prison there – but this time revealed it was actually over something to do with Melissa.

'But Melissa cared so much for me that she got me out of prison.' He gave no indication as to exactly why he was inside.

'We were staying in a room in Amsterdam,' he continued, 'when we finally split up.'

He appeared sombre and unsettled, unwilling to disclose much. Melissa seemed fresh in his mind. It was only that year that he had returned from Amsterdam, several months after leaving her.

His girlfriend must have been really nice-looking if she was a model. Does that mean I am nice-looking too, if he wants to be with me? I wondered. *Should I be flattered that he should choose me for a girlfriend, after being with a model?*

I stared at the attractive blonde in the drawing. *I hope that I'm not second best.*

Once again the unanswered question rose in my mind: *Why did he leave her?*

9

Several days after first showing me his artwork, John hung some of his drawings on the living-room walls. The roped-down girl with the miniature men sawing at her hung to the right of the door; the girl in the fishing bowl was placed next to it. A life-size self-portrait, with a real-hair beard made from cuttings he'd taken from his face, which showed him smoking a joint (the tip of it glowed ominously with red tinsel, to give the illusion of being lit up), completed the display. I was dubious about having such strange pictures displayed on my walls, but wished not to offend him, so I said nothing.

John drew a picture of me, too, and I was added to the collection of females he had committed to paper. It was adapted from a photograph; one I did not like. In contrast to Melissa, who seemed to have been recreated lovingly and appeared so vibrant in his art, he used sallow yellow colours for me, and emphasised the lines around my mouth. I looked ugly; it was not how I wanted to be depicted. But, as the artist, John had all the control. I had not been given the opportunity to see what he was drawing.

He also drew sketches of me doing my exercises, from memory. Every morning before dressing, I performed my ballet stretches. I had been taught the movements long ago in classes at The Dance Centre, Covent Garden, which

I had once attended regularly, before attending the Pineapple Dance Centre.

I held my arms arched over my head, fingertips pointing towards each other. While doing a plié I stretched them to the sides and bent forwards with a straight back while straightening my legs. My arms reached behind me and upwards, then swung forwards and upwards over my head.

My joints move so smoothly, they are so supple. Dance keeps my body in good condition, I would think to myself as I stretched and arched.

That winter of 1991, he started calling me 'honey', an Americanism not used by someone from England – he must have picked it up from Melissa. *Does that mean he likes me as much as he liked her?* I felt a little special. *It shows me how different John is from other guys; he's more interesting, more worldly.*

He also started calling me Dee. I never allowed my name to be shortened, but with John, although I wasn't keen, I let it go. He seemed to realise I had given him this unspoken privilege, and maybe I thought that he would appreciate me even more for allowing it.

Throughout those months, he went back and forth to Germany. Though I had by now started my therapeutic massage course, it was only a weekend commitment, twice monthly. The rest of the time I was alone. On his return, John would bring me not only his company, but also gifts. He seemed to know my tastes, and often surprised me with nice things. From Germany, he brought me a pink, silk pincushion shaped like a heart, about the size of my palm. In light-blue letters, on one side, was written *Ich liebe dich*. I never sewed, but I liked it in a funny sort of way.

He bought me flowers or chocolates. A basket with a long arched handle – a pink ribbon tied to it – contained a pot of flowers. I felt somehow silly to be given such things. Much later, when I discovered the word, I considered his gifts a bit twee.

One shiny, rectangular, gold-coloured chocolate box was the right size to hold my bottles of essential oils, so I kept that container for many years afterwards. He also added a rubber plant to my collection. He was also still making furniture, and constructed a wooden wardrobe with latticed doors. When he'd finished, he spread his few clothes all across the single shelf.

'You didn't leave room on the shelf for me!' I exclaimed in surprise.

Growling, he suddenly reached out a hand and threw all his clothes to the bottom of the wardrobe.

'You didn't have to do that,' I protested. 'I thought we were going to have half the shelf each?'

It seemed the obvious thing to do but he ignored my explanation and made me feel selfish. Nothing I said would change his mind; his clothes remained where they were. I never stopped feeling guilty all the time I used it.

Soon, decorating a handle of the wardrobe door was the first gift he had given me from Germany: the pink silk pincushion expressing the endearment *Ich liebe dich*.

I love you.

I hung it on the door with the words facing out.

Christmas 1991 approached. Even once the weather turned bitter, and John pulled a thick green woollen hat onto his balding head when he went out to work, we didn't change our habit of going to the pub and sitting outside. Adapting to the season, I placed a large plastic sheet over the seats to keep us dry when it rained, and held over us a large blue-and-white umbrella. No matter what the weather, we sat underneath it, drinking our pints of real ale, as John rolled joints – even in the heaviest rain.

'That umbrella keeps it feeling a little warmer under here,' he once commented.

I agreed, as I had dressed sufficiently to protect myself from the biting cold.

In January 1992, once John had settled into another job in Germany, he asked me to visit. I left a week later, after he paid for my flight.

When I arrived at Stuttgart airport, he was watching for me through the crowd of departing passengers, accompanied by another worker. But not until I stood in front of him and said hello did he look down and see me. I was happy, looking forward to my first visit to Germany.

We travelled together to the village where he was staying and entered a lovely hotel: a traditional chalet with wooden beams on its exterior walls. Inside, our room was small and cosy with a double bed. Best of all, a bottle of champagne was waiting for us.

I expected John to open the champagne at once in order to celebrate my arrival. Instead, his immediate desire seemed to be for sex. I felt dismayed, but obliged, perhaps because I was trying to convince myself he was giving me physical affection. At the same time, he seemed to have very little to say to me.

That night, we ate in the hotel's restaurant downstairs: the food, German beer and service were excellent. We were not alone: his fellow English workers who were labouring abroad joined us, and I found myself sitting amongst a rowdy bunch. As I listened to the guys talking, I was 'gripped by the knowledge' that I would not have chosen to spend time with these 'individuals'. They'd travelled to another country to work, and at first I'd been under the illusion that made them intelligent, but they soon proved otherwise. Afterwards, in a bar, they became more intoxicated.

The worker who had accompanied John to the airport

to meet me invited him to his caravan. He offered us a narrow wooden bench to sleep on, as he was ready to sleep, himself, on the only bed available. I wanted to return, this first night, to our warm hotel room. There was no means of my returning alone by foot; the hotel was too far away. But the instant I expressed my wishes, John whipped his head towards me. With his mouth open and teeth bared, he snarled at me angrily.

I was shocked. He had never shown me such anger before. And still we didn't leave the caravan. He was my boyfriend, yet he showed no concern for my comfort; his friends seemed more important to him than me.

Silently, we immediately bedded down together on the thin, hard bench. That night was so uncomfortable: cold and cramped, sleep sporadic. I felt dirty and unwell in the morning. My face was pale, and a huge painful cold sore disfigured my bottom lip – I often got them when stressed.

Completely disillusioned, I was unable to comprehend what had happened the night before. Nevertheless, I enjoyed good food and drink for the rest of the week.

The visits to the nice places that John had promised me on the phone before I arrived, however, never occurred. It was perhaps the first sign that he was a guy who could not be trusted. It was a sign, however, that I did not note.

10

John was holding in his palm a strong wooden handle, which curved over the back of his gripped fingers. On the back pointed metal studs covered the surface.

What is it? I wondered.

'This is a knuckle-duster,' he told me straight.

I had heard of a knuckle-duster before somewhere, but never seen one. 'What is it for?' I asked wonderingly.

He laughed at my ignorance. 'What do you think it's for? If you're having a fight, and you want to punch someone, you punch them with this, and it saves your knuckles from getting hurt.'

I made no comment, just wondered. *I have never heard him talk like this before, about fighting – does that mean he has been in fights? What does he fight about?*

I looked at the weapon wrapped around his hand. *If he already has this thing, it must be that he is expecting to be in a fight.* Hoping that was not true, I refused to imagine such a possibility. I blocked the unrest from my mind, and the knuckle-duster seemed to disappear after a short while; I never saw it again.

Despite all, John seemed so good to me, but I felt overwhelmed, somewhat strange. I was unable to fathom it . . . a subtle feeling, in the back of my mind.

I gave it a fleeting thought, trying to be objective.

This guy is always giving me flowers and chocolates. I know there are other guys who give their girlfriends flowers, chocolates and presents, and then become violent, I thought. *But no, I know this cannot happen to me. He would never do that, not John – I would know if he was like that, and I would soon be out of it. I would not allow myself to be with such a guy.*

Reassured, I dismissed my reservations.

As the spring of 1992 drew on, John continued to drop snippets of information about himself. He spoke to me about his very first night in the squat. The night he was talking of was the same evening he had first returned from Amsterdam, after splitting from Melissa.

He remembered seeing a coffin being carried out of a door onto the balcony opposite his house. He seemed to relish describing the scene for me and had a great laugh about it. Afterwards he spoke of it frequently, and seemed preoccupied when he did. One of the times he brought it up, we naturally got on to the subject of death.

'I've seen dead people because of my job,' I told him. I asked casually, 'Have you ever seen anyone dead?'

John grunted. 'Yes.'

'Oh, when was that? Where did you see them?'

'Never mind,' he answered curtly.

On other topics he was more verbose. Once, he spoke of his workmates in Germany.

'Remember the guy who dressed up and wore a suit when we weren't working?' he cackled one day. 'The one who brought a suitcase full of good clothes? The same one I told you dressed up when he was sent to court for fighting?'

I had seen him once, at some point in Germany, but it was not until John brought it to my attention that his workmate's sense of dress registered properly.

'Well, we all thought we would teach him a lesson,' he chuckled.

I can't remember the specifics, but they had destroyed all his clothes.

'When he opened his suitcase and saw what we had done, he laughed along with us – and said he wouldn't wear clothes like that again. He would be like the rest of us.'

It disturbed me. I remembered the workmate had once come to the flat; I'd noticed his admiration for my Japanese teacup, when he had held it up to look at its design. I was disheartened to see that in his free time he now dressed like the rest of them, very casual. The only redeeming factor of his sub-superior mentality had been eradicated.

John told me one day: 'I'm going to Liverpool for the weekend, and I'm taking you with me to meet my parents.'

I was excited. *He must now think me good enough to meet his family.*

The Sweeneys lived in Skelmersdale, a town thirteen miles north-east of Liverpool. John called it 'Skelmers-hell', but I couldn't see why. We took a local bus out into the country to get there, and walked a short distance, passing several rows of streets with modern terraced council houses. The homes were all two storeys high, looked recently built and each had a neat front and back garden. It seemed peaceful enough, and the road had a pleasant view of the hills in the background.

His mother appeared at the door and welcomed us in. The atmosphere seemed warm and I felt at ease. She showed me to a small bedroom while, 'chivalrously', John carried my weekend bag upstairs.

'This is John's room,' she said. 'You can sleep here tonight, John can sleep next door in his brother's room.'

John had two brothers, one older and one younger; the youngest was the only son still living at home. He carefully placed my bag in the box room his mother had indicated. Though she had described it as John's room, I took it to mean that it was simply the room he usually stayed in when at home. It appeared cosy and comfortable and had a single bed.

We entered his younger brother's bedroom, where there were two single beds. 'Hey,' said John, 'I've brought my girlfriend, Delia, with me.'

His brother mumbled a brief 'hello'. He was plumper than John, as though he lacked exercise, and appeared listless.

On the way downstairs, John filled me in: 'Tony doesn't work, he spends most of his time in the bedroom.'

His father was sitting on an armchair in the living room. His hair was turning white. Tall like John, though with a thicker build due to his age, he looked strong. He proceeded to 'hold court' on any number of topics; we discussed the poll tax, amongst other things. Later, John remarked that he was a good conversationalist, to which I agreed.

It was pleasant being in a family home, spending time with John's parents. Though I never really thought much about it, I think deep down I missed my own family in the States much more than I ever realised. I went back once a year to visit, but it wasn't the same as having them nearby. The distance between us – both geographical and emotional – added to my loneliness and sense of isolation. I think, looking back, that I courted my boyfriends in part in the hope of filling that aching hole, of finding something I'd unknowingly lost. That weekend, in meeting John's family, I felt a new sense of belonging: I wasn't alone anymore.

In the morning, I woke to find John kissing me on the cheek. He was tender as he rested his hand upon my shoulder.

'Are you all right? Did you sleep well?' he asked.

I smiled up at him. 'Yes, I did.'

As we spoke, I heard his mother's soft footsteps just outside, around the corner from the box room beside her bedroom door. She may have been near enough to notice his attentiveness. I felt secure. But, on our return to London, John was soon to disclose something of which I had hitherto been unaware. One afternoon, he said casually: 'I'm going up to Liverpool to see my two kids and my ex-wife. I'm leaving next Saturday.'

What?!

'You never told me you had a wife and kids!' I exclaimed.

I felt betrayed and hurt. I'd no desire to be with someone who had kids with someone else *and* who had been married before. I'd always felt like that; I wanted to be the only one, the person who came first. Had I known about this earlier, I *knew* I would have been swayed in the opposite direction when it came to John: I'd have been less keen to invite him to stay, to let him into my life so readily. I felt cheated.

John, however, seemed matter-of-fact about the whole thing, as if it was quite natural suddenly to visit a family never previously mentioned. I learned he had a son and a daughter; his ex-wife was called Anne. I grew more and more irritated as the day approached when he would be leaving me to be with them. A sensation of distance between us, and of my not belonging, unsettled me. I became aloof towards him, holding in some of my anger, but nevertheless letting bits of it show in my expressions yet my feelings didn't seem to bother him at all.

There is another story to John, I realised, *the dynamics of which I have no knowledge.*

On the appointed day, the flat door and then the house door closed behind him with a final, conclusive *click*. I stood alone in the bedroom, feeling abandoned and rejected. Gazing angrily around the room, my eyes stopped at John's large green canvas bag, which he had never completely emptied apart from odd bits of clothing, of which he had few. I felt spiteful and knew I wanted to get back at him somehow.

I know what I'm going to do. I'm going to look through his green bag and I'm going to find out more about him.

The bag reached the height of my shoulders when stood up. Stealthily, I began to remove the contents. Being very adept at remembering the exact order of things, I knew I could replace them as I had found them. He would never suspect I had been near it.

I worked quickly, with an air of suspense; myself like a spy, or a detective searching for clues, leaving no signs of disturbance that he might detect.

Probably I will find nothing much more interesting than a few of his hippie clothes, which are more like rags, and which will tell me nothing of great significance . . .

I dug deeper – and came upon something I hardly anticipated: pornographic magazines, full of naked girls. And not just one or two, but enough to fill both of my arms outstretched. I was taken aback – I had no wish to be with someone with such interests. I had thought he was so artistic, intelligent; above things like that. *Why does he want to look at these, and so many of them? Why does he have so many? Am I not good enough? It seems so strange. So many.*

I continued to pull them out of the deep bag, my thoughts now in fervour.

My next find was a book on the Kama Sutra. Then something even more alarming presented itself as I dug further into the bag.

My heart racing, I pulled out a light-brown leather belt – a gun belt. It had a shoulder strap so it could be worn hidden beneath a coat. From inside the holster I pulled out a heavy gun, yellow and gold in colour: a revolver. It was by no means an imitation – the belt and holster were too well made. The revolver looked too serious to be anything less than the real thing.

I sensed I had made a discovery that was not mine to know; the knowledge of which I should never disclose to John.

Why has he got a gun? What is he doing with this? It's real; it can't be anything other than real. What does he want it for?

Never having held a real gun before, its weight, its cold feel and the sight of it in my hands unnerved me.

With a heavy feeling in my chest, I replaced everything as I had found it. He would never suspect, and I would give him no indication of what I had done, and what I had found.

Despite the unsettling contents of the bag, I felt a certain satisfaction that my efforts had not been in vain. I had made discoveries far beyond my expectations. There was more to John than I had ever imagined. *What could it be?*

My detective work had raised far more questions than it had answered, and two questions in particular.

Who is the real John Sweeney?
And what else might he be hiding?

11

After John returned from his family visit, I remained aloof, festering inside about his betrayal. He never guessed I'd searched his bag and in the face of my irritation was the very personification of a reasonable man. I glared at him while he only smiled in patronising amusement.

'It looks like we're having our first row,' he said indulgently. He seemed to take my animosity in his stride and soon brought me a bunch of flowers as if everything was normal.

But 'normal' for John could still be very strange at times. On occasion he pulled up a floorboard in the kitchen or the bedroom; I cannot remember if he said he was looking for things hidden, or if he wanted to place something himself. Later, he often remarked on the possibility that a body might be hidden under the floorboards – specifically, in a cupboard located in the odd little corridor that led to the kitchen. I kept recycling bags and washing bowls in there, but he saw something much more macabre.

His reading tastes centred on the same lines. John read books about the imprisoned Marquis de Sade, and Doctor Crippen, who hid his wife's body in the cellar. Real crimes clearly engrossed him. On our way to Camden Lock, he would take a small detour to the police station to look at the 'Wanted' board outside, so he could marvel and chuckle at the crimes committed. I could never comprehend why he was so fascinated; I'd never even thought of looking at the board before I met him. I felt strange at a somewhat unconscious level.

That year of 1992, John shaved off his beard, his intentions unannounced. When he strode into the living room afterwards, I viewed a different person. With his chiselled jawline uncovered, he looked much younger. I was not displeased with what I saw; altering his appearance seemed a part of his artistry. Only much later would I appreciate what a useful skill it could be for him, that ability to make his appearance so different on demand, as though his face itself was simply a charade. John was able to change his image at will, becoming unrecognisable in an instant.

As part of my ongoing massage course, I had to find thirty people to practise my newly learned techniques upon, in order to record their case histories and receive feedback. With so few friends, I had difficulty finding anyone, but John came to my aid by supplying me with 'guinea pigs', as he referred to them. His fellow squatters received full body and face massages lying on the floor of their squat while I knelt to perform them. I brought towels for their discretion and used essential oils.

John gave his friends instructions that the massage was 'straight'. He wanted none of them 'trying it on' – or so he told me. If he had been out working while I'd performed a massage, he would always ask protectively, 'Was it all right? He didn't try anything, did he?'

'No, nothing happened,' I'd say. 'He just let me give him the massage and that was it.'

John had made it so clear to the others that I mattered to him that they dared not cross the line.

My massage tutors and the other students thought it hilarious that I was practising on a flat-load of squatters.

I suppose it was unusual; not least because of some of their requests. I'd asked each guinea pig to write feedback on his personal history sheet; the first time I did so, the client hesitated, pen poised, at the entry that asked for his name.

'Would it be all right if I changed my name instead of using my real one?' he asked.

The other squatters in the living room glanced at each other, waiting for my answer. I agreed. There seemed no harm in allowing them to use false names; the comments would still be authentic for the purposes of my course. I asked no questions, yet it was obvious they had something to hide.

The last of John's friends that I massaged was Ian. He lived with his girlfriend in a flat on a nearby council estate. According to the little John told me, theirs was a controlling relationship: Ian would not allow his girlfriend to do anything without his being with her and afforded her no freedoms. Apparently it was not unheard of for her to have bruises and, once, a black eye. She was quiet when I met her, and there was no opportunity to get to know her better.

I massaged Ian on the bedroom floor of his flat, while John relaxed in the living room. While I was massaging Ian's head and giving stretches to his neck, he reached backwards with his hands to try to feel my breasts. I backed away, offended, and soon told John what had happened when he later asked if everything had been all right. Yet, to my bewilderment, he gave no reaction, nor said anything to his friend. I couldn't figure it out: he had seemed so vehement, should anyone come near me inappropriately. It seemed to me his friend was somehow important to him, or that John might actually be afraid of him, or not want to upset him. *Why, when one of these guys did try something, did he do nothing?* I wondered. It was another example of him not keeping his word.

Often he would say we would do something, but it would never happen. He was always secretive and if I asked questions he became angry. So I stopped asking to avoid sparking him off. I got the message that there were certain things he didn't want me to know; it was best that I kept quiet, I felt. He was clearly a closed person and did not like anyone to know too much about him.

To my dismay, I soon discovered that extended even to basic facts. We were in the Stag one day when John went inside to buy a round and Tony, one of the squatters, teased me: 'Aw, Delia's got a toy boy.' Ever sensitive about my age, as well as the slight age gap between John and me, I was disturbed and later brought it up with him: 'Tony said I have a toy boy. Why, when you are only a year younger than I am?'

'No,' John said easily, 'I'm five years younger than you.'

So, he has even lied to me about his age. I felt betrayed.

One evening, we were leaving the Stag, walking towards Chalk Farm Road, when three girls headed in our direction. Dressed strikingly, they were slender and well proportioned, as well as expertly made up – not the usual kind of person you'd meet on the street. They strode towards us, walking tall.

As they grew closer, they all looked at John. A hint of sarcasm and amusement was evident when, simultaneously, they spoke: 'Hello, *John.*'

John grunted back sheepishly, 'Hello.'

The girls looked down smugly at me, dressed in my flowing Indian skirt of pinks, purples and blues, and wearing red leggings. They made me feel inferior, as though they were laughing at what John had with him.

I looked up at him with curiosity. He appeared unsettled, was silent, and kept on walking.

Who were they? I wondered. *Is he involved in some underworld that I don't know about? Has he got another secret life? Why did it seem to bother him when they saw him?*

I questioned whether they might be high-class prostitutes. Or – perhaps, more likely – could they be models,
and he knew them through Melissa?

It seemed a bad idea to ask.

Throughout our first year together, John travelled back
and forth quite regularly to work in Germany. His trips
lasted anything from three days to two months, often
never being as long as he suggested. At first, I was bewildered when he turned up again, so soon after he had
left. Later, I just waited for his unexpected arrival at any
time.

His departures could be equally unpredictable. He
always seemed to spring them on me at the last moment,
usually when my massage course was to happen the
following day. Somehow, his absence put a dampener on
it for me, so that I enjoyed the weekend classes less.

Nor was that the only time he spoiled something from
which I had gained satisfaction. The council gave me a
new sink and kitchen cupboards, and John helped by
completing the improvements. He made a set of new,
low cupboards that sat on the opposite wall to those from
the council. White, with a smooth surface (not real wood),
they looked clean and shiny and I was happy with them.
But, only days after he had completed them, John deliberately scratched the surface of the counter, using a knife
or some kind of sharp tool: a long, narrow scrape now
scarred the surface.

'What did you do that for?' I asked, upset and puzzled.

'It's all right, it doesn't matter,' John replied easily. 'It's
just a scratch, it's nothing.'

I couldn't understand it: he had made nice new kitchen
cupboards but now he'd ruined them. Yet I could say
nothing for John said: 'Don't make me angry.'

*He does this. And he did it on purpose. Why? Then he gets
angry with me for saying something.*

Yet I would not let this stop me from speaking out. Often John and I took tea while sitting on the large cushions in the front room, facing the window. One day, he began pouring tea from my elegant Chinese teapot into my colourful Japanese cups. I watched with alarm his deliberate carelessness.

'Hold the lid of the pot,' I demanded. 'It won't stay on and something will get broken.'

He continued pouring, as though my words had encouraged him to do so.

'What are you doing? It's going to fall off!'

'Don't make me angry . . .' he said. 'Be quiet.'

He poured, deliberately leaving the lid untouched. As I watched, the lid fell off and broke one of the delicate cups. I felt a twist of pain in my chest to see the damage.

'I *told* you that would happen! Why did you do that? What for?'

'Don't make me angry, I don't want to hear anything about it.'

I can't believe it; why is he doing this? He expects me to think nothing of it. I'm not allowed to object, or be angry, at something he did on purpose. Yet, I'm not supposed to make him *angry.*

I returned to the local hardware shop to replace the cup he had broken – I wanted to avoid collecting material objects, but I needed cups, and especially liked these. I didn't have a lot of belongings, but I liked nice things.

It would not be my last visit to the store. Once again John poured the tea and again he broke a cup, ignoring my protestations, instructing me not to make him angry while I seethed with frustration inside. This time, the shopkeeper told me he was unable to help as the cups were too expensive to order more from Japan. And, yet again, John allowed the teapot lid to fall off. This time, it broke in half – I knew I would be unlikely to find a replacement lid.

Several days later, John turned up with another teapot from the hardware shop. Not really my style, but cute; it had a drawing or painting of a grinning cat's face on each side, with green eyes.

Green eyes – just like John.

John phoned from Germany. I had some good news for him: Barbara, one of the other students in my massage course, had invited me to Kent to her house for the weekend, while he was still away. With John working abroad, her invitation offered me the chance to be with someone, as well as to get away from London for a break.

'What does she want?' he asked bluntly.

'What do you mean, "What does she want?" She doesn't want anything.'

'She must be a lesbian.'

'She's not a lesbian!' I exclaimed. 'Where do you get that idea? She is just a friend. She's married, with grown-up kids.'

But still John professed the same notion. He showed his displeasure so strongly that he discouraged me from taking up Barbara's invitation. In the end, I did not visit her.

Another time when John phoned, I told him I'd spent an afternoon with an Italian girl I had met in the Hawley Arms. We had gone to the squat she was staying in, along with some others who frequented the pub. One of the regulars, a guy who wore a black hat with feathers and a belt with studs in it, had put his hand on my thigh when we were sat next to each other on the couch; I'd shoved it off. I told John what had happened.

Unexpectedly, he uttered a rumbling groan of anger: 'I'll sort him out when I get back.'

I was shocked – I didn't think he'd take it so seriously. The guy had only been messing around; there were a few of us in the living room that afternoon.

'What do you mean?' I said. 'He didn't do anything.'

When John returned from Germany, he made no further mention of it. I forgot all about his irritation and what I'd told him. Then, one day, he said lightly: 'You know that guy with the hat? I saw him today . . .

'He looked in pretty bad shape.'

I froze, then shivered. I had a sickening feeling. *Was it because of what I'd told John? Did he beat him up?*

Until now, John had been all talk. It seemed he had perhaps decided that actions spoke louder than words.

12

In the August of 1992, I received an invitation from Elaine, a fellow nurse whom I'd met while training. Now and again, we had kept in touch, but I had not seen her since moving into my flat. She was turning forty that summer and invited me to her birthday party; when I told her I had a new boyfriend, she invited John as well.

Elaine worked as a Sister in an A&E department and had invited her nursing staff to the party. I worried about the impression John might make, as he clearly did not fit in with a group of conservatively dressed professionals. An expression of doubt greeted us when Elaine opened the door and saw John; he was dressed in his obvious hippie way, his marijuana brooch plainly displayed on his waistcoat. When Elaine greeted us at the door and saw him, she looked let down. Her eyes widened and her smile dropped briefly. She introduced me, and showed me around her recently bought flat, while John stood alone in the living room. No one attempted to speak to him; he seemed nonplussed. John and I drank wine and ate and watched the other guests mingling. None appeared keen to have any contact with us; rather, they avoided us.

Elaine invited us to stay the night; we could sleep in the living room, she said. The party eventually finished and Elaine's flatmate left for her room. John and I were alone; everything was quiet. He opened the door onto the small balcony: there was standing room only on it, and it was decorated with two or three pots of plants. He produced a joint and lit up. A tingle of nervousness ran through me, but I remained silent: any commotion might draw attention.

'I need a piss,' John announced. He took the stance of preparing to do so.

It was as if an electrical charge was zapping through me. I spoke in a hushed, hurried tone, in case Elaine or her flatmate heard.

'What are you doing? You're not going there, are you?' But I had no control, nothing I said mattered.

'Yes, I am,' he insisted.

'You *can't* do that,' I said. 'She is my friend, she won't like that.'

'I'll do it in the pot,' he offered uncouthly. 'She won't know.'

'Yes, she will,' I insisted. 'She'll see it in the morning, and it will smell.'

The splash of urine hit the plants in the pot. Panic-stricken, I tried to delay him, my throat becoming tighter. 'Don't *do* that! You know where the toilet is – go there!'

'I don't want to go there, it's easier to do it here,' he said obstinately.

My pleading was ignored. I watched in horror and dismay. *How am I going to face her in the morning?* John was showing outright disrespect for me and my friend. Did he not think that this might end our friendship, and probably would?

Or was that the point?

My chest was tight. I had let Elaine down and felt I had snubbed her. *When she finds out*, I thought, *I cannot ask her to forgive me*. I never considered standing up to John, who was over six foot tall and who had such a temper. Far from his strong build being protective of me, it was actually quite the opposite.

In the morning, I prayed Elaine would not open the balcony door. I was horrified when she did so almost immediately. I tried to distract her with whatever words I could muster, to draw her away from the open doors; I pretended to act normally but felt anything but. She stepped out onto the balcony and frowned, her annoyance penetrating the room.

'Who did *that*?' she said with disgust. 'Someone has passed urine on the balcony and onto my plants and pots.'

How could I say anything? The silence was awful. I felt terrified she would ask me about it. John, meanwhile, stood nonchalantly in the lounge, showing no concern or guilt whatsoever, as though waiting to observe whatever reaction he had instigated, and probably enjoying it.

To my relief, Elaine made no attempt to question me further. Nevertheless, it was evident what had happened; we were both aware we knew who was at fault. Kindly, she gave me some leftover food to take with me.

Although we still kept in touch infrequently, I never saw her again.

That wasn't the only time John scared off or simply alienated my friends. Another friend, Martine, whom I had met while working on the kibbutz in Israel, was a more regular acquaintance than Elaine; she was one of my guinea pigs for my massage course and she, John and I sometimes went out together.

When she first met John, they appeared to size each other up. Always humorous, Martine would tickle me with her spontaneous outbursts, and observations about life and people. Meeting John did not dissuade her from her usual jokes and entertaining chatter each time she visited. However, the more familiar she became with his character, the less she came to see me.

One time, the three of us went to a party at the Ear, Nose and Throat Hospital, to which I'd been invited by a Mauritian family, whom I had practised on for my massage course. It was held in the hospital itself, in a large room where they'd laid out tables for eating and drinking. A band played popular music at the far end, and the family went to dance and mingle with the other guests. When they left the table, John pulled out a joint and lit up.

Martine and I, both sitting near him at the round table, looked aghast: firstly at him, and then at each other. My eyes darted around, hoping no one had noticed. In a hushed voice, I exclaimed, 'You can't do that here! You will get us in trouble.'

Martine added in alarm: 'This is a hospital, you can't do things like that in here.'

We stared at each other helplessly, wishing he would stop. But he did not. Our eyes were fixed on John each time he raised the joint to his mouth. Martine and I shifted our gaze constantly to see if anyone had noticed yet, hoping no one would come close enough to smell it. We found it unbelievable how far John would go, not giving a damn about the people he was with.

I danced once to music I liked, but my movements were tense. Martine and I survived the evening without anyone suspecting, but the occasion was not a success. I was not surprised, therefore, that her visits soon lessened. As for me, I could only continue to endure whatever unforgiving behaviour came my way.

Occasionally, I would go out to stay with John in Germany while he was working there. My trips always seemed to end in some sort of disaster. John would drink too much and either ignore me, or speak to me in an aggressive tone of voice.

On one such trip, he and I visited the northern

boundaries of Stuttgart on his day off. He seemed distant and cold towards me: he made me feel unwanted and a nuisance, almost irritated by my presence, even though it had been his idea that I should join him in Germany.

Across a road, we saw a large cement wall and building, situated in the midst of barren fields.

'Look, that's a high-security prison,' John commented. He seemed fascinated, obsessed with it in a strange sort of way. He stopped and lingered to look at it. It was as though he had taken a special trip just to see it; there seemed no other reason for us to be in that location.

Much later, I discovered the prison to be Stammheim, once the most secure block in the world. For John, it seemed to hold some sort of appeal. Many years later, I wondered if his freedom that day felt like a kind of triumph.

John was inside himself and showed no interest in talking to me. We drank a beer in a small bar; he seemed not to want me there. He was sombre and the atmosphere was strained. I felt deserted, and wished I could vanish – I was beginning to feel increasingly unhappy about being with him, considering the way he behaved, and all the unpleasant incidents that occurred. But, still, I had yet to convince myself entirely that I should be without him. So naïve was I that I did not understand what was happening, and refused to acknowledge the obvious. I tended to persevere, as with a bad habit; to allow things to continue, even if I was uncomfortable – I had so little confidence in myself.

It was as though I was tied to him with invisible chains. One night, however, I woke to feel those chains tightening – or rather, not chains, but John's strong hands. They were fastened around my throat and he was squeezing tighter and tighter.

In the still of the night, I was being strangled by John Sweeney.

13

I was startled awake by the sensation of his hands around my neck. My eyelids shot open. I saw John's arms arched over me as he lay beside me. His hands were tightly gripped around my neck, pressing onto my throat. His eyes were closed, yet he muttered and swore, threatening aggression.

It's as though he's trying to strangle someone, but it seems as if he is dreaming, and it may be someone else, rather than me, being strangled.

Before I could even try to move away, or know if it was safe to wake him up, he settled back into a quieter sleep. I was shocked.

Why would he be dreaming about strangling someone?

The next morning, he appeared no different from usual; nor did my neck show any signs of the tight hold he'd had on me the night before. Did I dare ask him about it?

I bit the bullet. 'Last night I woke up in the middle of the night, because something was gripping me tight around the neck,' I told him. 'You had your hands around my neck, as if you were strangling me. It seemed like you were still asleep.'

He was blithely unconcerned. 'Oh, it was a nightmare. I dreamt that someone was attacking me, and I had to defend myself.' He didn't seem the least bit concerned that his deed might possibly have been seen through.

*

Summer transformed into autumn. An opening was knocked through a wall of the Hawley Arms; the same wall, in front of which, I had first seen John sat watching me. The door that had been created led into a vast room under the railway bridge. All manner of people came to drink and listen to the loud music – John and me included.

One night, the guy sitting next to us at one of the many picnic tables noticed how morose we were.

'This is the best pub in town, but you don't even look like you are enjoying it,' he observed.

I might have felt in the spirit of things had I been in better company. I merely accompanied John, who had nothing much to say to me. He drank and smoked, not getting involved with anyone sitting nearby. I amused myself by watching the many characters, and ignored his presence.

On one of our nights out, John brought my attention to a man standing at the door. Always on watch, he missed nothing, even though he kept himself to himself.

'See that man with the long raincoat,' he said knowingly. 'Underneath it, he is wearing a hidden gun belt with a shoulder strap and gun. He's plainclothes police.'

The man did have an authoritative air in his appearance and dress, and seemed to be surveying his surroundings. I would never have noticed him, had John not said something.

He seems so attuned to such things . . .

Before the year was out, John took me again to visit his parents in Skelmersdale. Unlike the first trip, with our relationship more tense it was a disagreeable journey and I felt subdued. He grumbled at me most of the way, and was still grumbling as we approached the house. Yet, when it came into sight, he suddenly grabbed my weekend bag from my hand and carried it to the door himself – just in time for his mother to see. He was pleasant as he followed her upstairs, still carrying it 'for me'.

I thought it wasn't for me at all, it felt like it was for his mother. *Oh yes*, I thought, *he knows how to put on a good show for her*. On our first visit, I'd heard her step on the landing outside the box room, on that morning when John had woken me with a tender kiss. Without doubt that had all just been for show as well.

Even his dad seemed less approachable than the last time. I sensed a certain distance and controlling nature in the way he spoke. It occurred to me that he and John seemed to have similarities in their behaviour. As with John, I felt less comfortable in his dad's presence.

During the visit, John and I went to a pub, in which I felt out of place. It was not the kind of establishment I usually frequented: there was no real ale, no one I thought I would like to speak to, and the pub rang with the overly cheery jangle of fruit machines.

A man stood at the bar holding a pint. He grinned at John. 'Every time you come here, you come with a different bird.'

This man had not shocked me. I was ready with an answer. 'Yeah, I suppose I'm just one of the latest,' I said back to him. Already I knew about Melissa, of course, and John's ex-wife, Anne, but it seemed from the man's comment that John Sweeney had still more secrets that he wasn't prepared to share, maybe more girlfriends that he had claimed for his own.

I had not expected the visit to John's family to be a success; I was only obliged to trail along with him. During phone calls with my parents throughout the previous year, I had told them very little about John – only that he was a carpenter, and that he was artistic. I'd sent a postcard of my first trip to Germany, thinking it might impress them, but I didn't tell them what had happened while we were there. I also sent one to each of my brothers.

When it came time for my annual visit to the States in December 1992, my parents allowed me to bring John with me. He went along with it. Before we left London, I had been becoming increasingly unhappy about him. I had an obscurely unfounded hope that this visit could change things between us, for the better. Subconsciously, I wanted my parents' reassurance that John was OK, and we were fine together. Despite everything my instincts were telling me, I was blind with my eyes wide open.

Sometime before we left, having a desire to show my cultured mother that John was artistic, I asked him to draw my granny from the old Victorian photograph I had of her. His sketch showed an excellent similarity. However, John's talent wasn't the only thing consistent about him, and despite agreeing to do it for me, he soon frustrated me in some other way; I forget now what had happened. In a rage, beside myself, I ripped up the drawing, screaming in frustration. I was dismayed, afterwards, but unable to stop myself.

I wanted him to see how he was bothering me, despite not knowing how he would react, so I told him what I had done. Yet he showed no reaction. I had wondered if he would get angry but, if he was, he didn't show it. As he had done when I'd been outraged about his ex-wife, he merely took it in his stride, cool and in control. He even obliged when I asked him to draw another. (The drawing was similar, but had a more modern aspect to it. Therefore, I lost interest, and my mother never saw it.)

I was not wary of his calm response; I should have been. Given the hours he spent watching his tarantula, I should have learned a lesson. For, like her, John would wait for the right moment: he would only get angry when he was good and ready.

14

On 22 December 1992, John and I arrived in the United States of America. My parents and two brothers lived in Texas. I loved the heat; and I liked my parents' house, which was nice and new.

I wasn't sure how the visit would go, and it was soon evident that the reassurance I'd hoped for would not be forthcoming. Nothing hid from me the fact that my mum and dad disliked John — both the way he dressed and his character. My parents were so polite, however, that they showed no outright disapproval towards him, nor did they say anything to me. He was my boyfriend, they did not interfere, but I knew that their disgust was smouldering inside them. Any expressions of disapproval were directed towards *me*, rather than John, through their body language. It was typical of them to say nothing when they should, and to interfere at the wrong times.

My mother was in a wheelchair by that time; she'd been diagnosed with MS when she was fifty. Mum had mousey-brown hair; she was quiet and very timid. Dad, in contrast, had hair so dark it looked black. He was in good health and was a full-time carer for Mum. Both of them, in their own way, tried at times to help me in my life, but we had our differences.

While we watched TV, John sat on the armchair

situated between my mother and myself, and slightly behind us. He produced a needle and some thread.

Oh no, he's sewing his old jeans here, in front of them.

I was embarrassed yet again. My mother's eyelids fluttered in annoyance.

Being in America also provided a chance to spend some time with my brothers, Gerard and Stewart. Gerard took us sightseeing to the dam between Oklahoma and Texas. On the Oklahoma side, we looked over the edge of the rails to where Lake Texoma had been formed. I clung to John's arm, and smiled up at him, hoping he would show reciprocal signs of affection . . . no response. I had wanted Gerard to look our way and observe something that was not there. It was obvious my brother was unimpressed; he turned his back and ignored us completely.

One day, Stewart took us to his apartment, where the three of us drank a bottle of wine and talked. I think my brother shared some of the sixth sense that had been warning me for so long because, out of the blue, he suddenly asked John: 'Have you ever killed anybody?'

John had the most peculiar reaction. His head tilted momentarily sideways and backwards, as though trying to rear away from the question physically and escape its charge. At the same time, his gaze remained fixed in the corner of his eyes. He soon regained his composure and gushed: 'In England, there is a lot of arson, but the newspapers cover it up.'

It was such a strange question for my brother to ask, but he had taken note of John's height and build, how he dressed, and his use of language. We both wondered at his response, and twigged something was behind it. But there was nothing of substance to act upon, should we even have considered there was any need to.

John and I were only staying with my family for a few days before heading on to Mexico, where I wanted to travel for a month. On one of our last nights with them, we were having dinner at their neat dining-room table. In his typically uncouth manner, John suddenly said, shattering the civilised setting, 'I'm going for a piss.'

As he pushed back his chair from the table, my parents looked at me in a telling sort of way. I wanted John and I to shrivel and disappear.

How could he say that in front of them? I thought in consternation. *Surely he knows they dislike that kind of language? How does he think I feel? Doesn't he care that I want my mum and dad to think I'm with someone nice?*

I think it took seeing John in the setting of my parents' home to realise: *No, he* doesn't *care.* The stark difference between what I had become used to and learned to accept, and the elegance and culture of my parents' lives, was striking. It hit me, suddenly, that I had got mixed up with someone completely inappropriate. Until now, I'd been blind. I had blocked it out, been largely unaware of the type of person with whom I was mixing. All along, I'd been trying to convince myself that he was the right person for me, despite all the obvious signs. But, now, I saw more clearly.

I wanted time to go backwards.

I choked on my wine at John's uncouth words, in front of my parents. A little of it sprayed and splattered over the beige lace tablecloth.

The red droplets landed like a warning.

From Texas, John and I took a Greyhound bus and travelled overnight to Laredo. Previously, I'd hoped that a vacation in Mexico might improve things between us. As we settled into our seats at 8pm for the night service, however, I was simply relieved to get him away from my parents' house.

During the journey, some passengers dozed, chatted or perhaps read. I sat at the window seat staring out at the darkness. John's hand suddenly squeezed inside the waistband of my skirt, my pants, and started groping between my legs.

I was frozen, or stunned into silence. Or was I? I just sat there and let it happen. A wave of self-repugnance swept through me. I screwed up my face.

A few seconds passed until he had achieved his goal. I was disgusted in myself for succumbing to it. He was intent on corrupting me, and he had managed it.

I am so weak – so much in need of physical affection, affection of any kind – and the need to relieve stress that I let him do this to me. Or am I just trying to give myself excuses? Am I the abhorrent person I appear to be, guilty of allowing inappropriate behaviour – and then responding to it, despite myself?

The trip did not improve as we travelled through Mexico. On my travels, I always carried a small light bag but John insisted that he carried everything. He put his heavy, bulky bag, now containing my possessions too, on the train rack above the seat. His actions sound so chivalrous, but in reality they meant I was unable to reach my things. When I protested, he said, 'Just ask me if you want something and I'll get it for you.' But he was so temperamental I was afraid to ask.

The cold sore around my mouth had worsened at that time; caused by stress, no doubt. My ointment was in my toilet bag yet I knew he would probably get annoyed and take it out on me if I asked him to fetch it. Frustrated, I seethed inside at my lack of control, even over my own belongings. Though John knew I needed the cream, he never once offered to get it for me.

In Mexico City we stayed in a cheap hotel not far from the train station, and the centre. Once we had settled in, John stopped us going out; we had to sit in the hotel room because he thought people were looking at him. We were there for an hour before he finally allowed us out.

After the first night, John woke, and bellowed. My eyes flashed open.

'It smells in here. I smell cockroaches,' he shouted darkly.

He shoved aside a picture frame, hanging on the wall by string on a nail – and, indeed, he was right. On previous trips I had spent nights there, but had put the damp smell down to the fact that this was an old building. I had thought I had done well in finding a hotel that was cheap, otherwise clean, and basic. And so close to the *Zocalo*, the central plaza of Mexico City.

There were two double beds in the room and, with little effort, John flung one of them up onto its side. He was enraged and his natural physical strength enabled him to do it with ease.

'What did you do that for?' I said. 'Put it back where it should be.'

But he did not. John hated cockroaches and his wrath persisted. I had no say in the matter; he was out of control.

Nearly every pleasure I'd had before in Mexico was denied me on that trip. John's behaviour remained unpredictable and he became angry at the least little thing. When we strolled through a traditional market, he saw a hooded Mexican top, and suddenly decided he wanted it. He seldom bought anything to wear, and his timing of that declaration ensured I had to spend hours in line at the bank to change money for him. I *knew* he had done it on purpose to ruin my enjoyment of the day.

Later in the trip, we headed to a beach on the Pacific coast, where I had previously slept in my hammock under a palm tree roof, a *palapa*. We arrived at nightfall, to an unsigned bus stop on the road, where I asked the driver to let us off. Some Mexican boys were waiting, to guide new arrivals to the beach. A family had a small house there, and cooked fresh fish and provided beer.

There was no running water or electricity, or in the small village nearby. A fresh spring water stream was close by to wash in. Only a handful of travellers were there at a time, and a few Mexicans on vacation.

The boys led us through the dark. John struggled, carrying the large bulky bag through the sand. He was sweating and stumbling, muttering and swearing under his breath. I feared another outburst. Already he had astonished me when he insisted on wearing his wool-lined leather boots, and not bringing sandals as I suggested – I had warned him about the heat he would encounter.

The beach may have been less than ten minutes away. John's irritation was increasing all that time. I sighed in relief when we arrived but was embarrassed to be seen in his company with his bulky bag, and fur-lined leather boots on.

Theo, an American I had met the last time, was sitting at a table drinking a beer. He stood up, greeted me and gave me a kiss on the cheek. A Mexican guy from the village, with whom we had spent a lot of time, plonked a bottle of beer on the table for me.

It is a pleasure to see them again, but at the same time I am anxious. John will be unhappy with their familiarity towards me. His eyes and ears were keen, as he watched and listened, looking for fault.

My voice was flat, almost apologetic for his presence.

'This is John, my boyfriend. He *would* carry this huge heavy bag here even though I told him not to. I wanted to carry my own small bag, but he wanted to carry everything.'

'Yes, it *is* big.'

Theo's expression was telling – he thought John peculiar altogether.

John had dropped the bag, and took off his boots. He remained barefooted.

We set up the tent my brother Gerard had given John to keep. Before we slept, John wanted answers.

'Who is he? Why did he kiss you? What were you doing the last time you were here? And the Mexican, what about him?'

'Look, they are just friends. They were glad to see me. We just sit and talk and eat, and drink beers together, that's all.'

John's strange behaviour became ever more apparent. Along the beach, the waves lapped around sculptured cliffs; one of them resembled a horse's head, bending over the water to take a drink. A steep, crooked path led to the top. John was reluctant to climb to see the view, although he followed me. He was nervous and hesitated every so often, to look behind him; he had something on his mind.

We had just reached the summit, but he was afraid to linger.

'Come on, let's go down now. Someone might come and try to push us over the edge.'

'But no one is going to push you over the edge here. Why should they do that? No one knows you here anyway. The view is really good, look at it.'

I glanced at the ocean spread below, in front of me, the cliffs along the beach and the palm trees behind. At least I had seen the view before. The warm, soothing breeze caressed me, the smell of salt in the air. Yet John wasn't soothed at all. Later, a Mexican lady, who was on vacation, tried to include him in our conversation, but while we laughed he was morose and appeared increasingly annoyed. His face stiffened; his body tensed. I tried to be light-hearted, but inside I was preoccupied with the fear he might explode with anger.

One afternoon, a few locals invited John out on their fishing boat. Despite our encouragement, he refused to go, seeming distrustful and threatened.

Another day, he was irritated by the little girl from the house, who had become annoying since the arrival of another baby: she was receiving less attention than the last time I was there, and playing up. Lying in my hammock that afternoon, trying to relax, I noticed John glaring at the girl when she ran towards us. Everything about him was draining me; I didn't want another scene. The female Mexican tourist nearby noticed my withering appearance and called the girl away. Our gazes met. I knew she understood the relief spreading over my face.

But, when the time came to return to London in January 1993, there was *no* relief. If anything, I felt increasingly stressed. I had hoped the holiday would improve things, or at least provide respite, but it had done neither.

15

Upon our return to London, I experienced the strong desire to finish with John, and for him to leave my flat.

But how do I tell him? What reaction will I get, considering his erratic behaviour and bouts of anger, often about nothing at all?

So I kept quiet. I knew not what to do.

The months passed. In March 1993, I started working as an agency nurse in the outpatients' department of the Chelsea and Westminster Hospital. The newly opened hospital had vacancies in the department to fill. I got on well with the permanent staff, including Sue, the sister in charge, and Rosie, an Afro-Caribbean nurse, who said what she thought and was easy to get on with.

While I worked from Monday to Friday, John continued labouring abroad in Germany for long stretches – and going to the pub at the weekends on his return. We continued in this fashion throughout the year. It seemed best I follow this routine rather than put too much thought into anything. At least I had stable work.

Since our relationship had begun, John had developed the habit of asking me: 'Are you happy?' Even after Mexico, I conformed to what was expected. 'Yes,' I would say, in a trance-like, sort of hypnotised, unthinking way, as though I had been programmed to do so.

Although my parents had clearly disapproved of John,

he made a point of staying in touch with my brother Stewart, a connection which he took care to maintain. In 1993, he sent him several postcards, therefore suggesting his closeness and his affection for me. It was almost as though he was attempting to infiltrate my life; a sensation that intensified when he unexpectedly turned up at my workplace one day. At the time, however, I didn't think about his motives; I simply thought it strange.

It was a Friday afternoon and Rosie and I were just finishing our work. The department had closed earlier at midday, so we were cleaning and organising things ready for work on Monday. Suddenly, John appeared.

It seemed odd to see him at the hospital, the last thing I would have expected. I could not imagine for what reason he had come there.

Rosie and I stopped what we were doing and gave him quizzical looks. I was a bit embarrassed that he should turn up, and felt rather strange. Rosie, of course, needed an explanation.

'This is my boyfriend, John,' I told her, introducing them. I turned to John: 'What are you doing here?'

'I came to find you to tell you that I am going to Germany later tonight. I've got some work there and I wanted you to know before I leave,' he replied.

It was a peculiar answer; he had gone off to Germany many times before without making a special trip to tell me.

I thought of how he always sprang the news on me at the last moment. He'd never been the least perturbed about doing so before.

Rosie mentioned that I worked hard, and so told me I could leave a bit earlier, as we'd almost finished anyway. Somehow, I'd have rather stayed at work with her. I felt a tinge guilty, but thought it nice of her to let me go, in order to be with him. Apart from that, I was looking for reassurance.

Now, at least, Rosie has seen him. Now she knows what he looks like.

She was a witness – though to what, I could (or would) not articulate to myself.

Upon returning from work one night that year, I encountered a jar on the kitchen windowsill. Its lid had holes punctured in the top. Inside, the jar contained several crickets. I looked away and sighed – another of John's distasteful ideas.

I avoided approaching him about the subject, now so used to his annoyance if I made any remarks about his odd behaviour. Instead, I waited, hoping he would take them away; wondering what he was doing with them. When I cooked in the kitchen, chopping with my wooden-handled knives, I deliberately avoided looking at them, but found it hard to stop my gaze drifting in their direction. My constant awareness of their presence over the next couple of days further revolted me so that I eventually gave in and demanded an explanation.

'What are you doing with those crickets in that jar?' I asked him. 'What do you want them there for?'

'It's just an experiment,' he said without emotion. 'I pulled their back legs off with tweezers, to see what they would do.'

I felt sickened. 'What for? That's awful, it's cruel.'

'Oh, it's all right,' he said easily. 'It doesn't hurt them, they don't feel it, and they can live without them – they don't need them.'

I looked at the jar and cringed at the sight of them. Just because they didn't need their legs, that was no reason for John to amputate them. His attitude was callous; I hated the idea of what he'd done in particular. I sometimes saw amputees at the hospital and I found their condition distressing; I didn't know how they handled it.

To have these dismembered crickets in the *kitchen* made it even more sickening.

'Get rid of them,' I demanded. 'That's like something some stupid little boy would do. I don't want them in here.'

He didn't snap back and I later found that his crickets in the jar had been removed. No doubt he had his own motivations for doing so. I felt ever more unsettled and wary of him, and my frustration at having him in the flat grew exponentially. The constant stress caused by his irrational behaviour and outbursts were taking their toll on me.

John began doing some carpentry on the side, though reluctantly. Upon discovering he was a carpenter, one of my friends had asked him to make a trellis for her garden. He did it, then returned grumbling from her house: 'She wants me to make something for one of her friends now. I wish she would stop finding jobs for me, I don't want them.'

I thought to myself: *Well, why don't you say, 'No, I don't want to do it'?* It wasn't as if John had a problem standing up for himself – though perhaps he did not want to let that side of himself show. I had watched him with my friend, silently listening to her next request and then agreeing to it. A heavy feeling would weigh me down as he did so. I would cringe, knowing that I would get the heavy end of the stick afterwards.

On one occasion, we visited a lady's house to discuss the work she wanted.

'Where will you do the work?' she enquired.

John picked up the planks of wood she had provided – 'I'll take them with me, and do it in the kitchen there.'

She looked relieved and satisfied, but my eyes widened. '*What?*' I exclaimed. 'I don't want you sawing wood up in my kitchen.'

The woman looked at me; John looked at me . . . and said nothing. I may as well have been invisible.

The planks were piled lengthwise in the corner of the kitchen, next to the sink and the window. I waited, boiling inside, feeling frustrated every time I looked at them. Though I hadn't yet managed to find the words to tell John to leave, I didn't want him in the flat and the planks only emphasised his presence. A week passed.

'Are you going to make anything for that lady?' I asked. 'Why don't you take the wood back to her house and do the work there?'

'Aw, I can't be bothered,' said John.

'Well, take it back, get rid of it! Why do you say you will do things when you don't want to? Why can't you just say "no"?'

In a flash, John started roaring at me. I simmered inside, but turned my back and walked away. There was no point in saying anything more – he did whatever he chose to do. My words meant nothing.

Weeks later, the planks still stood there. My eyes fell on them every day when I cooked a meal at night. They were layered on top of everything else that had happened: the broken teacups, my purple rug, the crickets in the jar . . . It had all become so maddening and I could hold in my deep frustration no longer.

Alone in the flat, I stared angrily at the planks, tension erupting inside me. I cried and screamed and started tugging at my hair, trying to pull it out. In the midst of my rage, I thought of how John liked long hair – all the girls in his magazines, and in his pictures, always had flowing luscious locks. Though I had always liked to wear my hair long too, on impulse I found some scissors and started hacking frenetically at my blonde tresses.

Afterwards, my hair was no longer below shoulder length, but at various odd angles – a complete mess. I felt *satisfied*: I had relieved some of the tension inside me, but still I felt inclined to cut more. Before I could do further harm, however, I looked in the mirror at the dishevelled mess it had become.

Oh, look at it . . . I couldn't leave my hair in such a state. *I'll have to go to a hairdresser now*, I thought. I never went, except for an occasional trim, because I usually wore it longer; once, it had been all the way down to my bottom.

It certainly wasn't now. I found a hairdresser on Fortess Road, around the corner from Leighton Road. I gave the hairdresser a brief idea of what I had done in frustration, and left with a becoming hairstyle.

When John returned from work that evening, he gave me an accusatory look as soon as he walked into the kitchen.

'Who cut your hair?' he demanded. He was suspicious; his displeasure showed.

I had thought nothing of having my hair cut. It was *my* hair, after all – but, whatever I did, it seemed John had something to say about it. From his reaction, it appeared that someone had meddled where they shouldn't.

'*I* cut it,' I told him defiantly. 'I was angry and so I cut it, and it was in such a mess I had to go to the hairdresser to have it straightened out.'

His gaze was fixed; he said nothing, then appeared to have let it go. The planks disappeared soon after. It was one small relief.

In the summer, there was a strange occurrence. Walter, one of John's squatter friends, and his girlfriend, a nurse, visited. I had only just got under the bedcovers, unsure whether I needed to. After letting them in, I pulled the covers over me again.

'Why are you in bed?' they asked.

'I'm cold.'

'But it's a hot sunny day outside.'

They looked at each other, puzzled.

It was then that I realised that John had spiked the coffee he had given me with acid, before he went out. On a second occasion, I felt strange, I cannot remember how, but I twigged he had spiked my coffee again.

I treated it as though it were an interesting experiment, and I had no ill effects. I was glad I had been able to figure out John's underhanded actions. He could not play with my mind so easily.

Time passed. My hair grew out. There were no more crickets in the kitchen; no more planks of wood. When John sent Stewart a postcard in late October from Bavaria, he told him that he missed me. I knew what he was playing at, and that my brother would not fall for it.

In December 1993, he was due to go to Germany again. This time, he said, he wanted me to go with him.

'I think we should start afresh,' he told me earnestly. 'Maybe not come back. I think that things might be better for us both somewhere else. It will just be the two of us.'

Always so mixed up and never sure of myself, nor of what I should do, always looking for change, and always eager to travel, I agreed to his suggestion.

I thought of all the nice places he had travelled to with Melissa; maybe we would do the same together.

16

John headed off first, taking his tarantula with him. He'd left it with his friend Ian when we'd gone to the States the previous year, and ever since then it had looked lethargic.

'I'm not leaving it with him this time,' he declared.

He placed the limp and faded spider in a small plastic travelling aquarium and concealed it inside a plastic bag. Then he took his leave of me. We would meet again in two weeks' time.

I arrived in Frankfurt as scheduled and took a bus to the hotel, *Landgasthof zum Rappen*, in the village of Oberickelsheim, as John had advised. We had stayed there before on a previous trip and the hotel staff remembered me. Their warm welcome comforted me, a sensation I seldom had. A member of staff smiled as she carried my bag up to John's room.

I spent the afternoon settling in. It was a small, cosy room with a double bed and some minimal furniture. To my surprise, the tarantula was not in evidence. When John returned that evening from work, I asked what had happened to it.

'The tarantula died,' he said, without a trace of emotion. 'I stuck the aquarium, with it inside, in a hole in a brick wall at the building site.'

I felt sorry for the poor spider and its fate.

Downstairs in the restaurant, I was disheartened to find it was not just the two of us as John had promised. His workmate Alex was waiting, already drinking a beer. As on my previous visit to Germany, they both ignored me during the meal, talking only to each other. When the opportunity arose, Alex asked why I was there: I shouldn't be there, there was nothing there for me. I felt as though it was my fault ... that I was imposing. I was too timid to say that it was John's idea.

The same thing happened night after night. While John and Alex spent all their time together, I trailed along behind them: an outsider; a nuisance. John got angry with me for no reason at all.

At the weekend, we took the bus into town, which was several kilometres from the hotel. Given it was December, there was a traditional Christmas market in full swing in the town square and I hoped to enjoy it; it had been snowing, and the scene was picturesque. But although we drank a hot mulled wine from one of the stalls, I was soon steered into a bar and given little time to explore. Instead, we spent most of the day drinking.

We were still in the bar that evening when John left me for a moment to visit the facilities, and I sat silently on my barstool. Alex was disinterested in my presence. But someone else was interested: a sturdily built German approached and stood close beside me. I felt uneasy. He started talking to me; maybe he was chatting me up.

John returned. Displeasure showed in his stiffened face. An air of tension could be sensed between the German and him. Other drinkers had stopped talking; all eyes focused on them. Alex was anticipating the next move.

The German returned to his friends, unconcerned.

Had he been trying to provoke John?

If he had, it had worked: John was wound tight as a

spring. He set upon me with accusations, towering above me on my barstool: 'Why were you talking to him? What did he say?'

I cowered in the face of his aggression.

After the upset, we soon left the bar – but only to enter another one. I had no choice in the matter; I just had to go along with them. We stayed in the second bar until midnight: closing time.

Yet John wasn't ready to call it a night. Earlier, he'd been speaking to two friendly, nice-looking German guys at the other end of the bar; now, he approached them to ask if they could find him some dope. The man he spoke to was reluctant, shaking his head and shrugging his shoulders, but John persisted until the pair walked away together, leaving Alex and me alone.

By this time, we were outside on the snowy street. With the bar now shut, the area was soon deserted and quiet. Alex and I stood on a walkway between the winding town paths, ignoring one another. Eventually, though, he started fidgeting and broke our silence.

'I don't like this,' he said nervously, 'they've been gone a long time. Something must have happened.'

Suddenly, we heard John shouting. They appeared from around a corner; John was snarling, his face twisted.

'You cunt, give me my money back, you've ripped me off! You said you would get me dope – where is it?'

'I don't have your money!' the German cried.

John raised his fist to punch him.

Horrified, I turned and ran before I could see the damage. I found it abhorrent that John should exert such physical violence towards someone. There was something wrong with him, but I had never expected something so extreme.

The hotel was five kilometres from town; I sped in that direction. I had to get away; to be near John was unbearable. Yet I was defeated. He and Alex soon caught up with me. John was still full of wrath; Alex looked uneasy.

'Leave me alone,' I said. 'I don't want to be with you.'

They coerced me into going to a nightclub with them. My alarm and disgust heightened when I saw John's right sleeve and cuff in the dim light: they were both covered in blood.

Time passed, seemingly never-ending. I wandered through the crowd in the club, trying to lose John, who followed me, muttering threats at my disobedience. No matter where I went, twisting between people, looking for escape, trying to dodge him, he followed. It was fruitless.

John and Alex wanted to leave. I refused to go. Alex eventually left by taxi on his own. Then it was just me and John.

There was no chance of getting away. Everywhere I went, he followed. In the end, I fled the club and hurried along the left side of the deserted, snow-covered country road. John tracked me, close behind, on the right.

The more distance I can keep between us, I thought, *the better*.

He snarled and swore, possessed: 'You slag, you fucking bitch, you whore . . . *Slut!*'

John didn't sound like John anymore, even though I knew it *was* him. His tone of voice had transformed into something deep and devilish. Distorted words tumbled from his lips. My terror was all-consuming; there was nothing I could do but keep walking.

Then . . . headlights on the snow. A solitary car, carrying a couple, appeared from behind me. It was the early hours of the morning and they were seemingly concerned to see a lone female at that time, so far from town; they didn't spot John, prowling behind me on the other side of the road. I think they were worried something might happen to me; they didn't realise: *it already had*.

The lady wound down her window. She spoke to me

in German; I gathered they were offering me a lift. *How good of them to stop*, I thought. *How much I would like to accept their offer* . . .

But it was not to be. John had sprinted across the road. They turned their heads and saw him. From behind, in the car lights, he looked dishevelled and manic, snarling with intimidation: a madman on the loose.

Their eyes widened in alarm. They shot off in their car. These people had been so kind to stop, but I could hardly blame them for deserting me – I feared they would think I was as deranged as he was. The small hope I had of escaping John, even for a short time, vanished as quickly as their car.

I felt chained to the inescapable terror. John continued snarling and swearing, now at my side, keeping pace with my steps; the two of us leaving tracks in the snow that didn't tell the true story of that long walk home. He walked with me all the way, until we reached the hotel: it was such a relief to finally see it, after that frightening walk on the deserted country road.

Together, we approached the door. John became more subdued: a return to comparative normality. When he spoke, now, his voice was his own again. He spoke to me as if he cared about me. I knew it was quite the opposite, one of many acts that I could no longer deny.

In bed, he tried to hold me.

I stiffened: 'Don't come near me, keep away.'

He let me be.

I woke to the smell of John's cooking: boiled eggs and toast. He kept a small campfire burner in the room to make breakfast and went about his tasks with a normality that hardly surprised me, considering the side of him I'd seen the night before. It was evident he had the ability to switch between the two sides of himself.

I was not at all interested in his affectionate attentions.

The threatening aura of last night still haunted me. Frightening images and sounds – the punch, the blood, that demon tongue – were not so easily dispersed in the sunlight as his behaviour seemed to suggest.

Until now, I had been angry and frustrated with John. The previous night, I had been scared – it made a difference. That night had given me the push to tell him what I had for so long wanted to demand of him. For the first time, I was ready; I took courage.

'I don't want to be with you anymore. I don't want you to come back to my flat.'

It was the first time I'd ever said it. I listened in anticipation, already realising whatever response he gave might hold no truth. He would not dare snap, not here in a hotel with other people nearby, I sensed.

He was cool and casual; no hint of the heat of yesterday's violence.

'OK,' he said, the words tripping easily off his tongue. 'When we get back to London, I promise I will leave. I'll go back to Liverpool.'

That was all he said. No explosion; no devil; not even an angry roar. He continued making breakfast,

He is so cool about it. Is it true? Can I believe him? I wondered cautiously. *I expect him to leave, now; it* is *my flat, after all.*

Only time would tell.

17

That evening in the hotel restaurant, John and Alex had little to say to each other. Some German guys sat nearby, at a table opposite, their gaze directed towards us. They mentioned 'English pigs'. Uneasy, John and Alex mumbled about what they had heard, and what trouble they could be in. They avoided eye contact with the Germans.

The village we were staying in was so close to the town where John had assaulted the other German that the news could easily have travelled fast. He and Alex refrained from their usual after-dinner drinking. In our room, John told me that we would be leaving very early in the morning for Frankfurt.

A moonlight flit.

It was expertly arranged, almost as if he had done this before. They asked a young Eastern European guy they knew from the building site to take us to the train station in his car. In the early hours of the next morning, we sneaked downstairs and out into the darkness. Alex was already there with the chatty European, talking and laughing as though nothing was amiss, but his body language told me different; he was edgy, and I could read his desire that this guy stop talking.

I could also sense John and Alex's relief when the car finally pulled away. They were in such a hurry to leave, I presumed the hotel bill was left unpaid. I suspected they wanted as few people as possible to know their plans.

The Eastern European was friendly, but innocent and naïve. He was under the impression that John and Alex spoke the 'King's English', and showed his admiration for them. I wanted to enlighten him but Alex made a point of not allowing me to be alone with him – I felt badly that he was being used for an escape.

When we reached Frankfurt train station and the young guy dropped us off, the three of us went to its elegant cafeteria for breakfast. I should have found it a pleasure to be there but under the circumstances, and with the company I was in, there was no chance of that. Alex was uptight and fidgety; John remained quiet, apprehensive.

Two well-dressed men, in suits that gave an air of importance, sat nearby to begin their meal. They were conversing.

John and Alex surveyed them out of the corner of their eyes. They were unnerved, and whispered, trying to avoid the men's attention.

'Do you think they are plainclothes police?'

We left before finishing our breakfast.

John and I shared a compartment on the train with some Germans, while Alex went his own way. We journeyed through the Rhône Valley; the train followed the river and passed the castles on its bank. It was such a wonderful sight; I had never expected to see it.

But what should have been a beautiful journey was a nightmare. John sat opposite in a foul mood; we never spoke. I was in hell – and that was a sensation that continued even back on UK soil. For, despite his easy promise, John made no effort to leave the flat.

'In Germany, I told you not to come back to my flat,' I reminded him. 'You said you would go to Liverpool, but you are still here. When are you going to leave?'

'Oh, I'll go next week,' he said airily.

Every day I asked John to go, but he made excuses for not doing so. He kept stalling.

'I'll go next week,' he promised.

But 'next week' never came.

He made another excuse: 'I can't leave you, I can't be without you,' he declared, in a tongue-in-cheek manner. But I could not be deceived. His underhanded objective was now so obvious to me. But even though I could see clearly the character of the guy with whom I'd ended up, I was powerless to make him leave. I felt frustrated and angry. Would I ever get him out?

How stupid I've been to let him come here in the first place, I thought with concern. *I've really got myself into a mess now.*

Over the next few months, John's trips to Germany became less frequent, meaning he spent more and more time in my flat with me. *Why does he not go so often?* I wondered. Yet I thought I already knew the answer: *No doubt to make sure he gets to stay and never leaves*, I surmised; *that I will find no means to keep him out.*

One afternoon, he left on what may have been his last visit to Germany. I was sitting on the large cushion in the living room, my back against the wall, feeling despondent. The door closed behind him and I slumped forward, my chin on my chest.

The heavy sound of my breathing stirred me awake. I heaved myself upright. It was only then I realised: *John is draining all the energy from me. He is like Dracula, sucking the life and blood out of me.*

John had used another ploy to weaken me, long before this, which I had not understood at the time. I woke in the night to find something hard pressing against my head.

His head was migrating onto my pillow, until he no longer settled on his own. I slept on the right side of the bed, against the wall, but John pressed his hard head against me until I reached the edge; there was no further for me to go. In frustration I pushed at him – and 'woke' him up.

'Look!' I exclaimed in irritation. 'Your head is on my pillow, I have no pillow because you are on it. Go back to your own. I can't sleep because of you, and I have to work in the morning.'

He was unlikely to be bothered, I knew that. And I was right.

'Fuck off, shut up, don't wake me up for nothing.'

He returned to his own pillow, but the same thing happened again; that same night, and other nights, until I no longer said anything – but it did not stop there. I woke to feel his whole body shoving against me, taking up my side of the bed; I pushed back.

'I have nowhere to lie!' I told him crossly. He was taking up my space. 'Wake up! You're taking up my whole side of the bed. I have nowhere to lie.'

'Shut up,' he replied gruffly. 'Don't disturb me.'

He heaved himself back to his side, but continued to deprive me of space, his verbal aggression increasing each time I woke him up. Things escalated gradually, throughout the nights we lay together. Deliberately and roughly, he pushed himself into me as he took over my side of the bed, so instead of waking him, if indeed he was fully asleep, I kept shifting away.

But I could go no further: I was on the edge, my hand and foot on the cold floor to support me, from landing the short distance to the floor altogether. There was no point; I got up, and lay down on *his* side, where I could find room. Many nights passed, when half-asleep, I was compelled to move.

At work, I told Rosie that things were bad with John.

'He keeps swearing at me,' I confided.

She took in that information. Rosie had some

knowledge of domestic violence; she asked: 'Has he ever hit you?'

'No,' I replied directly.

John was clever that way. He made his aggression felt, but not with his fists. Not for him the black eyes and bruises that might have people pointing fingers. He flew under the radar. But while he didn't hit me, I told Rosie what he was doing in bed – 'He keeps waking me up by pushing me hard until I have to move to the edge of the bed, and then I have to go to the other side because I have no room.'

She nodded sagely. 'That's the start.'

I was tired after work, and had no desire to have sex with him anyway. I started to resist his demands; I realised I had been allowing him to do it with me for a long time before now when I really did not want to.

In the face of my resistance, he became verbally aggressive once again: 'You cunt, bastard, fucking *slag*!'

When I objected to his abuse, he said the names meant nothing.

'Well, they mean a lot to *me*,' I told him, 'and I don't like it.'

His words insulted me. Although I opposed him, he continued to have sex. It was pointless saying anything, I just gritted my teeth and bore it. What else could I do, if I wanted to conserve what energy I had left?

In March 1994, running alongside my continuing work in the outpatients' department, I started an aromatherapy course, which ran twice monthly on a Saturday and Sunday. It coincided with something else that happened that spring; something rather unexpected.

18

John stopped swearing at me and calling me names.

One afternoon, he bounced back from Camden Lock Market wearing an Indian embroidered pillbox hat from Manali. It was similar to one I had, procured on my travels to India, but his was green and yellow. He made an enthusiastic announcement: 'I'm going to be a different person, I'm going to change.'

This, I knew, was highly unlikely: it was just another of his deceitful attempts to persuade me that he could rise above the unsavoury character he really was. Unimpressed, I made no comment. I'd had *enough* – no matter how hard he tried. Of course, he was *not* trying, he was just 'trying' *me*, and I was well aware of this. I knew there was something inside him that would never change, something dark and evil, and all this was just some kind of front.

Around this time I had mentioned that my massage tutor had given us instructions for making a massage table. This prompted him to make me a wooden fold-up massage couch. After he'd busied himself creating dovetailed joints that slotted into each other, and twisting the large screws into the hinges that would support the folding legs when upright, it proved very sturdy and solid; so much so that it actually looked a bit forbidding when erected. He left his signature on the underside, claiming it: 'John Sweeney, London, 1994'.

No matter how many times I told him to leave, John persisted in pretending that everything was all right. It was like a game to him, but I did not want to play.

He will not go, I thought in desperation. *I don't know what to do.* I felt there was no one I could turn to for help: when I'd been having trouble with Tyler, neither the police nor the council had stepped in to assist; my family was in the States and could do nothing from across an ocean; I rarely, if ever, saw the few friends I had; and I was not on good terms with my neighbours. I couldn't get rid of John myself, but neither could I think of any way to tip the balance.

As was his habit, he still kept asking me: 'Are you happy?'

It occurred to me how I was responding.

Wait a minute. I keep answering 'yes'. It's a form of control he has been having over me. I was angry that I had been duped into conforming.

If I say 'no', he will know that the game is up, and that I have seen through him. But I am not playing his game anymore.

'Are you happy?'

Anger heaved up into my chest.

'No, I'm *not* happy.'

He glared, as though I had spurned him. His head butted forward.

'Whaa? Whaa?' he said, his Liverpudlian accent commuting the 't' in 'What?' as effectively as an axe.

On yet another occasion, he asked again: 'Are you happy?'

'No, I'm not.'

'Whaa? Whaa?'

In the past, I had accepted his Liverpool dialect. Now, it had become intensely irritating. I could hold myself back no longer, so, although knowing it would antagonise him, I glared at him and barked: 'Whaa? Whaa?'

He growled at me, but I stood my ground, my eyes fixed on him.

We started rowing a lot. I was increasingly unhappy and worried, but no matter how many verbal fights we got into, he remained living in my flat. I made a point of standing near the bathroom when we had our rancorous exchanges – a location where the neighbours would be able to hear me through the wall.

'Look, I am not happy,' I repeated for the hundredth time. 'Why do you stay here? You said you were going to leave. Why don't you leave here, and do something about yourself? I can't get on with my own life, with you here.'

I hoped the neighbour would hear my raised voice, and realise something was wrong. But John, characteristically, was clever, and remained silent or spoke only in a low voice. This might give the impression that I was the one creating trouble.

He was clever, too, whenever we left the house. I noticed, now, that every time we did so, walking out of the front door and then down the seven concrete steps to the pavement, he gripped my hand. At the time, I'd wondered if he was holding it in case I tried to run away from him; another form of control. Later, I mused on whether he was deliberately giving the impression to the outside world that everything was all right; already setting up an alibi of sorts, if ever I should try to speak out.

He pretended everything was all right, telling me *I* was the problem in our relationship: 'You're not trying.'

But I had no intention of trying, and had not fallen for his empty accusations.

The May bank holiday came around; the anniversary of our meeting, three years before: something I had forgotten entirely. On the Friday night, before leaving for the pub, we rowed. On the Saturday morning, just before leaving, another row. I stormed from the house alone, the first time I had ever done so. But he was soon by my side, sticking to me as closely as he'd done when I'd tried to flee from him in Germany. We went to a restaurant in the Camden Lock area; I had no choice. *This is the only entertainment I'm going to get*, I chose to reason in an utterly absurd way. During our meal, we argued again. John kept his voice down to avoid attention, and I kept mine down too.

The next day, Sunday, before leaving for another restaurant, we fought once more. This second time, I escaped alone. I strode off, wishing fiercely that I could leave him behind. Yet I knew full well that he would be following me. *I will soon not be on my own*, I thought. The knowledge antagonised me. *I am so frustrated and enraged, I have no freedom or choice. But there is no point trying to escape; he will soon catch up with me.*

I had almost reached the pub. To my strong surprise, he had not yet appeared by my side. I had no idea what to do, but I needed to use the Ladies', and did so.

John was not waiting for me when I came out.

A sudden thought: *I am alone, he is not here.* The freedom unfurled in my mind like a rope from a helicopter, offering a chance of escape. *I know what I'm going to do. I'm going to visit Martine in Hackney. I'm not going back to the flat, I'm just going straight there.*

I gave no thought to the fact that I would need to return, and that John would be waiting for me, or to what consequences might ensue, I just revelled in my brief period of escape and freedom. After I boarded the bus, and sat looking out the window, I couldn't believe it: there was still no sign of John. The bus trundled along its route to Hackney. I felt elated that I was actually coming closer to my destination unhindered by his sudden appearance. Eventually, I rang the bell for my stop and alighted.

I am all the way here. How did I get away with this?

It had been a very long time since Martine had visited me; hardly surprising given what John was like. When I turned up on her doorstep that day, she was pleased to see me, and ushered me inside. I was so glad to be there. She knew I wanted rid of John, and that he had refused to leave. That afternoon, for the first time, we talked about him properly. She said she had sensed he was dangerous.

'I can't look at his eyes, when I look at them I see evil.'

'Yes, I know,' I agreed. 'I see the evil in his eyes too.'

The day was warm and sunny. We drank a few beers outside some real-ale pubs. I had been denied such simple enjoyment, outside of John's presence, for a long, long time. For a change, I felt free.

Martine's room in her shared house was small, bright and comfortable.

'Would you like to stay the night?' she asked. 'Then we can go out again tomorrow.'

At this I blossomed. 'Yes, that would be great!' I added: 'I'm having a good time with you. I don't want to go back . . .'

On that May bank holiday Monday, Martine and I breakfasted on tomatoes, cucumbers and a soft white cheese. It reminded me of our days on the kibbutz. Already it was warm and sunny on the back garden patio, where we ate and drank our freshly ground coffees. It felt idyllic.

We ambled through Broadway Market at the end of her road, and then began a pub crawl. Refreshed after having such a good time, drinking and laughing, eventually I became downhearted: I had to return to the flat, ready for work on Tuesday morning.

I had to return to John.

I knew nothing was ever going to change.

I wasn't concerned as I walked the short distance along Leighton Grove towards the flat, thinking about my return to work in the morning, and not wanting the weekend to be over. If John was annoyed with me – tough. I thought: *If I want to visit my friend, why shouldn't I be able to?*

It was about 7pm when I opened the flat door and entered quietly. I'd expected John to be out, still drinking at the Stag throughout that bank holiday evening – as he would normally do. Instead, I found him lying on the bed, a can of beer in his hand. I was nonchalant; my sense of freedom still lingered.

He followed me into the front room when I walked in and sat on one of the cushions with his beer and a joint. Glaring at me suspiciously, he then began interrogating me, more intensely than he had done when I cut my hair.

I remained standing, showing my impatience for his unacceptable attention.

'I've been waiting for you to come back,' he began. 'Where have you been?'

'I've been with Martine.'

'What were you doing?'

'What do you mean, "What were we doing"? We went to the pub for a drink, we had a nice time.'

'Where were you during the night?'

'I was with Martine, I stayed the night there. Why shouldn't I? She's my friend, and we wanted to have a nice time again today.'

It was only as I spoke that a realisation hit me: all this time, he had allowed me no friends, and had attempted to see off the few friendships I'd tried to maintain. Though he had been nice to Anne the first year we'd been together, she lived so far away that she must not have been a threat; perhaps she was even a useful aid for him to suggest he was more relaxed than was the truth.

All along, I thought, *he has been keeping me to himself, discouraging contact with other people.*

It struck me: *I am his possession.* That was how he saw me. And possessions are in their master's power ...

I was still wearing the clothes I'd headed out in on the Sunday morning: a red knitted top with short shoulder-length sleeves and my black Lycra skirt that ended about three inches above my knees; underneath it, I wore black leggings. These clothes clung closely to my shapely dancer's body.

'You are wearing that short, tight skirt,' John pointed out. 'You wore that to attract attention, didn't you? Did any guys look at you?'

'I don't know, and it doesn't matter anyway,' I replied. *Who was he to talk to me about clothes?* 'I am wearing these because I *like* them. Why shouldn't I?'

He'd never brought up my clothing before, but then again I wore a nurse's uniform most days. As had happened with my haircut the previous year, it seemed he took issue with my having any control over my own self. It made me angry. I was listening no more to his interrogation and his stupid accusations.

'I'm going to bed now,' I told him briskly. 'I have to go to work tomorrow.'

I turned on my heel and walked out of the room. In the bedroom, I lay down upon the bed. No sooner than I had, the door opened and John strode in.

In a heartbeat, he dived down and seized rope concealed at the bottom of the bed. With practised ease he grabbed my left ankle, then my right. I tried to pull my legs away, but he was too strong for me. Within seconds, both were tied to the bed, the rope looped through those gaping bed boards he had crafted so long ago.

I shot up into a sitting position, my arms supporting me. 'What are you doing?' I demanded.

He lunged towards my arms, and pushed me down

with unwavering purpose. My left wrist was tied. I struggled – but soon learned not to. It seemed he knew exactly what he was doing, for the rope became tighter and tighter – more painful, cutting into me – the more I fought against my bonds. I soon realised: there was no escape.

I had no choice but to stop resisting. My right wrist was placed in its noose. I was now splayed out on the bed, my arms and legs tied as though on a horizontal crucifix. He had me exactly where he wanted me, and he had prepared his next move.

Without missing a beat, John reached behind my suit-case, which was lying on the floor to the left of the bed. He had hidden things there that he now wanted to show me. As I watched, my heart pounding, my mind in turmoil, he retrieved his hidden gun and my sharp kitchen knife with the neat curved end. The silver blade shone, as big as my hand.

He knelt on the low bed in front of me, holding the weapons high above his head.

'Don't scream,' he threatened. 'Or I'll cut your tongue out.'

19

Motionless, silent, my eyes wide, I waited. I dared not think what might happen next.

'Who is that guy you are in that picture with?'

Steadily, I looked in surprise as John held up an old photograph from years past, taken in a booth in Leicester Square. A female friend and I had encountered two guys and the snapshots were forgotten mementoes of an insignificant evening. I kept my many photographs in a plastic bag in the big box; John must have been going through my things.

'He's just some guy who wanted us to have our picture taken, just for fun,' I replied. 'I don't even know him, and I never saw him again.'

Next, he produced a tin tobacco box. A former boyfriend had given it to me and it was engraved with his name.

'Who is that who has written this in here?'

John displayed the offending underside of the lid.

'That's an old boyfriend; I never see him anymore. That was a long time ago.'

After further unreasonable and preposterous questioning, John seemed satisfied. But for how long?

I waited for his next move, my heart pounding. *I hope he cannot hear it; it might provoke him further.* I tried to hide my panic even as I lay stunned, my arms and legs tied.

As I watched John knelt before me, a look of pure evil spread over his face, the pupils of his green eyes shrinking to a pinpoint. He snarled, waving the gun and knife frantically above him. He seemed possessed, just like a madman.

He spat his next words from his mouth: 'I suppose you wonder what happened to my American girlfriend, Melissa.'

I was thrown; Melissa had been furthest from my mind. *Why, suddenly, should I find myself tied to the bed; and he feels it's time to tell me about Melissa?*

He ranted and raved, waving the gun and knife high above me.

My eyes remained focused on him, taking in every action, wondering what might happen next. *This cannot be true.* I glanced towards the left-hand corner of the ceiling, trying to will a movie camera into being there. *Surely I'm only acting a part in a movie, in a psychological thriller?*

But the camera was not there.

Instead, I remained an unappreciative, literally captive audience for John. At last, he seemed ready to share his secrets; secrets that had been submerged beneath his showmanship all this time but were now rising, unstoppably, to the surface. I had no time to ponder over his remark or whether I wanted to hear about Melissa, I could do no more than just listen.

'We were in our room in Amsterdam,' he continued. He was ranting and raving as he spoke. 'Melissa was there, and there were two German guys.'

What he had to say next astounded me.

'I killed them all,' he said, 'I sat with the bodies for three days. I didn't know what to do; I didn't want the police to find me.'

He waved the knife in the air, slicing through it, the blade swishing left and right.

'On the third day,' he confessed to me, 'I cut up their bodies, and put them in bags, and threw them in the canal.'

The words gushed out of his mouth in a frenzy. There was no way it could not be true. His story was so explicit, and his body actions so frenetic. *It had to be true.* I had no doubts at all. It felt as if his speech was an eruption of something kept hidden inside him, which could no longer be contained. It poured forth like lava, hot and scarlet and destructive, flowing like blood from a fatal wound.

My heart was pounding. I endeavoured to keep calm and collected. Instinct told me that, if I faltered, it would trigger him into doing something worse.

John lowered his arms, still holding the gun and knife. He was kneeling closer to my left shoulder now, the side of his face silhouetted in the darkening twilight. He stared aimlessly out of the window behind my head, completely motionless.

Through the corners of my eyes, I looked upwards at his profile. Empty eyes, bottom lip pouting: he was lost in a world of his own. A slight film of sweat covered his pale face.

It is as though I'm no longer in my bedroom. I'm in a padded cell with a completely dangerous and unstable person; and there is no escape.

Gradually, John re-emerged from whatever dark world he had entered. He suddenly switched on the radio at full volume, and returned with a can of beer as the music blared.

'Here, have a drink.' It was more a command than a courtesy.

He held the can to my lips and I awkwardly raised my head to drink – I knew it was better to obey, to keep quiet and follow his orders, than to risk doing anything else. I was terrified. *I'm living with a serial killer.* It sounded like the psychological thriller again, but it was absolutely real.

John rolled a joint and put it to my lips while he smoked and drank. He gave the appearance of being completely in control of the situation; and indeed, he was controlling me. And he soon took that further. He left my arms tied up, but released my ankles to have sex. No doubt he released them to make it easier for him; I might have found it too painful had he not. If I were to scream, it would draw unwanted attention.

But I did not scream: instinct kept me silent. While I lay pinned under John's heaving bulk, his face directly above me, I saw the malice in his eyes, and his determination to see his wicked deed through.

I lay there silently, enduring it, waiting for him to finish. What else could I do?

Afterwards, when it was over, he rolled off me and went to sleep.

My wrists remained shackled, my arms outstretched. Unable to move, I tried to think of some way to escape, but I knew such thoughts were futile. My only hope was that the still-booming music would attract attention, so that somehow my plight would be discovered.

By now, it was late on the Monday night. Sure enough, as the radio continued to blast out at top volume, there was soon some heavy knocking on the main front door. My heart leapt with hope.

John woke, and left the flat to answer the door. *Should I shout or scream?* I wondered desperately. *What do I do?* In the eye of the storm, in the midst of my panic, I tried to calculate the consequences.

'Turn that music down!' I heard from the front door. 'We can hear it and we can't sleep.'

It was the neighbour from the basement flat, once occupied by Tyler. He and his girlfriend and I were not on speaking terms. We didn't click and I had nothing in common with them. Despite that, I hoped he would somehow sense that something was wrong, so I might be saved.

Yet John was the epitome of a calm and reasonable man. 'OK,' he said.

I considered shouting for help, but I was lost for the correct words to say. Too many words might not be able to match John's swift actions, even if the neighbour was willing to help. In that split-second of opportunity, I determined: *No.* I could not shout; the attention I so longed for might be more to my detriment. It would be taking a huge gamble and I didn't want to play those odds. I was in no doubt: my life was at stake.

The door closed with a decisive click, a sound that signalled an ending. My closest contact with the outside world was lost.

John returned to the bedroom. He lay down next to me, still in my trussed-up state, and went back to sleep.

In the middle of the night, I needed to use the toilet. I waited as long as I could, but soon my bladder was bursting. Unable to hold it any longer, I squirmed towards the edge of the bed, my bound hands still stretched uncomfortably to the sides, hoping to pass urine onto the floor, but I could not reach: I had no choice but to wet the bed.

I lay in it for the rest of the night, the only comfort being that I had, at least, relieved myself. The dampness beneath me remained warm due to my body heat, and some of that from John, but stuck to my skin with the minimal movement I was able to make.

It is possible that I dozed a little throughout part of that long night, but I never really slept. I lay, exhausted, both dreading the moment he would wake up, and yet hoping he would do so, and that I would be released.

Again I tried to plan my escape, but I knew it was

hopeless. Worry about the possibility of John killing me was not on my mind. There were more immediate things to consider, and I could not waste my sanity on the possibility of murder. I had to keep my wits about me and think only of tactics that might lead to my continuing survival.

In the morning, my left hand was swollen and purple: the tightened rope had constricted all circulation. I told John how desperate I had been for the toilet.

'Why didn't you wake me up and tell me you needed to do it, and I would have let you go?' he replied evenly.

His answer astounded me. Would he have actually undone the ropes, in the middle of the night, so that I could do so? *He is so matter-of-fact about it*, part of me realised, *as though it is quite normal that I need to ask to be loosened to use the toilet.*

'I need to go again – *now*,' I added quickly.

'OK.'

I thought maybe he was going to untie the ropes on my wrists and let me go through to the bathroom, as he had just intimated he would. Instead, he left me lying there, still bound, and returned with a small round orange bowl that I used for washing the floor.

'Here, you can go in this.'

'But how am I going to do that?'

'I'll hold it under you.'

Indignantly, feeling demeaned, I bent my knees and raised my hips. He placed the bowl underneath me; my arms still outstretched, and my wrists still tied with ropes. With difficulty, I tried to pass urine while holding this awkward position. My thigh and buttock muscles held tight to keep me above the bowl – I felt like collapsing into it.

'I can't do it.'

'Keep trying.'

It took several minutes before I could finally let go,

and pass urine in such an awful situation of tension, and in that cramped position. All the while, John watched. After I'd finished, he took the bowl away and I eased back down.

While I remained tied to the bed, he spoke about the night before. Today, there was no sign of the madman who had ranted and raved while evil secrets spewed forth from his mouth like vomit. Instead, he was direct and blunt, matter-of-fact and forthright.

'Look, what happened last night, it's all a joke, it was just a game! It didn't really happen.' On edge, I watched him lie through his teeth. 'Look, I'll show you the gun,' he enthused, as though it could provide proof.

Suddenly, the revolver appeared in his hand; it must have been hidden close to him all along. I cringed as I tried to turn my eyes away, but I could not help but look.

'See, it's just a toy.'

He swivelled it around with a finger at the notch, where the trigger also was. This deadly-looking weapon was in the hands of someone so volatile: *anything* could happen. John seemed to really know how to handle it, I observed; his dextrous movements reminded me of how a professional gunman might handle a weapon in the movies I had watched. He opened up its chamber, which contained a few bullets, and even took one out to show me. The bullets were gold-coloured on one end, more copper-coloured on the other.

Try as he might, John could not convince me that this serious-looking gun was not real, and was just a toy. Yet I kept quiet; I said nothing.

'I didn't mean that about Melissa, Delia. It was just a joke.'

He stated it as though it was a fact, indelible as ink, trying to cover up what he had said and pretend it was not for real. But he had shown me his true self, and I would never have unseen the monster behind the mask, anyway.

Suddenly, that monster started, disturbed by an unexpected noise. He looked towards the front room. The noise kept on, interrupting the hostage situation that he had engineered in the bedroom. I lay still in my ropes, listening in expectation.

In the living room, the phone was ringing.

20

Moving quickly, John went through to the living room to answer it.

It was a Tuesday morning; I should have been at work. I knew it would be the hospital agency office staff, wondering why I was absent.

As he did so well, John lied: 'She had to go away, it was an emergency. She had to leave London, she'll be back next week.'

As I listened, I was surprised when they seemed to accept his excuse. He came back through and I said nothing, just stared at him. But – to his surprise and consternation – the phone soon rang again. This time, he barked down the handset aggressively: 'Oh yeah! Whaaa? You're going to do whaaa?'

He banged down the phone. Panicked, he ran back and forth, from the front room where the phone was and back into my prison. Then he leaned over me, his hands and arms supporting him, gazing into my face.

'It was Rosie. She said, if you aren't at work by 12 o'clock, she's going to phone the police.'

Rosie. I was pleased; she had not accepted what the staffing office had told her John said. *Now, at least somebody knows . . .* Having met John, she hadn't been fooled by him. She had borne witness, after all, and she had put the clues together.

'I feel sick,' John announced. He spoke rapidly, the words tumbling out of him in panic. 'I don't know what to do. What am I going to do? What am I going to do?'

Glancing at his sweating face, I showed little emotion and was unimpressed with his apparent need for advice. I spoke slowly and moderately, almost shrugging my shoulders, though the ropes prevented it: 'I don't know.'

He ran back and forth several times more: saying he felt sick, sweating, and leaning over me, asking me what to do.

'I don't know . . .'

Suddenly, he calmed down a little: a decision had been made.

'I'll untie you so you can go to the phone. Call Rosie and tell her that everything is all right. Tell her there was an emergency, and you had to go away, and that you'll be back to work on Monday, next week.'

He bent to my bonds and released me. My left wrist was red; my hand swollen purple. Yet really it wasn't a release at all: it did not mean I was free, I had to do what he said.

The phone was on the floor near the bay window. I knelt down to it, and John knelt close beside me. He was right there, listening to every word, making sure I didn't try anything.

I pressed the numbers. Rosie picked up. I was so glad to hear her voice, but nothing could stop the trembling in my own. I told her his lie. She accepted my message, but I knew she was playing along with the game: she was well aware that something was wrong. She did not phone the police – because she knew they could make things worse. But she had at least twigged how he worked, and she knew I was in danger.

If something happened, Rosie would *know*.

After I replaced the beige handset in its plastic cradle, John did not tie me up again. Instead, as we sat in the front room on the large cushions, he began talking to me about the bad times he'd had when he was a boy.

I found myself enveloped in a make-believe world that he was creating. I had a sense that there was a struggle and I had become a part of that struggle. Whatever he had done to me should be put aside. His father, after all, had hit him, he revealed. He took off his T-shirt to show me a scar: a thin white line across his back.

'Look at my back – see? My dad hit me with a belt. See the mark? My mum wasn't there, she was at work.'

Having viewed the scar, I had a strange notion that I belonged; we were in this together. Pain and punishment: scars had been inflicted on him by his father, and John had inflicted on me a punishment. So we had a certain kinship in this together. Perhaps I felt closer to him for it; perhaps, then, he accepted me as being at one with him, and belonging.

I was initiated.

We spent the whole day talking. He continued to give me a sob story until, eventually, he gained my sympathy – though only to a degree. For underlying that sympathy in my subconscious was a desperate desire to escape; although, at the time, I did not realise the subtleties of my feelings: I *wanted* to believe him, as it might be my only means of escape.

Then he began to talk about the murders again – and how much they bothered him. It was another sob story, though I tried to believe what he was saying was true. Contrition, or at least an awareness of the fact the murders rightly troubled him, could be my first step out of this hell.

'I need to tell someone but I don't know where to go, who to tell,' he told me. 'You are the first one I've ever been able to talk to.'

'Well, why don't we go and talk to a doctor, who might

be able to help you?' I suggested. 'Or maybe a counsellor – or even a priest?'

John seemed unsure about seeing a doctor or a priest.

'Well, you say you need to talk to someone, so what about a counsellor, maybe they can help you?'

'OK,' he agreed at last. 'We'll go later tonight.'

Sitting on the cushions, pondering the delay, I wondered: *why later tonight, why not now?* But I had to believe that he had made the decision and back off: if I pushed it, it might not happen, I felt.

After that I felt more at ease, and John seemed more approachable, more subdued. He genuinely seemed to *want* to confide in me as to how troubled he was. We had reached an agreement, and he was going to try to do something about himself.

Then afternoon arrived; nothing was happening.

'I thought we were going to see a counsellor,' I said inquisitively. 'It's getting late now, when are we going to go? It will be too late soon.'

But John had changed his mind.

'We'll go tomorrow.'

I had to satisfy myself with that, and hope the visit would materialise.

In the meantime, another night sleeping next to a multiple murderer lay ahead. As though it was just a normal evening, John and I both got under the covers and lay side by side in the dark. There had not been an opportunity to change the sheets: they remained slightly damp, and the odour from my urine lingered. There was no point dwelling on it, though; and my mind was otherwise occupied anyway.

I didn't try to run that night; didn't steal away while he slumbered beside me. His watchfulness extended into his rest time: I knew, from my intimate familiarity with his sleeping patterns that he never got to sleep easily and often woke in the night; he was too edgy, always on alert.

It was too risky to try to slip out for fear he might wake, as he always did at the smallest, softest noise. Instead, I just lay there as the hours ticked by, a killer spread out beside me.

In the morning, he led me to believe that we would go to the counsellor that day. I felt reassured.

Having lain uncomfortably in it the night before, the damp bed, soiled with my urine, was preoccupying me. I placed the stiffening, yellowed sheets and sleeping bag in a plastic bag, and cleaned the mattress with water and bleach as best I could.

John was in the front room. I had my back to its door, and was putting on my pink coat in the bedroom.

'John,' I called, in as normal a voice as I could muster. 'I need to go to the launderette to wash all these, everything is wet.'

His response sounded rather pleading, and had a sense of hidden alarm.

'No, don't go! You might tell someone. We'll go out together later.'

'No, I won't tell anyone,' I promised. 'I just need to get these done.'

'Don't do it, Delia, don't go!' He sounded anxious rather than controlling.

'It's all right,' I said reassuringly. 'I'll be back as soon as it's done.'

I pulled the other sleeve on, my back to the living room. So I didn't see him coming. I didn't hear him, either. The first I knew of John's presence was when I felt something pressing into the back of my head: I didn't know what it was, but it was hard against my skull.

I turned slowly, and whatever it was moved around my head as I did, until it was pressing into the side of my skull. By the time I had finished my half-circle, I was facing the small pine-framed mirror that hung on the side of the wooden wardrobe that John had constructed in the early days of our relationship. Within the mirror's neat rectangular border, I could see my reflection.

Held firmly to my left temple was a big black gun.

I did not try to 'will' a movie camera and a psychological thriller into being, as I had done before. What was happening was all too real, and I was well aware that, without doubt, I was truly living such a thriller.

Another extremely sensitive situation had arisen. I knew I must be very careful how I reacted.

I was transfixed by the weapon, noticing neither John nor me, my eyes fixated on its fluted barrel, my brain focused only on its unyielding pressure against my skull. Yet I saw one thing clearly. As I watched in horror, John touched the trigger. I heard the gun click once, as though to signify a bullet was now engaged.

I knew, if he clicked it again, that he would blow my brains out.

Slowly, I turned to face him, the gun now at my forehead. I knew I had to be so careful in what I was doing and saying, so I moved cautiously, lifting my gaze to his.

I witnessed a change in his eyes that I had not seen before, but which reflected the state of his unstable mentality. His eyes were dark, black and empty; his pupils constricted to pinpoints. The embodiment of evil, his face had distorted into wickedness again, with a twisted smile. His voice resumed as a deep snarl, low pitched and with certain threat.

'I'm going to have to kill you, Delia,' he announced.

21

He hadn't finished.

'And if Martine comes at the weekend, she might have to go too. And Rosie . . . she'll have to go too if she gets the police. *I know where to find her.*'

I suddenly appreciated why John had *really* come to see me at the hospital that day, when he had unexpectedly turned up to tell me he was going to Germany: he had been checking up on me, gaining intelligence that he could later use against me. Anything was a weapon in John Sweeney's hands – and that included information. He had left nothing to guesswork in case it should be of further use to him.

With the gun still pressed against my forehead and John's eyes as black as his soul, I knew I had to be very careful in how I reacted now.

Any second could be my last.

I worked on instinct, trying to use psychology, but really making it up as I went along. I returned his gaze, direct and steady, without flinching. After a slight pause, I spoke in a gentle and soft tone; yet, inside, my heart was pounding.

'John, you're changing again . . . you're changing.'

John's hand, still holding the gun to my head, began trembling, before he dropped it to his side, the weapon falling away with it, though he kept the gun held in his shaking hand. I felt no relief – this ordeal was not over, not by a long shot – but it removed the instant threat in that immediate moment. I couldn't think about the future; I was thinking about the now, it was enough to focus on.

His face softened, the evil left his eyes, and his pupils dilated to normal. He began to cry.

'Delia, I can't let you go out. I'm scared of the police, they would put me in prison.' He added, as though he had no choice, 'I don't want to do it, but I'm going to have to kill you.' The reality was he was not concerned for my welfare, but he was concerned very much for his own fate, should he be caught. As before, I stayed calm: it was best not to think or feel, I just had to take it from minute to minute.

After that incident, I was not permitted out of John's sight. He even followed me to the toilet. Another night passed; still we did not go to see the counsellor as he'd promised. On Thursday, the fourth day, he allowed me out with him to a small café just around the corner. I felt frustrated in the sunlight, rather than free, because I knew I could not escape. Instinct told me I dared not try to get away; his mental state was too finely balanced.

It was a break of sorts, nonetheless. We sat and drank our coffee in the tiny, quiet café. There were only three of us in there: me, John Sweeney and the man who ran the place. As John settled the bill and we returned to the flat, I felt I had missed an opportunity – if there was one.

After our brief sojourn, he made a suggestion: 'I would like to get rid of my gun. Would you come with me to Hampstead Ponds, later tonight, to throw it in the water? If you come with me, you will see me throw it away, and know that I don't have it anymore.'

I considered what he was saying carefully. A self-confessed triple murderer, who had dumped his victims in a canal, was inviting me to a body of water late at night with a gun so he could 'throw it in the water'.

Instinctively – understandably – I disliked the idea of being alone with him, in the dark, on the Heath, with a lethal weapon ... At that point in my imagination, my mind blanked out. I refrained from thinking just what he might do to me up by Hampstead Ponds.

'No, I don't want to go there.'

I fell silent.

He must not twig that I know he is up to something else sinister.

He did not push it. There was no reaction to my refusal; he did not say anything more about it. I think, now, that was another part of his psychology: even though I had instinctively realised it *was* a plan, he wasn't going to show me that he'd had one. He liked to leave things blank, so no one really knew what was going on inside his mind.

I certainly couldn't fathom what was happening the next day, Friday. John suddenly announced that he was going to leave; to leave the flat, just as I desired.

To leave me alone.

I felt no sense of relief at his words, however; he had said the same in Germany, five long months before.

Throughout that day, I waited. As usual, nothing seemed to be happening.

'When are you going to pack your bags?' I demanded. People might think it brave of me to ask the question, but I wanted him out, and to see proof of his departure.

It took him a few hours to get his things together. In the end, I started packing for him, as I was growing more impatient.

It was early in the evening by the time a minicab arrived. As the squat had broken up by now, John told me that he was going to stay with his friend, Tony, in Archway. He left with all his things. Before he did, however, he made one final gesture: 'Here is the set of keys to the flat.'

The ones I had given him when I had first let him stay.

I clutched them in my hand, two metal keys on a single ring, finding it hard to believe my luck. But as he walked away, carrying his big green bag and his workman's trolley, and shut the door behind him, I realised it was true.

He had actually gone.

It was over.

The next morning, after a somewhat restless sleep, I woke up around 8 o'clock, hearing someone opening the door to the house. I lay still in bed, waiting. It was uncustomary for the neighbours above me to be entering at that time, and I was suspicious as to who it might be.

I heard a secondary catch of metal on metal, and a key turned in the lock of the flat door. My body became limp.

The door opened, and John entered.

'What are you doing here?' I asked numbly. Then I stated the obvious: 'You've got yourself another set of keys.'

'I couldn't bear to leave you,' he lied. 'I couldn't stand the idea of someone taking you out for a meal, and then going to bed with you.'

My heart dropped to my feet. I wanted to scream in frustration, enraged. *Does he really think I believe that?*

John went into the kitchen and made breakfast, unabashed, as though he had every right to be there.

I was still lying in bed – the bed he had tied me to, the bed in which he had humiliated me, in the bedroom in which he'd pressed a gun to my head – trying to take it all in.

I can see now that I'm never going to get rid of him. He is never going to go.

John acted as if everything was just fine, and that we would just carry on as usual. He made no mention of Melissa, or a counsellor, or the fact he'd held me hostage for five days, repeatedly threatening to kill me. Then again, to him, such a situation *was* usual. In his twisted mind, everything *was* just fine.

Lying in bed, I stared up at the ceiling.

The whole thing is hopeless, I have absolutely no hope.

Where on earth could I go from there?

22

'Why don't you go to the police?' my colleagues asked on Monday morning, when John finally allowed me to return to work. They all gathered round me anxiously – Sue, Rosie and the care assistant Claire – as I showed them the red mark surrounding my left wrist from where the rope had tightened; as I told them everything that John had done.

Of course, to most people that would seem the obvious thing to do – but I knew otherwise. My colleagues hadn't been in that bedroom with John; they hadn't seen his eyes go black and empty, nor heard him rant about Melissa's murder. But *I* had. I knew this was far more than domestic violence, this was the extreme: I was dealing with life and death. Death, in all probability, unless dealt with in the correct way. Could I trust the police to protect me? I knew that I could not.

'No,' I replied, shaking my head. 'I can't go to the police. They won't do anything. And *he* will do something if he knows I have been to them.'

Although I didn't necessarily think of it at the time, the police had already proved to me with my old neighbour Tyler that they would fail to act. I'm sure I had read in the newspapers, too, of how females were often killed despite so-called 'restraining orders' against their violent partners. All the police would do was give John a piece of paper and say, 'Keep away.' But that, I knew, would *not* keep him away.

That would only make things worse.

My colleagues advised me not to tell the temporary staffing office what had occurred; they might think me unreliable, likely to fail to arrive for work again, in which case I might lose my job. I wanted to continue working with them; it was the only sense of security I had. So I said nothing to the office personnel.

Meanwhile, John stayed in the flat, and his things began to trickle back: his art portfolio, his big green bag. He went to work, just as he had done before anything happened, and as if he had every right to be there. We went to the pub on the weekend.

About two weeks after he'd held me hostage, John showed me two tickets.

'Look, I've got some plane tickets for us to go to Madrid next week! We have a whole week there.'

I least expected this sudden gesture; it gave me no excitement or happiness. I was very reluctant to go with him, though I was not afraid; not thinking of how he had once gone abroad with Melissa, and then she had disappeared from her apartment. Instead, I thought it was a scheme to give the appearance of being good to me, in an attempt to fool me and others into thinking he was generous. But I was not easily fooled.

I discussed his plans with my colleagues.

'Well, I suppose you'd better go,' Sue said in the end, 'just to keep him quiet.'

I agreed; I didn't want to go, but neither did I want to antagonise him. We visited no sights of interest that I can remember, apart from passing them on the street. We did, however, take a train to the historic walled city of Toledo and spent the day there. Ultimately, it proved an uneventful trip. But there was no pleasure in it because I was with John.

When we returned, he continued his pretence, trying to create the illusion that everything was all right. Often, I asked when he was going to leave, but he just kept stalling, *all* the time. I tried everything to get him to go – being nice to him, getting angry, ignoring him, I stopped going out with him – but nothing worked.

I had no idea where to go for help. I was afraid to go to the police; I knew they would do nothing, my instinct told me so, and I had no confidence in the police. Even if they made John leave my flat, he would obviously come back for revenge and then I would be in worse trouble. Only if he were locked up would I be safe. Yet I knew the police would be unwilling to do that; nor were they likely to believe the serious danger I was in. And I *knew* that, if the system that was meant to protect me did not listen and take me completely seriously, I would be in the utmost danger. I was certain my life hung in the balance but I was on my own. I continued to work and carry on as best I could, under relentless strain. My life was filled with fear. One morning, while changing into my uniform in the staff room, I displayed my frustration with a bout of crying. The few others that knew my situation listened, but could do nothing to help me. Apart from those closest to me at work, no one else knew anything; I was too scared to tell anyone. I thought about running away, but was quite sure he would find me.

I was afraid of what might happen if he did.

Still, I kept asking him: 'You said you were going to leave, so when are you going?'

Finally, he declared: 'I might leave in December, or maybe January next year.'

On the surface, I had to content myself with that. Inside, I needed to plan. *What am I going to do? John will never leave, I know.*

I have to find some way of escaping him.

I considered methods to get away. One evening, I was cycling back to the flat from work. My attention had previously been drawn to a storage place that I passed on Goodge Street. This time, I stopped and went in. The price seemed reasonable; I needed only a small space for my few belongings. I pondered over how I might execute my escape.

Should I just leave the flat during the day, while he is at work? Gather only those possessions that really matter to me, leave everything else, and simply disappear?

Where would I go? Of course, I would not be able to stay in this country. I knew, wherever I went in the UK, John would be able to find me. He was so terribly cunning – and clever. I could take no chances; I would have to go abroad.

But where? To my mum and dad's house in the States? Instantly I realised: *No! I can't go there; he knows where they live.* I couldn't take the chance that he might come over there too, following me; and that he might kill them as well as me, and my brothers also. *I have to save them, I have to stay away.*

Spain? It was a possibility, especially because of my fluency in the language, but it wasn't that far away, and it was somewhere we had been together. He might think of it too.

What about Australia? This was the other option I knew I had. *That is far enough away; he has never been there.* I could go there for a while at least, to visit my friend in Sydney or my two aunts near Perth. *I would be safe there*, I thought, *until I figured out what to do.*

The aromatherapy course I had started earlier that year was not due to finish until the first week in January 1995, when I would take the exam. I had paid a lot of money for it and I wanted to finish it; I didn't want John to mess up everything that I had going for me. Sue had already told me that my job in outpatients would finish on

22 December, as they were recruiting a permanent member of staff. What with John's supposed 'answer' for when he would leave, and the dates of my job and my course, everything seemed to be pointing to the same timescale.

If I can just see it through until the end of the year, I thought; *if I can just finish these two things that matter to me . . . If I just let John go along with his game that everything is fine – keep quiet, say nothing – I hope I can get away with it until then. Then I will disappear.*

But still the situation preyed on my mind. I was taking a huge gamble in trying to hang on.

23

That summer of 1994, the weather was good. As I cycled to and from work each day, a journey of one hour, I often thought how the commute was probably helping to relieve some of the extreme stress I was under, preventing my mind and body from cracking up altogether. I had cycled many miles on my gold-coloured Claud Butler touring bicycle; I loved cycling and had cycled from London to Dover, taken the boat, and then cycled from Ostend to Amsterdam during one trip. I liked the freedom it offered, not having to wait for things, always able to transport myself away . . .

Of course, the one thing the bike couldn't help with was transporting me away from John Sweeney. Despite the minimal relief of that one-hour commute, as the weeks passed the stress of everything that had happened caused me to live in a state of constant nerves. My face was so tense it hurt, the facial muscles held tightly. The edges of my tongue were red and raw, with deep indentations from the way I was pressing my tongue so hard against my teeth. I had a perpetual feeling of butterflies in my stomach.

The pain in my face, around my cheeks and jaw was so bad that in the end I went to the doctor, looking for some kind of relief. If I was to hang on for the next six months, I could not fathom doing so in such unrelenting agony. He sent me to The Eastman Dental Hospital on Gray's Inn Road, where, as it happened, they were carrying out a study on facial pain.

My appointment was on Monday 13 June at 9.30am, but I left my flat at the usual time, so that John would be unsuspecting. I pretended I was cycling to work as usual, but instead went to Café Delancey in Camden Town until it was time to leave for my appointment. There I sat outside at a table at the front of the café, enjoying the sun, and drinking a cappuccino.

I was wearing a jacket I had bought in Camden Lock Market. I felt good in it: it had bright rainbow colours on the outside and a thin blue-and-white striped lining. A windbreaker, it seemed to me to be the sort of thing one might wear on a yacht, which gave me pleasure as it made me think of travelling. By that time, any small comfort made the world of difference to my living hell.

I closed my eyes and let the sun's rays warm my face as I finished my coffee. This innocent pastime was so relaxing, but it was something I never experienced anymore. I felt pleased with myself that John had no idea what I was up to.

At the Dental Hospital, I saw the dental consultant, with whom I immediately felt at ease. I was aware my facial pain was derived from no dental foundation, however, and as we discussed it, I found I could hold back my secret no longer and burst out crying. I narrated my experience of being tied to the bed during the spring bank holiday and John's threatening behaviour. She was understanding; of my ultimate dilemma, too.

'Well, you could go to the police,' she observed. 'They would probably get him to leave your flat, and give him an injunction to keep away. But that is only a piece of paper, often does not work, and will not stop him from doing something.'

'Yes, that's right,' I agreed, gratified she comprehended, 'and I *know* he will want revenge. I will be in *more* danger.'

I felt a slight relief that I had told her, even more so when she said she would arrange an appointment for me with their psychologist to see if she could offer any suggestions about how to deal with John. Finally, I thought there might be some hope.

While I waited for the psychologist appointment, life continued as I resided with a confessed killer. I ate but did not notice eating. My energy seemed to derive more from my highly tuned nervous state, rather than from food. At the same time, I felt exhausted. John, however, seemed true to form. He bought a refrigerator, and enthused to me about frozen orange-juice lollipops. I made no comment – it was best to keep quiet about everything.

One afternoon when we were both in the flat, John cut his finger. His face looked pale, as though he was going to faint. Although I had no feelings for him, I administered to the wound, telling him to sit on the edge of the bath. My first thought was that I didn't want blood dripping everywhere. My second: *Why does he react so badly about himself when he has drawn so much blood from another?* After all, he had chopped Melissa into bits; he'd told me so.

On Monday 25 July, at 9am, I attended my appointment with the psychologist at the Dental Hospital. Beforehand, I was anxious, thinking she might be my only hope of surviving this terrible ordeal. I didn't know if I had the ability to hang on until December; would she be able to help?

My name was called in what was perhaps a German accent. From the beginning, her serious and stern manner made me feel uncomfortable; the dental consultant had been much more approachable. I entered her office feeling absolutely desperate. It had been nearly three months since John had pressed his black gun to my head and told me he would kill me, and the pressure was unbearable. Words gushed from my mouth from the moment she led me into her office, and I could not focus on what I should say.

'My boyfriend, I am in danger from him. He swears at me. He says "fuck off". I can't get him to leave me—'

My distress showed so strongly; I was frantic. Yet she gave me a disapproving look, making me feel like some sort of unsavoury character, as if I had come to her under false pretences. I had been under the impression that she would have read my medical notes and would, therefore, have had an insight into my problems. But I was wrong: we had not even sat down, and already she was showing me to the door.

'That is enough. Please go now.'

'But didn't you read my notes? They told me that you might be able to help me know what to do about him.'

'No, I have not seen your notes, and I cannot do anything for you.'

I pleaded with her to hear me, but by then I was outside the door.

'What about my next appointment?' I asked in desperation.

'It will be sent to you.'

She closed the door promptly, allowing no further explanation.

I waited and waited, and worried when the appointment never arrived. In the end, I telephoned the dental consultant – but she now sounded rather cool and dismissive.

'There is no further appointment for you. This is a study for facial pain, and I am afraid you do not fit the criteria.'

My heart sank; I felt rejected, more vulnerable, and

even ashamed because it seemed I had wasted their time. It bothered me so much that I wrote to her to explain what had happened while I was with the psychologist, but I never received an answer.

What can I do? I thought frantically. *I'm on my own again. The only way I will be safe is if John is locked up. But the police won't put him inside.*

Then an idea: *What if I go to the doctors' practice? Maybe if I tell the doctor about John, I can get him sectioned. It might not work, but it is the only thing I can think of.*

My decision was instant; I made an urgent appointment for the same evening.

The general practitioner, who was perhaps in his mid-thirties, sat at his desk opposite me. Next to him sat someone younger: a new GP whom he was mentoring. I was asked if I'd mind him sitting in on the consultation.

'No, that's all right,' I said.

I had more immediate things on my mind anyway – but I felt embarrassed, and was unsure how to start. I smiled and became apologetic, hesitant in my explanation, wondering if the doctors would take me seriously.

'Well, look, you see . . . I'm having a bit of trouble . . .'

I paused, laughed nervously as if to lighten the situation, looked at each of them, and then said nothing. The doctor raised his eyebrows impatiently.

'Would you please tell me what is wrong? This is my last consultation, and then I must hurry to make a home visit. I haven't got time to wait.'

At this I felt like hiding under the table with humiliation and embarrassment. I felt stupid for not already having explained myself, the words stumbled from my mouth – but not necessarily what I had intended to say.

'It's my boyfriend, I'm having trouble with him. I'm in danger. In the spring, he tied me to the bed, and threatened me with a gun and my kitchen knife.'

A look of alarm crossed both their faces; their eyes widened, their mouths opened, aghast. They sat more upright. Before I could continue and ask for what I really hoped for – John's sectioning – the doctor intervened, urgent in his response.

'Here, take this, and go there immediately.'

He handed me a card and I was ushered out of his office. My heart sank. I had been given no opportunity to explain properly what I really wanted. *Why did I have to be the last patient; and he in such a hurry to leave?* I felt like everything was stacked against me.

Dejected, I left for the address shown on the card: the office of an organisation in Camden (now no longer in existence) called First Step. *What is this?* I wondered. *It must be a place for advice. Oh well, I'd better go and see what they have to say. If I don't, the doctor will think I'm not trying to do anything to help myself.*

Within a row of offices was an unsigned, frosted-glass door. Off-white vertical Venetian blinds hung over large glass windows to conceal the inside view.

When I rang the bell, a lady answered. In her late forties perhaps, she was conservatively dressed in a neat blouse and skirt teamed with polished high heels. She looked quite the part, but I was not swayed by her appearance. Somehow she did not seem to fit whatever role she was playing. In a way, I felt intimidated by her.

I feel like I'm being roped into something.

With a brisk attitude, she ushered me into a room full of desks, with phones on each as well as scattered paperwork.

'My doctor sent me here,' I explained. 'I told him I was having trouble with my boyfriend.'

Before I could enquire what purpose her organisation served, or outline the complexities of the life-or-death situation I was facing, she started making plans.

'You must leave your flat immediately,' she announced

brusquely. 'I will make some phone enquiries to see where you can go.'

'But that's no good!' I protested. 'He'll still be in my flat. I went to the doctor to try to have him sectioned, that's the only way I will be safe.'

'We have a solicitor here; I will speak to him about that.'

She disappeared into a small office, but soon returned. 'No, he cannot be sectioned,' she told me.

They refuse to take me seriously.

'The police will have to remove him from your flat,' she continued, with a sense of self-importance, 'and you will have to stay away from there, until further plans can be made.'

As I sat there, voiceless in the maelstrom of her brisk efficiency, she made more phone calls. My life was not my own. Everyone was planning it for me – John, this female ... I was not in control of my own destiny.

The lady busied herself with an air of satisfaction and eventually turned to me again. 'I have found a bed and breakfast in King's Cross for you, it was all that was available.'

'I don't want to go to a bed and breakfast in King's Cross,' I said angrily.

I just want to be safe. Going there is not going to stop John Sweeney – nothing *can stop him.*

But she hadn't finished. Her next words filled me with fury.

As though it didn't matter, as though it didn't put me in mortal danger, she added breezily: 'I have informed the police at Kentish Town police station.'

24

Oh no . . . I had managed, despite everything, to keep myself safe until now. Had this female blown everything with one ill-advised phone call? I was in danger, I knew it – and she had just made the situation ten times worse.

'Go there,' she persisted, 'and they will take you to your flat to collect a few belongings.'

I was astounded. 'But that's no good,' I told her bluntly, 'he will still be out there!'

She looked down her nose at me and spoke coldly: 'We don't want to be giving you get-well wishes if you end up in hospital, you must go.'

I frowned, but could say nothing: the damage had been done. A lump of irritation and frustration bore into my throat, and into my chest, as I made my way to the police station. *This is not what I wanted*, I thought. *This is no good. He will be in my flat, and he'll destroy everything . . . and then he'll find me, and he will destroy me too. I just know it. They can't see what serious danger I'm in – none of them. This isn't just plain domestic violence, this is a different extreme. The only way I will be safe is if he is locked away – and they are not going to do that.*

I was right: they didn't. A uniformed policeman and woman, and two plainclothes detectives, received me, asking for details. I sat in a drab, poky and dimly lit room to the right of the entrance and, as they all stood in front of me, I recounted how John had tied me to the bed in the spring. I told them about his sexual demands too. I did it all unwillingly, convinced I was putting myself in danger.

I'd gone out asking for help that day. As I gave my statement, I felt I was asking for trouble.

Afterwards, the plainclothes detectives escorted me to the flat. Two uniformed policemen accompanied us. As I knew he would be, John was at work.

'OK, find what you want . . . a change of clothing you can put in a bag,' they told me airily.

I looked around me in alarm, at all my belongings that John would destroy, before he found and destroyed me. A 'change of clothing'? What about work? I needed my uniforms, my shoes. I didn't want to leave my photo of my granny, nor the souvenirs from my travels. I didn't want this to be happening to me.

I was not having it: 'No, I don't want to go to King's Cross.'

The uniformed police were sent away. I had one last chance to make the plainclothes detectives appreciate what was really happening here. Before they could leave, I tried to highlight the seriousness of my case. Even as I did it, I was wondering how I dared.

'He killed his American girlfriend, Melissa,' I said urgently. 'He cut her body up, and threw her into the canal in Amsterdam.'

They merely scoffed. 'Oh, come on now, that's carrying it a bit far! He's just trying to scare you.'

Scare me . . . how could I convince them? I felt a horrible, twisted sensation of knowing I'd been right all along: *I* knew *they would not believe me.*

There was one last roll of the dice. 'Let me show you the drawings he has done!' I said in desperation. 'It will tell you a lot about him.'

They're as crazy as he is . . .

'You see that one on the wall,' I said urgently. 'That is one he did of himself.'

I pointed to John's portrait with the real hair for a beard, and the joint with the tinsel flame hanging out of his mouth. Both guffawed in amusement.

Why did I show them that one first? I thought in anguish. *Now they don't take me seriously. They won't even give me time to tell them that he drew it as a piss-take.*

Frantically, I knelt down and scrambled to open John's portfolio, which was lying in front of the low table. I had to be quick.

But it was too late: they had lost interest.

'Wait . . . Look . . . You have to see these.'

The first picture was that of the girl tied to the ground, the little men working on her. *It is all so apparent, if only they would look.* I pleaded with them, but they did not even glance. They joked with each other as they sauntered from the room.

The door closed behind them with a dull thud. *Alone again. Alone again, but left to live – or die – with a madman.*

I had reached the last resort. Nothing was working: not doctors, not refuges, not police. Now, I began to plead, to pray; but not to God – to whom, I was unsure. I simply whispered my words to the empty room, feeling helpless, always hoping and waiting for an answer.

'Please, whatever energy there is, whatever force . . . please, help me.'

25

After visiting First Step, I hid their card in my bicycle bag. At the first opportunity, I transferred it to my locker at work. I felt assured I had smuggled it out of the flat in time, but two days later, John confronted me.

'You have been to First Step,' he announced accusingly. 'I know what it is . . . and where. I found the card in your bicycle bag.'

He never misses anything, I thought wryly. He didn't blow up at me about it, but it didn't mean the damage hadn't been done. Now, he would be even more on edge: hoarding the information like treasure to use against me later, and becoming ever more vigilant in keeping track of my movements. I regretted that the 'authorities' had become involved. Already, it had got me into trouble. The only good thing was that John never found out about the police.

July became August. The sun was still strong every evening. On my commute home, I cycled past the sunbathers in Regent's Park and, once, I stopped to sunbathe too. The heat of the rays soothed my tense body; the smells of greenery uplifted me. I dozed in the peacefulness, and to the sounds of the twittering birds: a small escape from the turmoil in my life. *John need not know about this.* But, as I soon found out, I could no longer trust that, when I was alone, he wasn't watching.

On 3 August 1994, it was my birthday. It was another lovely hot evening as I cycled home from work. *It's my birthday*, I thought as my legs powered the pedals. *I know what I'm going to do. I'm going to the Stag for a drink, and I'll sit outside in the sun. This might be the last birthday I ever have; I want to enjoy something, at least. Surely I can get away with it; John won't know.*

While I basked in the sunshine, drinking my pint of real ale, 'Dad', John's former roommate from his old squat, arrived, and joined me at the table.

I sort of trusted Dad more than any of them. I needed to tell *someone* what was happening; I wondered what he might have to say about it all.

I was cautious. My gaze swept across to the park, and onto the street. *No one to be seen.* I crouched forward across the picnic table, and spoke in a hushed tone.

'Look, this is my birthday, and it could be my last,' I whispered urgently. 'John is dangerous, I have to get away from him somehow.'

'Aaah, Delia, you can't get away from him,' Dad replied. 'Look at Ian's girlfriend, he won't let her go. It's the same with John; he will never let you leave him.'

A swirl of anxiety ran through me at his words.

Yet there was worse to come. Back at the flat, John confronted me, accusation in his eyes: 'I saw you at the Stag, talking to Dad.' His words read deeper: *I've been watching you . . . I know where you've been . . .* But I had not seen him at the pub. Could I ever really know for sure now when he wasn't stalking me?

In the face of his confrontation, I replied: 'Yeah, well, it is my birthday, and it was nice and sunny, so I just thought I would go for a drink. Dad happened to turn up.'

I tried to appear light-hearted, unconcerned that John had seen me. Inside, my thoughts were in panic. *He never misses anything. How did he know I would be there? Does he go there anyway every day at this time? How am I supposed to escape in January if he is following me without my know-ledge?* It added urgency to my thoughts.

Consequently, I now reconsidered visiting First Step, especially in the light of John's heightened surveillance. Nothing else was working, what else could I do? Reluctantly, I retraced my steps to their office.

When the lady answered the bell this time, she blocked the entrance.

'Look,' I began, 'I have thought about your offer, and now I am wondering if you can help me. I wasn't ready then; it was so unexpected. It was a shock. I had to think about it.'

But her eyes were cold, her expression was hard, aloof.

'No, you have had your chance. You can go now.'

'But wait . . . !'

My eyebrows knitted together in a frown, my mouth ajar, as she closed the door in my face. *I can't believe this*, I thought desperately. *Is this really the right way to treat someone in my position? Give me only one chance, not give me any breathing space to think about whether it is wise or not, and then turn her back on me?* I had taken the 'first step', but it appeared she would not now help me to take another in my attempt to escape. Once again, I was left alone, feeling more abandoned to my fate than ever.

Living with John day in and day out was so stressful – and increasingly so, the more time passed. Though he wasn't directly threatening me, I knew only too well that he could snap at any moment. One day, for some reason, I experienced an impulse to get him to see himself for what he was.

He was flipping through the drawings in his portfolio – all images of sex and violence. *Why hadn't the police looked?* I thought in frustration as I saw the gruesome images. They were as strong as a confession: a visual journal of his inner thoughts. Over and over the Devil appeared, the numbers 666 a habitual refrain. These drawings were a portrayal of his nature and his mindset.

I blurted out my thoughts: 'If anyone saw your drawings, it would tell them an awful lot about you.'

As soon as I spoke, I wanted to snatch back my words. He looked up at me, blankly. Though he was quiet, and said nothing, I worried that I had now enlightened him.

In late August, my annual trip to Texas to see my parents loomed. John knew I had bought the ticket. It surprised me that he had not concocted some scheme to prevent me from going, but he was such a cunning person he knew not to. To anyone unaware of the truth, everything in our relationship would look normal. It would prove useful to him that I went alone. Surely, if he were not with me, I would be more likely to tell all. But he was so self-assured he knew I would say nothing to my parents – I dare not take the chance.

Yet it was an opportunity to get away from him for a little while. I would just try to block him from my mind as much as I could while there. But the day before I left, he requested casually: 'Give me the phone number of their house so I can talk to you when you are there.' Somehow, I had sensed already that any contact with him could cause even more trouble. So I lied and said I did not know their number, even though I knew, damn well, that it was written in my diary. He did not press the issue.

The following morning, he accompanied me, carrying my suitcase to the Underground station. I'd wanted to go alone, without him. On the Tube, he seated himself on the outside, next to me. *It's as though I belong to him – and he is unwilling to let me forget it; not until the very last minute, when he finally has to get off at his stop for work.* His presence felt domineering. We remained silent throughout the journey.

Upon my arrival in America, as John had known I said nothing to my family about what I was enduring. I was simply glad to be there, free from his constant menace.

But John had other plans.

One evening, when I returned from a day trip with my brother Stewart, my mother announced: 'John phoned to speak to you, but I told him you and Stewart had gone out for the day, so he said he would phone again tomorrow.'

I was alarmed. '*What!* How did he get the phone number? I didn't give him it.'

'He must have got it out of the phone book, then.'

'But you never put your number in the phone book.'

'Oh well, it's in there now.'

'Well, I don't want to speak to him anyway.'

I was seething inside. *Never before have they put their number in the phone book!*

But now, when it matters so much to me, they have done it.

The next day, Stewart and I returned from a second day out. My mum was watching TV in her wheelchair.

'John phoned again. I told him you didn't want to speak to him.'

'*What?!* You told him *that*? What did you say *that* for?'

'Well, that's what you said.'

I glared at her. *Why can't she keep her big mouth shut? She's always got to say the wrong things. She's stirring trouble for me, and she doesn't even know it.*

Yet I couldn't tell her or my dad anything, in case they made things worse. I couldn't risk getting them caught up in this; there was no telling what John might do.

The following week, Stewart and I returned in the evening. As soon as I opened the door, Mum announced: 'These flowers arrived today for you, from John.'

In front of the television was a lovely arrangement of flowers, with blue, purple and red petals.

'*Aaagh!*' I exclaimed in undertones, merely glancing at them, perturbed.

The next day, when Stewart and I returned from another outing, Mum reported: 'John phoned again today, I told him you didn't like the flowers.'

Nervous sparks tingled through my body. '*What?!* What did you say that for? I never said that.'

'Well, yesterday when you came in, you just walked past and ignored them, so I thought you didn't like them.'

That's really blown it, I thought desperately. For the past few months – outside of my private attempts to get help – I had just kept a low profile, hoping to make it to January, when I planned to run away. *Now I won't be able to go back and pretend to play the game that everything is fine!*

I was speechless with frustration and anger; not that there would have been any point in saying anything anyway. *John really knows how to do it*, I fumed. *Making me look bad in front of my mum and dad; making it look like he cares so much about me, and that I'm snubbing him. He knows they will fall for it, and will take sides with him, instead of me – even though they don't even like him.*

Mum and Dad saw only what they wanted to see; I had got myself mixed up with this 'character', he was living with me, and therefore I must take the consequences. No matter what they thought of him, any focus of disapproval was aimed towards me. Anything that ordinarily might be seen as rudeness was seen so regarding myself – as that is what they wanted to believe. They did not choose to consider that there might be underlying issues unknown to them.

John phoned again when Stewart and I were out late, informing my parents he would phone the next day. When my mother told me, I said: 'I'm not going to be here when he phones, I don't want to talk to him anyway.'

But at that point my dad intervened: 'Oh yes, you are.

You are going to be here to answer his phone call; I'm
not making excuses for you.'

Dad was stern; I was shocked. When Stewart then
phoned to say he'd soon be there to collect me, to take
me to Dallas Zoo as we'd planned, I told him: 'Dad said
that I can't go out because John is phoning today – but
I don't care, I'm going with you anyway.'

My dad insisted: 'Oh no you're not, you are going to
be here for that phone call!'

'No, I'm *not!*' I cried. I felt rage and injustice boiling
in my blood – and a little bit of truth slipped out. 'I can't
do anything without him stopping me . . .'

26

'Well,' my father replied, 'you got yourself into this, so you're going to have to put up with it.' His tone was sharp. I knew Mum and Dad cared not to have a clue what was going on, and they would not open their eyes to see even an inkling of it.

My heart sank. Even from across an ocean, John was trying to control me. He knew damn well that Stewart and I always went out on his days off. He'd been with us, himself, when we had done the same thing on previous visits. Cunning as ever, he knew he could use my parents' obstinacy against me – and that they would play the game.

Astounded, so angry and tormented, with my mouth wide open I almost swore. I stopped myself just in time. *He is my dad, I can't use such a word in front of my dad; they are both so respectable. I would never hear the end of it.*

Yet my throat was twisted into knots and I had to release the frustration and anger somehow. Instead of swearing, I burst out crying.

My father sat down pointedly in his armchair. He was unsympathetic: 'Boo hoo hoo, big baby!'

I ran past him and upstairs, howling wildly. Frantic, I pelted into the bathroom, closed the sliding door and remained there, distraught, for an hour.

Eventually, Mum called from downstairs; my sobs became whimpers. I tried to prevent the wooden door from rumbling as I slid it open; I wanted to be invisible.

My mother's voice carried up the stairs: 'Your dad says you can go to Dallas Zoo with Stewart, you don't have to wait for John's phone call.'

Stewart drove us there. I was fragile. A fine tremor lingered in my body, a pain in my chest, and waves of tears were welling in my eyes ... I was desperate for comfort. We ambled through the zoo in the heat and humidity. So soothing; I felt caressed by the warm air, surrounded by the large green tropical trees and plants. The animals helped me to feel closer to nature, and to innocence, away from the threats and danger I usually felt back in London.

'I'll take you back to my apartment,' Stewart announced when we were done. 'Stay there tonight, and I'll take you back to Mum and Dad's in the morning.'

I was so relieved. I didn't want to go back to our parents' house. It was a comfort to stay with Stewart after what had occurred that morning; I slept on a bed of sheets and blankets that he made for me on the living-room carpet. I felt less vulnerable, and it distanced me from my agony.

On Monday afternoon, by which time the previous events seemed to have settled, I was sitting on the deck of my parents' house taking the sun, absorbing the heat I loved so much – I was seldom warm in London, except on the hottest of days. It was peaceful, quiet; as usual. Only the birds chirped in the trees surrounding the house, a cow mooing as it grazed in the field across the country road. An occasional car passed.

I was concentrating, reading a clinical nursing article from one of the journals I had brought with me. During the past couple of years, I found I was always studying;

it was a way to block things out of my mind . . . all those awful things that plagued me. For even in America what had happened in May 1993 disturbed me. It was always there; that kind of experience doesn't leave you. There was no vacation for my mind.

Suddenly, the door opened behind me with a sense of urgency. With a start, I turned my head. My father's face was ashen grey, his expression troubled. A feeling of dread swept through me.

Oh no, now *what's wrong?*

'Delia, come in here. We want to speak to you.' His voice was stern.

My arms felt limp as I dropped my journal. I rose stiffly from my seat, my legs having difficulty carrying me. My feet felt as if they were stuck to the deck.

My mum sat in her wheelchair, a stiff look of disapproval on her face, her lips pursed: 'Sit down, Delia.'

I felt as though I was in a place of judgement. Ripples of anger stirred in my chest. I didn't want to sit down, but I obeyed. Mum waited as Dad took his seat. Then the interrogation began.

'Delia, John just phoned.'

A pause: their gaze upon me.

I waited, paralysed, sat on the edge of the chair and seething inside. *There I was sitting outside, and they didn't even bother to tell me, they just let me* sit *there while they talked to* him.

'Delia, John said there is something wrong with him, but he says there is something wrong with you, too. Is that right?'

'What? No.'

'He told us you have a drug problem. Is that true?'

'No!'

A grave look on my mother's face; her gaze fixed on me. Her next statement oozed disgust and shame.

'He told us that you have herpes, and that he caught it from you.'

'Well, if he did, that's his own fault.'

They looked at each other uncomfortably, shifting in their seats.

My father intervened, demanding an answer: 'Do you have herpes down below?'

I was mortified. *John has really put me in it.*

'Here! Here!' I shouted out. Frantically, I repeatedly hit my lip, where my cold sores bloomed, with the tip of my index finger.

What do they want to do? Whip me? Throw me out? I'm so disgusting!

Eventually, they got off my back.

'I told John to stop telling me all those awful things,' my mother said. 'I told him that I am ill, and that it's not good for me.'

In exasperation, I drew a heavy breath. *What did she tell him that for? Does she think he cares? All that's going to do is rile him even more. I can imagine him thinking – 'Does she really think she can sway me to feel sorry for her? How dare she?'*

'All right, you can go outside now, Delia,' my mum finally said.

I felt as if I had just been taken off the rack.

I obeyed their command, feeling humiliated, as though they had just deigned to give me mercy. Underneath, I was enraged, but dared not show it. *John knows how to play with their minds; he knew they would fall for it. Their first thought was not for me, but what John said. They are so frustrating.*

Back on the porch, I slumped into my chair, stunned.

Here I am, outside, studying . . . and I'm supposed to have a drug problem, and something wrong with me. I can't believe it. It's like something out of some crazy thing on TV, something that shouldn't really happen. But what kind of programme could it be? I know . . . a stupid soap opera.

Was there no end to John's depravity, to the reach of his power? He seemed able to pluck his fingers inside my mum and dad's brains – as though their heads were those in his spaghetti picture. Once inside, he simply played about to his heart's content.

As the days wore on, I tried to enjoy what little time I had left away from John. My brother Gerard had a water-skiing boat at that time and together we went out onto Lake Texoma, the sun blazing hot as we darted across the sparkling water. Later, I dropped over the edge of the boat and swam in it, my dancer's arms propelling me lithely, the fingers of each hand parting the water with precision. I relished the sensation, and the feel of my body as I used my strength to heave myself back onto the boat after my swim.

Towards the end of my vacation, Stewart and I took a day trip out to Arbuckle Mountains and Turner Falls in Oklahoma. It has picturesque scenery – hills and a river. As we walked over the rocks beside the flowing stream, I felt the need to disclose my secret. Stewart was the only one I could tell.

'Look,' I began. 'I have to tell you something, but don't tell Mum or Dad, or Gerard, or it will make things worse.'

I told him all about what had happened in May.

'He threatened me with a gun and my kitchen knife,' I confided. 'Then he told me about Melissa, his American girlfriend: how he killed her and two Germans, cut up their bodies, and threw them in the canal in Amsterdam.'

In detail, I told Stewart the whole story. He fidgeted nervously, in a state of shock; alarmed.

'What are you going to do?' he quavered, appearing helpless himself, beyond any suggestions. But I already knew: there *were* no suggestions that could save me. Worry permeated his expression; he was on the verge of tears.

'I don't know,' I admitted. 'I can't stay here; I haven't got the Green Card anymore. And you know what Mum and Dad are like; they might interfere and make things worse.'

'Yeah, I know.'

'I can't take the chance anyway . . .' I went on. I then expressed my very real fear: 'John might come over here to get me, and you never know, he might kill them too. I don't know how far he would go.'

We continued along the rocky path, the water from the river gurgling past, birds chirping as the sun shone down. Yet the peacefulness surrounding us was cut with an air of doom.

'Don't tell anybody, will you?' I added.

Stewart frowned, troubled. But: 'No, I won't,' he agreed.

The day of my return arrived: bright sunshine in direct contrast to my black mood. Dad and Gerard took me to Dallas Fort Worth Airport. My nerves were in turmoil during the whole seventy-mile drive there.

I want to scream out that I'm in danger. I want to tell them that I can't go back. But if I do, I'm afraid of what might happen then. I don't know what they would do; how they would handle it. It might make things worse.

And if John were to come over . . . ?

I have to sacrifice myself for them.

At the airport I was frantic with desperation, hoping they would somehow realise my precarious situation, but at the same time trying to hide my alarm. I thought: *I would like them to see it, to grasp the danger, to say – 'Don't go back.'*

'Do you think I should leave London?' I finally said, in agitation. 'Should I go to Australia and see my friend, Lynn? Maybe I could go to Mexico and stay there for a while?' In a roundabout way, I was trying to tell them the threat I was facing . . . but they never caught on.

'Oh well, it's up to you, Delia. I don't know what to say,' Dad answered.

Gerard simply shrugged. 'Do what you like, it's up to you.'

An agonising fear gripped me inside as I left them. *Should I go back?* My feet took me in the opposite direction from where I wanted to go.

Throughout the night's plane journey, I tried to block everything out. I watched the movies, and drank red wine all the way back. No sleep – I would feel like I had arrived there too soon, I wanted to 'enjoy' what time I had left of my journey; what safety and freedom I still possessed. Yet I was frantic with anxiety and fear all the way there.

Upon landing back in the UK, I felt flustered, a heavy headache boring through my brain and my stomach turning somersaults with wine and worry. I collected my luggage at Heathrow, then hung around the airport, afraid to leave, wondering what to do. On impulse, I bought another pair of 'wheels' from the luggage shop.

I might need these extra 'wheels' to carry more, if I take flight from the flat.

I dawdled, without purpose, before forcing myself to return on the Underground. The morning was bright and warm on my arrival in Camden. I stood frozen, helpless. Conflicted thoughts fought in my brain.

What am I going to do? I don't want to go back to the flat. Should I go to the police?

No, I can't go there, they won't do anything. It would cause trouble.

I'll go to a friend's house; maybe she can help.

So I phoned Kim, a friend. No answer. I walked to her house and knocked on her door. Still no answer.

I have no choice, I have to go back.

John was sitting on the cushion in the front room, swigging a can of beer; keeping guard.

As I entered, I immediately noticed that the portfolio containing his drawings was missing. *That's unusual, it's always with him. What does it mean?*

The police, even if they'd wanted to, had missed their chance to see the evidence.

I stood before John, waiting. I knew it was coming. Sure enough, the interrogation began.

Pointing to the new 'wheels', his eyes remained focused on me.

'Why have you got another one of them?'

I know he thinks I'm up to something, he misses nothing. I need an excuse.

'The other one is getting old, and so I just thought I might as well get another one.'

'Martine sent you a letter while you were away,' he went on. Obviously, he had opened it. 'And a pamphlet about domestic violence, with contact numbers for help.'

He paused, his eyes fixed on me, looking for my reaction.

'What have you been telling her?' he asked coolly.

'I didn't tell her anything.'

Why *did she send that?* I thought wretchedly. *I know she was trying to help, but that was such a risk . . . and now he thinks he's onto something.*

'What did you tell your parents about me?'

'I didn't tell them anything.'

'Your mother told me you didn't like the flowers I sent.'

I frowned. 'I didn't say *that*.'

John scowled; his words were caustic: 'She told me that she is *sick*.'

As I had anticipated, Mum's comment had riled him. He was annoyed that she had dared try to gain his sympathy.

Is it my fault she blurted that? I thought.

'Well, she *is* sick,' I simply said.

Why did she have to say that? I knew he would use it against me.

Wanting to get away, I told him: 'I'm going to sleep now, I feel awful. Don't bother me, I want to be left alone.'

In the bedroom, I lay down on the futon and shut my eyes, hoping not to be disturbed.

But I was back with John Sweeney now. Hope was redundant.

The door opened. He removed his clothes.

'I don't want sex,' I protested. 'I feel sick. I have a terrible headache, and my stomach feels awful.'

His weight fell on top of me, the pressure causing pain to my already queasy stomach. My head felt like it was going to burst yet I knew too well: John never took no for an answer.

27

After I returned from the States, in September 1994, things became really bizarre. I knew that my mother's words had got me into trouble. John became extremely possessive and jealous; his sense of reasoning was the completely opposite to reality. Apart from the obvious rows that invariably occurred, he found fault with what I did, questioned me and accused me of alleged transgressions where there was no fault.

Hoping to try to get into his head, I offered to give him a massage, as part of my continuing aromatherapy course. As my massage tutor said: 'Bare the body . . . bare the soul.' For a long time he refused, and I sensed a sort of fear or mistrust, but eventually, that same autumn, he agreed. I erected the folding massage table he had built in the living room, and he stretched out on it.

His height meant I had to take several steps to reach another part of his body, while trying to maintain my flow. Using my arms, hands and dextrous fingers, I pressed into the knots of his back and shoulders. At first, he was very tense, but then began to relax. I used lavender oil, which was intended to bring the mind and emotions under rational control, and ease inappropriate feelings of anger and hostility. I was still trying to hang on, to stay safe, in any way I could.

I offered to treat him several times afterwards, and he

acquiesced. On subsequent occasions, however, I did not enjoy it. In contrast to every other person I had ever massaged, I received a sense of emptiness or coldness from him; a feeling I can't quite describe. I rubbed his skin with cypress oil, which is said to help manipulative individuals relinquish their neurotic need for power; orange oil, to calm his mind; lemon, to lighten the spirit. Yet the relaxation John had previously taken seemed beyond him now.

I was using a side-to-side stroking movement on his neck, unsettled by this empty feeling emanating from him, when his neck muscles suddenly became very tense and rigid. I had the sensation that I had struck a nerve, and had touched something held deeply inside him – a grief, perhaps, that he could not let go of. A strong sensation of fear, and of being unable to cope, seemed to stem from him.

I became slightly agitated and impatient, for some reason. Though I asked him to relax, and continued stroking his neck, I sensed only pain and sadness. I thought: *Whatever it is he is holding inside, it seems neither one of us can help him with it.*

In my quasi-official role as his therapist, I brought it up with him. As I had done back in May, I suggested that he sought help. I advised him to see a doctor for his emotional needs – but he would not comply. He said no one could help him.

Unexpectedly, John then offered to massage me in return; I thought it better to consent, rather than risk antagonising him. I guess I felt no more vulnerable than usual, spread out before him on the table. The massage was adequate, but seemed somehow mechanical to me, devoid of the human sensitivity with which we normally touch others.

After we had finished, John suggested that instead of folding up the table we left it open all the time. Something made me desire not to, but I allowed it.

Each time I sat on a cushion, I had a creepy feeling as I stared at the forbidding wooden table. It stood there, in full view, as if waiting for something.

I imagine him standing in front of it, cutting something up . . .

We began going out for meals a lot more often than normal. Initially, I took this as another sign of John's act: he was supposedly giving me what I wanted, being good to me, but I knew I couldn't trust anything when it came to John. He'd also begun the practice of telling me he was going – 'This time for good' – and leaving me a set of keys as 'proof'. Yet he would always return soon after, with a new set cut. So many sets of keys . . . some worked well, some not. I was unable to keep track of them all, with no time or energy to sort them properly; John would only mix them up again anyway.

Sitting opposite him in the restaurants we now frequented, I chewed the food mechanically, not really tasting it, feeling uneasy and sensing something was wrong – beyond the usual anxiety. Yet I was unable to define quite why. One evening, we ate tender rabbit at the restaurant situated by the bridge going across Camden Lock Canal; since I had come back, John's extravagance had become increasingly excessive. I sat quietly, pretending to enjoy it; afraid of his wrath, not knowing what else to do.

At the conclusion of the meal, he threw a generous tip, far more than ever before, onto the small silver tray. I became suspicious, and a dreadful misgiving settled in my stomach.

I was anxious to find out if my suspicion was correct. Back at the flat, I frantically opened my unlocked green suitcase, which always rested at the bottom of the bed. I searched underneath the things I had gathered on my travels and felt for the plastic bag I had stashed secretly underneath.

It feels thinner.

Oh no!

When I pulled out the money that was left inside I was mortified. The cash my parents had sent me at Christmas, and for a few birthdays, was almost gone; around $800. I had been saving it for something special because it was from them. John had been dipping his paws into it, spending it frivolously on meals and giving waiters big tips. All those occasions when we had eaten out, he had been using their money, laughing at me and them the whole time.

I felt so guilty; that I had let my parents down. All my dad's hard-earned dollars ... *John has done this to spite me and to spite them.* I felt as though I had betrayed them. The only silver lining was that I wasn't reliant on the money to escape, but it was a bitter blow and I blamed myself.

I never deserved to have that money, I thought. *John has such guile; why did I not catch on long ago? I'm so stupid.*

Not long after, I was at work, changing to leave when an urgent thought flashed through my mind: *I must act quickly.*

I pushed hard on the pedals of my bicycle.

I hope I'm not too late.

Back home, I headed straight for my Indian embroidered purple-and-red passport bag, which I had bought in a bazaar in Jerusalem. It hung from its strap on the pipe of the boiler, above the corner of the bed.

I unzipped it, and breathed a sigh of relief: my passport was still inside.

I felt fortunate that, at work, I had my own small locker in the changing room and my own padlock. I had to be discreet. The following morning, I smuggled my passport out of the flat and left it in my locker.

A day or so passed.

'Where is your passport? What did you do with it?'

'Why? It's my passport. What does it have to do with you?'

John gave no answer.

He never misses a trick, he knew I was onto his game.

This time, I had won a bout – but still the game went on.

I believe it was in October when John chastised me for yet another supposed misdemeanour. He was in a foul temper one morning, shouting at me as I hurried to get ready for work; no matter how I tried, I consistently ran five minutes behind schedule.

'You're going to be late for work,' he told me, adding: 'It's that bread you eat.'

I liked to take care of my body and always ate whole-wheat bread for breakfast.

'Who do you think you are, telling me what to eat?' I exclaimed crossly. 'If I want to eat that bread, I will eat it; that is my business. You never cared if I was late for work before.'

I glared at him.

How dare he? He is even trying to control how my body works now.

I had finished my breakfast and went to collect my bicycle from the living room. I wheeled the bike through and went to open the front door. When I reached the front door of the flat, I saw John was in the kitchen.

John, it seemed, was not prepared to take my defiance that morning. I glanced along the corridor – and saw his face. It had contorted; he had changed. That evil, menacing look was back; his eyes penetrating and potent, as though capable of disintegrating me with a single stare.

He was snarling. I was glued to listen in disbelief – because the language he spoke was not of this world. I had a flair for languages; I had travelled – I should have been able to recognise it as coming from *somewhere* on this earth. But I did not; I'd never heard anything like it.

The words and language were such that I shuddered to hear them, as though a curse might enshroud me. The very tone, the very pitch, the very articulation seemed to emanate pure evil. *Is he speaking in tongues . . . tongues of the Devil?*

It sounded like it. His snarl was spitting; his delivery intense. Though I could not understand them, the words he said *were* words. There was meaning there – meaning I would never discover. As I stared, aghast, beside the front door, my hands occupied by my bicycle, his whole being contorted into a devilish, dangerous presence.

As though he was about to transform into the Devil himself . . .

28

I could remain transfixed to this sight no longer. Desperately, I flung the front door open. It did so inwardly, hiding my view along the corridor; hiding my view of him. I rushed out with my bicycle, and then out the main door and down the concrete steps. Throwing myself onto my bike at the bottom, I pedalled away, gasping, wondering what I'd just beheld.

I don't recall telling them at work. What could I have said? They would fathom as little as I. Maybe I was beyond words anyway. It was perhaps the worst I had ever seen John look, and bore a resemblance to the night we walked back to the hotel in Germany.

I dreaded my return, wondering what to expect.

But what else can I do? Where else can I go?

I crept into the flat with my bicycle, almost wishing I had none – in case I had to turn and run. As I closed the front door, I looked with dread along the corridor to the kitchen . . .

John was there.

He smiled, as though nothing was amiss; as though he was not the same man who had become a devil that morning and cursed me in an untranslatable tongue.

'I'm making dinner,' he announced inoffensively. 'I'm roasting a chicken for us tonight.'

I sighed, the breath coming out in a rush of relief. *Well, at least he is acting normal – for the time being, anyway.*

But who knew how long that would last?

One afternoon that autumn I returned to the flat to find that John had his green Barbour on.

'I'm going out now,' he announced.

A sense of relief swept through me. *My own space; a little peace.* It was unusual for him to leave me there alone, but I did not want to question it. His sexual demands had become increasingly voracious of late; I could not do the things he expected me to do and to be free of him was a relief.

'OK,' I replied. 'Well, I need to go to the toilet.'

I expected him gone, when I returned.

But he was not.

Nor was the green Barbour still in place. Instead John sat naked on the edge of the low bed, masturbating. He held his head level, his haunting eyes leering upwards at me.

I turned my back to him, a frail, abject being, and pleaded in a hushed, nervous whisper: 'Oh, John, don't do that.'

It hit my conscience with a huge blow: that I was involved in something I had never dreamed of; never realised was happening to me.

Something is very wrong that I should be here in this. How can this be? What am I in?

John sat behind me, yanking my right forearm, abhorrence in his grip. He meant business: he wanted sex.

He wanted sex, no matter what.

In that moment, as I stood there in the bedroom, a thought came into my mind as though I had been awakened; electrified into sudden realisation. For so long, I had believed his physical contact was because he cared about me, up until a point, in whatever twisted way. But, like a clap of thunder that jarred me, now came the horrendous truth. Suddenly, all the so obvious signs displayed themselves, as though I had been unaware of their existence before. No thought was required; it was crystal clear now in split seconds: I *knew*. I had been blind, my eyes wide open and unable to see. I had been fooled. *I have been used, yes – but more than used, something much worse*. I felt so ashamed of myself, for so long having believed his physical contact was because he cared about me; distraught that I had let myself down.

John grappled with my clothes; I heard my blouse tear. He had no interest in what I had to say. I resisted; he became rougher, more aggressive. He continued ripping at my clothes.

If he keeps doing this, I will have no clothes left. He will not stop.

It seems I have no choice.

I made a bitter request: 'Wait, if you are going to do this, let me take my clothes off. You are going to do this anyway, so I might as well still have my clothes left, or I will have nothing.'

Humiliation crawled through me while I stripped – corrupted.

His face was above me. 'This is the way it is going to be from now on, so you better get used to it.'

While he had sex, I lay motionless, a lump in my throat, silent, tears trickling down my cheeks. *There is something about me that has led me into this situation, this situation I thought I could never allow.*

I was numb; I had no feelings. The numbing was not a conscious effort. It happened without my awareness. There was no time for feelings anyway. All I could think about was 'the moment', 'the now', in order to survive. If emotions had infiltrated my mind, no doubt I would crack up.

The next day, John presented me with a bunch of flowers.

What is this?

And then I understood; I could see the pattern.

'What are you bringing me flowers for?' I asked in disgust. 'You make me have sex, and then you bring me flowers. I see what you are doing: every time you have sex, you bring me flowers. I like flowers, but I don't want flowers because you have had sex with me; especially when you are making me do it.' I told him straight: 'Don't give me flowers anymore, I don't want them.'

After that, he became more and more physically aggressive.

'I want sex now,' he would demand.

It was understood I had no choice in the matter.

He said it once just as I was changing the sheets on the bed. I'd removed the orange sleeping bag that cushioned the mattress, in order to shake and air them both, when John suddenly appeared from the front room. He was insistent.

'Wait a minute, then,' I said with no emotion, 'until I put the sheet back on. I'm not lying on a bare mattress.'

I flung on the dirty sheet, sensing I had scant time to do even that – forget the sleeping bag first. My insistence on this small comfort, it occurred to me later, had given me a minute amount of control over my situation.

Before John could tear my clothes off, or demand I remove them, I proceeded to strip. He watched, as I let my clothes drop to the floor in a pile.

I lay motionless, my body straight and my arms by my sides, staring up at the ceiling. He threw me around, rather like a rubber sex doll. I allowed my body and limbs to remain limp, flailing. Throughout, I remained silent.

He cursed me for not showing any response, and became rougher.

'Why don't you *do* something?'

Yet I remained flaccid: not a word, not a whimper, not any sound came from me. He continued to throw me around with increasing intensity.

That time, he did not return with any flowers.

29

Time and again that autumn, John forced me to respond to his lecherous impositions, assuring that I felt further defiled and disgusted in myself. What before I had allowed because I thought he cared about me now became agonising self-deprecation and shame.

What would my parents think of me if they knew – especially my mum?

After sex, John would scowl at me: 'You smell. You stink. You are so dirty.'

I knew that his intention was to disparage me, in order to enhance my sense of filth. But I would not allow myself to accept such an insult: John Sweeney could enter my body with force, but he was unable to influence my mind.

One night, I was tired after work when John demanded sex. This time, despite my exhaustion and previous bitter acquiescence, I thought: *I'm going to refuse. I don't care; I'm going to try. I am not going to let him think that I am just going to let him have it, just like that.*

He lay on top of me; I resisted.

'*No!* I don't *want* sex! I don't want you to do that to me, get away from me.'

John suddenly slapped his palm over my nose and mouth, his left hand grasping me at the shoulder and holding me still. I could not breathe. My mouth moved involuntarily against the closed pressure of his fingers;

I was gasping for breath. I felt as if my face could burst like an over-inflated balloon.

'Don't scream,' he told me.

Scream? I am trying to breathe! How can I scream anyway? I'm being suffocated!

His hand pressure increased. My teeth were digging into my gums. My jaw and mouth moved again; not a conscious effort of mine to do so, but through necessity, fighting for breath by any means.

'*Don't scream.*'

He sounded even more threatening. The pressure of his palm was firmer still, my teeth digging yet more painfully into my gums.

I can't last much longer . . .

Abruptly, he released his hold over my nose and mouth. I gasped for air, breathing heavily, rapidly, gulping it in.

John watched for a moment, holding my wrists down at the sides of my head, about to have sex.

I looked up at him, and into his eyes. I remembered the lies, all the times he had said he loved me, which I had long ceased to believe; if I ever really *did* believe. Bitterness rattled me.

'*You* don't love *me.*'

My hands began to tingle, due to his tight grasp over my wrists. His face, scowling above mine, contorted. The furrow above his eyebrows deepened, his teeth bared – his mind preoccupied with what he was about to do.

'I do. I do,' he sputtered, glaring in my eyes. He said the words quickly, almost spitting them at me, as though I was wasting his time. It was just a matter of impatience. He was trying to shut me up, to stop me interrupting, so he could get on with his sexual deed without my irritating intrusion.

'No, you don't,' I insisted.

'I *do.*'

He thrust himself upon me, savagely.

He did so time and again. There was nothing I could do to stop him. On another occasion, John was attempting to have sex while I was adamant I wanted him nowhere near me. He grabbed my arms and pushed them above my head. Then, unexpectedly, I felt cold metal against my wrists. I looked above me to see handcuffs attached to the bedframe by a length of chain. As he had done before with the rope, back in May, John had planned ahead and had the tools there ready to bind me.

He threatened, 'This time it's going to be metal.'

'No!'

He secured my wrists; I struggled. Pointless. I lacked enough strength to release myself.

'I will let you loose,' he told me, 'but you have to have sex with me.'

It was no kind of freedom at all.

Once I was released, he threw me around the bed. I let my body flop otherwise I would have had broken bones. He spread-eagled my legs with purpose.

I can't let myself go completely – but I can't be too strong either. If I hold myself too tight, he will dislocate my hips. But if I let go, he may dislocate them anyway. I have to work it out, so he won't damage me. I must gauge how much to hold myself either way.

John's attentions were ever more aggressive.

Later that same day, we went to Camden Lock Market. He carried the handcuffs with him in an empty tobacco pouch.

'Give me the handcuffs,' I demanded. 'I want to get rid of them.'

I didn't like the idea that he had them; that he could keep me captive at any moment.

I was surprised when he actually handed them over – but then, anything was possible; he always had another scheme.

Quickly, I ran down to the canal with the handcuffs, leaving John on the street, waiting. An acquaintance of mine from the aromatherapy course had a stall nearby, which backed onto Dingwalls restaurant. It faced onto the path just before the railings, in front of the edge of the canal.

A sudden thought: *This is my chance to give someone some proof.* I raced towards my friend frantically and displayed the handcuffs.

'Look, Maura! See these handcuffs, he used them on me. I just want you to see, so you know. I can't wait, I'm going to get rid of them.'

She had no time to respond to my abrupt and strange appearance. I rushed off, running around the railings to the water's edge. John had already known my intentions, and I wondered if he would allow me to get away with it. I hurled the handcuffs into the canal. They sank beneath the surface: another secret now submerged.

Two teenage boys watched me do it and commented, disapprovingly: 'You shouldn't be throwing things into the canal.'

Of all times, it would have to be two respectable types, not the usual kind who would not give a damn . . .

I turned to face them. 'It's not something I would usually do, but I have no choice.' I added hastily: '*It's a matter of life and death.*'

It sounded melodramatic, but I knew there was truth in what I said. They were left wondering as I hurried away – back to John.

Two weeks later, I was making the bed. As I stripped the sheets, I found my stockings and suspender belt under John's pillow, while under the mattress, between the wooden slabs of the bed's base, was another set of handcuffs.

I confronted him. 'You have another pair of handcuffs

under the bed! And what are you doing with my stockings and suspender belt under your pillow?'

He scowled. 'You should have gone for a bath, and I would have taken them away without you knowing.'

I went for a bath as I had intended to do anyway. When I returned, the handcuffs had gone.

But where? And for how long?

On Friday 4 November 1994, John made a new demand: 'Give me £500, I need it to leave.'

Over the previous few weeks, he'd been speaking about going to Germany again. I half-listened, wishing such a departure would materialise.

His demand was a new development; John had not asked me for money before.

If I refuse to give him it, he may do something. Yet, if I do hand it over, he will treat it as an insult, as though I'm paying him off to get rid of him. He has me snared.

Reluctantly, I handed over the cash.

'So when are you going?' I asked yet again.

'I'm going on Saturday.'

Saturday 5 November arrived, and John got ready to go to the pub.

'You said you were going to leave for Germany today,' I pressurised him.

'No, I'll go tomorrow . . . or maybe it will be Monday.'

Will he really?

Sunday came; as I expected, John got dressed and made no attempt to pack his few things. We went to the pub, instead.

His words are empty, he is not really going.

On Monday, I returned from work, expecting to find John there. But the rooms were quiet; his belongings gone. He had left the latest set of keys.

But what does that really *mean?*

The only sign of his presence lay in front of the low

table on the floor in the living room: it was junk mail, open for immediate attention, the words standing out prominently: a pamphlet advertising something for people who were getting old. It was a deliberate stab, aimed at my preoccupation with age.

John has left it there to get at me. He knows how much it bothers me. He misses no opportunity to hurt me, and he knows how to do it well.

In the bedroom, the pink silk pincushion he had given me so long ago still hung on the doorknob of the wardrobe. But it had been turned around, to conceal the words *'Ich liebe dich'* from view. Out of spite I flicked it around to show them once again.

All week, I was wary. *Did John really leave for Germany?* Somehow, I sensed his presence still lurking, somewhere not far away, in London. Nevertheless, I made adjustments as though he might have gone. Recently I had stopped using the nicer of two hand towels that Mum had given me — I had been leaving out the towel with the hole in it instead. Now, I took the risk of placing the best one in the bathroom, hoping he would not return.

I wrote a short letter to Martine, telling her John had left, but only that. She still did not know what had happened in May, or since, and I wanted to avoid scaring her.

Each night when I returned from work, I noticed the pincushion had turned around, back onto its plain side. I was confused. *Am I sure I have not done that myself by mistake? Or is my mind playing tricks on me?* I shivered, then flipped it back.

With John *seemingly* gone at last – not returning within a day as he usually did – I pondered my whole situation. *He is out of the flat; how can I keep him out?* I arranged for a council workman to change the lock to the flat door on Thursday 10 November. He gave me the new key; one John Sweeney did not have.

I considered having the main door lock changed too, but it was too complicated because of the neighbours in the house. Time was crucial; John was probably already in possession of his latest set of keys.

At least he can only let himself into the house now, and not the flat.

I had to take my chances.

The next day, Friday, I rose at 6am, ate my breakfast of wholewheat toast and boiled egg, and left at 6.30. *Anything can still happen*, I thought anxiously, *but at least John will be unable to enter the flat*. I gave no thought to what his reaction might be to my changing the locks, if or when he came back – I was living from minute to minute, simply struggling to survive.

That evening, I returned from work between 5 and 6pm after cycling the usual hour. As was my habit, I first left my bike by the brick wall while I walked up the concrete steps to open the front door; then retraced my steps and pushed the bike up and into the house.

I was hesitant as I entered; hesitance had become even more of a ritual that past week. I was hesitant, too, as I unlocked the flat door, twisting the key cautiously, as though I might ignite it. After closing the door, I quickly looked towards the kitchen. I scanned the bedroom; the living room. *Nothing.* My breath held; I could not be sure yet. My surveillance continued into the extension at the back.

Fearing I might provoke something, I crept along the short corridor and into the kitchen. At the far end, the bathroom door suddenly flung inward. John burst into the kitchen, glowering.

I did not have time to think. Instead, instinctively, I opened my mouth and screamed.

171

30

He lunged for me, plunging me stealthily downwards. Unable to control it, I wet myself. I knew screaming would antagonise him even more, so I instantly stopped.

'What did you do that for?' he growled.

'Whaaat?'

I knew perfectly well he meant changing the locks.

Thoughts flashed through my mind. *What an odd and absurd position to be in, lying on the floor, looking towards the kitchen cupboards.*

I was lying on my side on the floor, a particular drawer behind me.

Oh no, the kitchen knives are in here . . .

This could be it.

There was no time to anticipate his next action. John thrust his fingers into my mouth. He dug. 'Are you going to stop screaming?' he snarled.

Although he knew I had already stopped screaming, he thought he would ask again just for the hell of it.

His fingers still in my mouth, I uttered the only response I could make, and gave a slight nod.

'Uhhh . . . huuh.'

The pain was excruciating. He dug twice again, more deeply each time.

'Uhhh . . . huuh.'

It was like having a horrific throat operation without anaesthetic.

John removed his fingers from my mouth, and raised his hand. His fingers were covered in blood; he was furious.

'You've bitten my fingers.'

My head was turned to the right. I felt something smooth, warm and semi-solid sliding inside my mouth. I opened it. Three or four large thick clots of blood, about the size of a dessert spoon, spilled out onto the floor: it was my blood, not his, I knew.

The pain was extreme when I tried to whisper; the blood gurgled in my mouth.

'You have damaged me inside.'

'I was trying to pull your tongue out.'

He rushed to the bathroom, and grabbed the hand towel my mum had given me. On his return he used my mother's towel to wipe up the blood clots, then wetted it to remove the rest of the stain. I was dismayed.

Why couldn't it have been the old one I put out, rather than the good one my mum had given me?

John shoved the bloodstained towel into a plastic bag and dumped it somewhere in the bathroom. Aggressively, he yanked me up by the wrist and dragged me through to the living room. There, he pulled me down beside him, our backs against the wall, onto the two large cushions. No one would see us, through the bay windows, sitting here.

'You, you are so mean,' he chastised me. 'You couldn't even buy some milk for a cup of tea.'

I thought how exhausted I was: trying to work, trying to keep myself together, always wondering how close he might be. Afraid to be out, or to go out to buy milk – or do *anything* – lest he should appear: this 'guest' for whom I had no milk.

He reprimanded me for having a new lock fitted.

'I got in through the main front door; the neighbour let me in. I saw that you'd had the lock changed on the flat door, so I left and went around the back. I climbed in from there.'

'But how did you get in there, it's so high above the ground?'

'I used the old ladder that was in the garden, and climbed in through the toilet window. I've been sitting in the bathroom all day waiting for you.'

I had left the small window slightly open on its catch. Although it was on the narrowest gap, it was not fool-proof; anyone could have lifted the catch from the outside and still squeezed in.

Why did I leave that window open? I berated myself. I'd *known* that old ladder had been there, and that it was long enough to reach the window.

Yet John continued: 'It wouldn't have mattered if I couldn't get in, I would have waited outside, and you wouldn't see me. I would have waited for you to get back from work. Then, after you left your bike at the bottom of the steps, to open the front door, and then went back to carry it up; *that's* when I would get you.'

By now, he was becoming bored with our little 'chat'.

'I want sex; we might as well get it over and done with. This will be the last time.'

He dragged me through to the bedroom and had sex, twice. My throat hurt; I felt weak. He was not interested.

Afterwards, I was desperate to get out of the flat and away from him, but I knew there was no chance. I was so scared of what he might do to me if I tried. He watched me all the time.

'I need to use the toilet,' I said.

'All right, go then.'

He followed me to the bathroom, stood at the toilet door, and watched.

That night, in bed, he *appeared* to have fallen asleep. While I lay next to him, I thought how I would like to try to escape. I looked at him, then at the flat door; its noisy metal chain was latched. It was only a few metres distant, but such an attempt seemed futile. I had no way of knowing how deeply asleep he was and was far too scared to move; I might disturb him. If he caught me, who knew what he might do?

I lay, hardly moving, and slept little, fitfully, my throat so sore. Every swallow required concentration. I tried to manoeuvre what felt like a rigid lump of thorns, the size of a golf ball, slowly down my throat. It was so exhausting, I gave up trying most of the time. The saliva dribbled from my mouth and down the side of my face, onto the pillow, until it was wet against my neck.

On Saturday morning, 12 November, John sat on the cushion, watching me lying in bed through the door of the adjoining room.

'I'm making some tea, do you want some?' he called out, as though everything was normal.

'No,' I whispered with difficulty. 'I can't swallow, my throat is too sore.'

He soon returned, holding his teacup. Bemused, I watched as he sauntered back into the front room. My ashen-grey, silky suspender belt, trimmed with lace, dangled from the back pocket of his jeans.

I lay in bed until late morning, feeling terribly ill and weak; my throat painful.

I would like to have a bath, I thought. *Dare I ask him?*

'When we were in the kitchen,' I began, 'because of you, I wet myself. I want to have a bath, let me have a bath . . .'

I held my breath. *Would he allow me such a privilege; the only chance of comfort or normality I could think to find?* I tried to hide my desire, in case he should deny it me to punish me even more.

'OK.'

I sighed inside, trying to conceal my relief.

In the bathroom, I soaked, attempting to soothe my aching body and my tense mind; somewhat, at least . . .

Clack! Startled – my body jumped, sending splashes of water around me – I heard the bathroom door fly open behind me. He had been keeping guard, sitting outside the door on the stool he had made.

'Just checking, you were too quiet. Making sure you are not trying to escape.'

I seethed when he opened the door to see what I was doing.

Escape. How? Even if I did try, the only way I could do it is by climbing out of the bathroom window. If I do that, I will have to jump and I will die anyway; the window is well above ground level at the back of the house.

After the bath, we sat on the cushions near the wall for a couple of hours as John smoked. He had taken the small pipe I had bought as a souvenir in the flea market in Amsterdam. Normally he smoked his hash in a joint, now he was smoking it neat from my pipe.

I'm glad he is smoking, I thought. *Maybe the 'dope' will subdue him . . . act as a sort of valium.*

Many times I pleaded with him to leave.

'I will, I'll go later,' he repeatedly replied.

His annoyance increased as time went by. 'I didn't want to spend the day here,' he said crossly.

Somehow, it was my fault, and therefore he had no choice but to stay.

'Neither did I,' I retorted.

His next words I found hurtful and demeaning: 'I didn't want to be farting around with you all day.'

So that is how you feel about me? And yet you spent the last few years with me in this flat.

Over time, John became macabre: 'If I had a syringe, how much air would I need in it to kill myself?'

'I don't know.'

His manner was matter-of-fact – 'I am thinking about killing myself. Do you want me to kill you too?'

I made no attempt to hide my indignation at such a suggestion: 'No, I don't.'

'I might as well; I'd only get three years for doing this to you, so I might as well kill you and get fifteen years, and then they'll let me out.'

Several times he asked me: 'What are you going to do when this is over?'

Over? Would it ever be over?

I was beyond thinking what I was going to do; I could only think about the moment.

Why is he asking me anyway? I wondered. *If he has his way, whatever that might be, will I ever be able to do anything ever again? Maybe he is asking me to give the false impression he will release me.*

Knowing how his mind worked, I realised he would then use that assumption against me: how *dare* I think I could do anything after this; who did I think I was?

The phone rang several times during the day, but I was not allowed to answer it. I knew better than to even try – I was afraid to make any wrong move, in case he snapped.

I was extremely thirsty, as though drying up inside, but too scared to drink anything. The pain in my throat was relentless, and swallowing so difficult – I was unable to know what damage he'd done.

I had not eaten or drunk anything since Friday; the last drink I'd had was a coffee on my morning break at work. I knew there was no food or milk in the house, yet I needed liquid; some kind of nourishment. There was only Miso in the refrigerator. At some point that afternoon, I mixed it into boiling water. I sipped the cooled Miso, concentrating on how I swallowed, aware of every pain.

*

I remained hostage until early evening. John's temper alternated from being angry with me and calling me names to being nice.

'Look, if you go for a drink with me, it will make it easier for me to leave you, and I won't come back, I promise.'

'No, I don't want to go.'

I want to be nowhere near him. Anyway, if I go with him, he will use that, I thought. *He will make out that I do want to be in his company; that everything is normal between us. People will be unaware I'm being held hostage.*

No one will suspect, if I go missing soon after, it will be at his hands.

John persisted.

I thought about it – *It is the only way to get him out of the flat.* I would at least feel safer out in the open with people around me; people who were normal. Even if it was only for a short time.

'OK, I'll go,' I agreed. 'But I *don't* want you back here.'

By asserting myself, maybe there was a slim chance he would take notice – though my doubts were high.

'By the way,' John said, as we prepared to leave for the pub, 'my bag is hidden under the bath behind the bath panel. I wanted to freak you out. I was going to take the fridge and some of your clothes, but it all went wrong because you changed the door lock.'

He went to the bathroom, unscrewed the panel on the side of the bath, and pulled out his large green canvas bag and his red workman's trolley. Just before we left the flat, he warned me about something else.

'Now, don't be scared. I have a hammer and another tool hidden in the electricity cupboard above the house door. I'm going to get them from the cupboard and put them in my bag.'

I was inquisitive. 'What are they in there for?'

'I put them in there,' John explained, 'in case I had to break into your flat.'

'But that's stupid, everyone would have heard the noise.'

'Yes, I didn't think I would do that anyway, because it would have made too much noise, and you would have seen the damage as soon as you got in anyway.'

He reached up to the electricity box, removed a hammer and another tool, and placed them discreetly in his big green bag.

At the pub, we sat outside at the picnic tables, just as we always had; as though nothing untoward had happened.

John went in to buy the drinks, and left me sitting outside at the table. Here was my opportunity to escape, it would be surmised, but I thought better of trying it.

He is too quick for me.

I know John would hardly have left me outside on my own had he believed there was the slightest possibility of my escape. To try it would undoubtedly incite much further danger.

Upon his return, John drank some beer; rolled a joint. No sooner had he settled himself than he began to go on about coming back to the flat.

'Look, I won't bother you; I'll sleep on the cushions in the front room.'

'No.'

'I promise I'll leave you alone after that.'

'No.'

'Just let me stay one more night.'

'No, I don't want you there.'

His words were hollow. Although I insisted 'no', my wishes, of course, went forever unheeded. He pleased himself and did what he liked anyway; that had always been his way.

My only moments of peace were when he went in to buy another pint, for all the time he sat at the table, John continued pleading. I would have nothing of it yet I knew he would eventually insist – one way or the other.

What are my chances? Is there any way out?
I was afraid to think.
Most likely I will end up hostage in my own flat again, I realised. *What will happen then?*

It was the weekend; no hospital would be calling to find me and in so doing disturb his plans. He had the hammer, his saw, his fists and fingers . . .

What can I do? I thought desperately. *How can I get rid of him?*

One thing was certain: I did not want him back in the flat with me.

If I have one at all, I realised, *my only chance is out here in the open.*

31

Closing time.

'I need to go inside the pub to use the toilet,' I told John. I held my breath.

Will he allow me?

'Go on then, I'll wait outside here for you.'

When I came out from the Ladies' and into the bar area, I stood, surrounded by laughing, chatting people. I dared not go outside, despite knowing John would be angry. This was my only chance, here with people, away from him, but I was at a loss what to do, so I simply stood.

An eternity seemed to pass, but it was only a matter of a few moments while I wondered what to do, or if I could do anything. I was caught between comparative freedom and safety, and an utmost grave and dangerous situation.

John appeared. With large green canvas bag and trolley in hand, he looked down at me sternly.

'Are we going?' he demanded with a deep gravity in his voice, and with a sense that I had no right to choose otherwise.

'Look, I don't want you back at the flat. You said you would leave, so leave.'

A threatening scowl flashed over his face, his mouth twisting, teeth bared, and his eyes bore into me. It was an intense, fleeting expression; something he would want no one else to see. Abruptly, he turned and walked out.

The pub started to empty, but still I remained. The barman told me it was closing time and time to leave. For the first time in front of people, I began to cry. In John's presence, I never allowed myself to cry; I wished to deny him the satisfaction of knowing that he controlled me. To cry in front of other people while he watched was not an option either.

The barman knew me from having drunk so long at the pub; and he knew John to talk to as a customer. A puzzled expression was on his face.

'What's wrong?'

'Look, I can't go outside. John is out there, and there is another side to him you don't know about. I'm in danger.'

I was unsure if he would believe me – he knew John to be an easy-going guy who never caused any trouble. I was relieved when he seemed to take me seriously.

'I'll go outside and see if he is still there.'

Soon, he returned.

'It's all right now; he's not there, so you can go now.'

'It's no good; he'll be hiding somewhere, waiting for me. I know what he's like. I can't go out.'

And so he went behind the bar to get the pub manager's son to phone the police. When he returned, his answer made my heart sink.

'We phoned the police, but they said they will not come to the pub, they are too busy. They said you would have to go and find the police yourself.'

'But I can't do that. He'll be outside somewhere hiding, waiting for me. I won't have a chance to get any police.'

'I'll walk down to Chalk Farm Road with you. Then go to Camden High Street, where it is busy. Wait until you see some police there.'

Together, we walked the short distance to the end of the road from the pub.

'Look, you only know one side of John; you only see the nice side,' I explained. 'There is another side to him; he is not what you think. He is dangerous. He stuck his fingers into my throat and damaged it; and he has had me hostage ever since Friday. He only let us out today because he wanted a drink.'

I hurried along Chalk Farm Road, and crossed to the other side. Then I stood at the corner near Park Road and Camden High Street, in front of Barclays Bank. People were everywhere, out to have a good time; the atmosphere was filled with a buzz of excitement. I had never seen it before; never been out this late.

For one hour, I scanned the crowd for sight of the police: not one to be seen. By now, it was midnight.

The later I wait, the more danger I may be in. There will be fewer people out on the street near Leighton Grove. It will probably be deserted; if he finds me, I know I will be lost.

I considered taking a different route, the long way round, but I would arrive much later. Still, I knew I had to leave; had to take the gamble following the usual path. I ducked and dived behind doors, and through shadows. With my back towards walls, I peered around corners and darted across more well-lit areas, to avoid being seen first.

Kentish Town police station was on the way back.

At least I have got this far. I am reluctant to involve the police, but I have no choice now. They may do little to keep John away from me, even if I do tell them what he has done to my throat. Though I know it could make things worse, I can see no other option.

Behind the front desk stood a policeman.

'I need help,' I told him. 'I am in danger from my boyfriend. I need to get back to my flat on Leighton Grove, but I can't take the risk on my own.'

'There is no one available,' he said bluntly. 'We have more important things to do. You will have to find your own way back.'

'But I am not safe!'

He looked at me with contempt and made no response. I glared at him, and with a hard feeling in my chest turned my back on him and walked out the door, and then down the few steps. I was astounded at his answer, and his treatment of me. Was it the way I was dressed? My pillbox hat from India? My Mexican top? Is that why he did not take me seriously?

Or was it bècause I was female?

Bewildered, I stood motionless, as if stuck to the ground: hopeless. *No, I can't do this*, I thought. *I know what is going to happen.* I re-entered the police station, took a firm stance, and made a sharp demand: 'Can you give me the phone number of someone who might be able to help me?'

His scornful look complemented his grumbling tone of voice: 'Just a minute, I'll go and get someone to take you there.'

The two policemen he summoned looked put out. They ordered me to sit in the back of a white police van. I had expected to be accompanied by only one, and that he would escort me by walking back. Now I felt even more of an encumbrance.

The policeman in the passenger seat shouted back at me: 'This is Saturday night, we haven't got time for this kind of thing; we're busy.'

At this I cringed and clasped my hands. I felt small, such a nuisance, and the police treated me like I was stupid. They were busy; I didn't matter. I felt so vulnerable that this time I thought I might crack: the police were my enemies too.

I fumbled with one set of keys I'd now acquired thanks to John, trying to unlock the door. My hand trembled with fear; my frustration and anxiety increased. The policemen's impatience caused me to fumble even more.

I whispered: 'I'm having trouble opening the door because he had so many keys cut, and I don't know which the best ones are.'

'Why are you whispering?' one of them shouted.

'Because I'm paranoid.'

Actually, I had used the wrong word: I was not paranoid, but terrified. His loud outburst had helped me to say the wrong thing. There was every chance John was lurking nearby, and would hear.

Finally the door opened, and the police searched the flat: 'You see, no one is here so you can lock your door now.' They made an abrupt departure.

I had expected them to look up both flights of stairs leading to the neighbours' flats, and, most importantly, to look outside the window, onto the roof extension of the kitchen and bathroom, where John might well be hiding. It was the most obvious thing to do.

I felt such a nuisance, I dared not ask them. Besides, I should not need to tell the police how to do their own job. I had to satisfy myself with the fact that I was inside the flat, and might now be safe – at least until tomorrow. I put the chain on the door, making as little noise as possible, although it was a bit too late for that.

My throat was still sore and I slept fitfully. *The bedroom is so close to the outside door and stairs, I'm certain to hear anyone coming in during the night.* I knew, already, that it was unlikely the upstairs neighbours would come in; they were never so late.

No one came through that door that night.

On Sunday 13 November Martine phoned in the morning, having received my letter. I made no requests of her – I wished to avoid her becoming involved in something awful, and for that to be my responsibility.

'He's gone, Martine,' I said. 'He's taken all his things with him, but I don't think he will be very far away. He told me he was going to Germany, but I know he is still lurking around somewhere nearby, without doubt.'

'Look, I won't come to your flat,' she replied, 'but I'll meet you at the Bull & Gate pub on Kentish Town Road at 2pm.'

'OK, that's a good idea, the best thing to do. I'll see you then.'

It was a relief she had agreed to meet me; I needed so much to see her. Even though I knew it was a bad idea, I wished she had said she would come to the flat: the idea of walking out of it alone terrified me.

As the time approached, my apprehension increased. I tried to prepare myself for any eventuality. The worst could happen.

If I open the door, he might be there, and then I will be hostage again. What should I do? Should I climb out the front window, so I don't have to go through the door?

But that's no good. If I do that, he will get back in that way; and he will get me when I come back.

What should I do?

It was almost 2pm. After putting on my light-brown leather jacket, I stood with my ear against the door. That was futile, of course; I would hear nothing.

The chain was still on its catch. Making the least possible noise, I opened the door and listened, then peeked through the narrow crack. It was impossible to see anything.

On the brink of exiting, I hesitated.

Well, here goes. I am free in a way right now, but this could change everything again.

I shut the door, and released the chain from its catch.

32

As I opened it, I held the door firmly, in case I needed to push it shut. But if I had to do so, it would hardly be likely I would manage it in the face of John's power and determination, should he be there . . .

Already visible through the crack of the door was the green colour of his Barbour coat. With all my strength, I tried to shove the door against his push.

He was too quick, too strong.

'Go away, get out of here, leave me alone, I don't want you here!' I broadcast for all to hear.

He stuck his finger down my throat, but this time I continued screaming. My throat was still painful, but if anyone could, I wanted everyone to hear.

His left hand gripped my right shoulder, and pushed. His one finger in my mouth guided us as I fell backwards, and we landed on the bed. He withdrew his finger from my mouth. My screams continued.

In a flash, he turned, darted the few steps towards the door, closed and chained it. He returned with the same haste and held me down by the wrists. I lay hanging over the side of the bed.

With an agitated tone, his hushed words rushed out: 'Keep quiet, keep quiet! Don't worry, I just want to speak to you. Don't worry, don't worry. It's all right, everything is fine. I just want to talk to you, then I'll leave.'

I stopped screaming, but raised my voice, hoping the neighbours would hear my protests.

It is taking a risk, I know, it could trigger him off, but it might bring attention. Part of me also thought: *Martine will know something is wrong when I fail to arrive.*

He wrenched me up, into the front room, and sat me on the big cushions near the wall, where nobody could see us if they looked through the window.

'One of the neighbours let me into the house last night. I heard you talking on the phone to Martine this morning; I know what you said. I heard the police inside the flat last night. I was upstairs outside on the roof and I could hear everything. What did you tell them?'

I cannot remember what I told John, but probably tried to make my answers as vague as possible. Watching him, my gaze settled on his teeth: small for someone his height, and grey, giving the aura of death, like those of a long-dead man.

After questioning me, he went to the kitchen and returned sipping tea – 'I will only stay ten minutes.'

Ten minutes never came; only more excuses.

When the phone rang, I fixed my gaze on it. I knew I would not be allowed to answer my only connection with normality.

John listened to the continuous ringing. 'That will be Martine,' he said sagely.

The ringing stopped and he started pacing up and down, looking out of the bay window. He peered around its corner.

'There's Martine.'

The doorbell rang. His tone of voice seemed reasonably diplomatic: 'Wait till Martine leaves and *then* I'll go; I don't want to get her involved in this.'

When Martine left, John gripped my arm and led me into the bathroom. I sat on the edge of the bath.

'Be quiet, I don't want anyone to hear.'

I didn't want anyone to hear, either; it might prompt him to take some fatal action against me sooner. I considered my position.

I don't like being in the bathroom, it is too near to the kitchen with the knives. I'm scared.

John made himself more tea, then led me back to the cushions. He rolled and smoked one joint after another. A fetid odour of sweat and dirt, but also pure evil wafted from him.

Time passed. I dared not even think of escape. John seemed so tuned into my mind I felt he could read my every thought, as though whatever thoughts I had might prove fatal. So I tried to numb my mind, to leave each next moment a blank. However, I feared he would sense my terror.

John was becoming impatient. He directed his anger at me; it was entirely my fault.

'I didn't want to be stuck in here with you all day, you slut! If it wasn't for you I could be out there, I could be at the pub.'

'Well, I don't want to be stuck in here either. This wasn't my idea, it's *you* who's doing this,' I told him.

John's appearance alternated between one of complete menace and instability to one verging on normality. His face, his eyes, drifted in and out of that penetrating look of pure evil.

I dared not look at him, at the evil in his eyes. Those eyes, piercing, penetrating, laser-like ... If I continued looking at them, I would be obliterated into small fragments, I felt. All I could do was avert my gaze from the sight of him; the only way I could try to salvage something left of me, of my fragile mind.

He continued hurling abusive words at me. With my knees drawn up, my hands covered my face and supported my head.

There was knocking at the front door. John looked out the window.

'The police are here now.'

He sat next to me again, waiting.

It is all like a game to him, as though we are in hiding for some necessary cause. As if it is them *that is the problem – not* him; *as if he has been set up.*

The doorbell rang; I heard voices, and tapping on the front window. Sweat covered John's anxious face.

'I feel sick.'

'Well, if you don't like feeling like that, why do you do these things? What for?' I implored.

'I feel like being sick,' he repeated several times, while rubbing his face with his hand, as though it was some unnecessary bodily response, caused by police presence.

'Well, why do you keep doing things like this if you don't like what happens?'

'When the police have gone, I'll go, I promise.'

They kept knocking, until the neighbours upstairs let them in. They persisted knocking on my flat door. John planned our next movements.

'Delia, just go to the door and tell them that everything is all right, we are just having a talk, and as soon as we finish, I am leaving, I promise.'

'No.'

I was still holding my face in my hands.

He repeated his request. I refused.

I dared not think or plan any immediate action. *If I follow his request, my lot will be lost, my only hope gone. I will be left at his mercy, in all probability. But if I say something, make any attempt to show my precarious position . . . I dare not think what might happen.*

On John's third request, I said nothing but stood up – mechanical, my mind a blank lest he should read my thoughts. I placed one foot in front of the other. *What happens next could decide my fate.* Sensing John's presence behind me, I took the chain off and opened the door.

Instantly, my eyes met those of the policeman to the left in front of me, and of the policewoman to the right. Without contemplation, without any plan whatsoever, the words burst from my mouth: *'Help me . . .'*

My body took flight, outside my mind's control, not sparing a second. I screamed and cried in hysterics and absolute terror. I glanced behind me, once, to ensure I was escaping – that he was not following.

I ran down the street; I needed to be out of sight. Martine seized me in her arms, but I wrestled to get away from her – nowhere was far enough away.

'Martine, let me go! I can't stay here.'

We ran to the end of the street, near the shoe shop around the corner on Leighton Road. There we hid in the doorway, and peered around it: John Sweeney was being escorted into a police van. I wanted him not to see me, nor I him, as though that alone would put me in further danger.

Martine held me while I cried.

The short, dark-haired policewoman, Sarah Hill, wanted me to return to the flat.

'No, I don't want to go! I'm too scared, I don't want him to see me.'

'It's all right. He's not there now; the police have taken him away in the van.'

Although I had seen him physically escorted, I remained petrified as Martine held me.

In the flat, the tall, sturdily built policeman, Jim Anderson, was waiting.

Martine and I sat on the edge of the bed. I was questioned first, then Martine, as she had raised the alert.

When I spoke of the spring bank holiday and being tied to the bed, Martine exclaimed: 'Oh, God, I didn't know that!' She sounded shocked.

I told the police everything, including about John's forced sexual demands: *'He* had sex,' I explained.

After the police had finished with us, they agreed with Martine's suggestion that I should spend the day in Hackney with her.

'Give us your phone number so we know where to contact you.'

Martine and I spent the afternoon hashing through all the events. It was a relief to get away from the flat. The modernised period townhouse, where she had her room, was like another world I thought I would never encounter again.

The police phoned that same evening: 'We need Delia to come to the police station to make a statement.'

Martine agreed to accompany me with the two uniformed policemen. I was glad she was with me; I felt uncomfortable with police presence. We sat in the car's back seat, silent.

It was when we were passing Hackney Town Hall that Martine could hold her composure no longer: 'Let me out, I'm not going!'

My heart sank: I needed her, but I could hardly drag her into such a situation when she did not want to be involved. She flung herself out of the car as soon as it stopped, and I was alone again.

At the police station, I was escorted upstairs into a large room full of desks scattered with papers, and people on telephones. I felt uncomfortable; this was never what I had wanted and it was a shock to have the police involved.

Sarah Hill arrived and I asked to use the toilet. 'I will show you where it is,' she said. When I entered a cubicle, I was disconcerted that she waited inside the room for me.

What is she waiting in here for? I feel like a criminal. It looks like they won't let me out of their sight.

We re-entered the large office; two plainclothes policemen stood before me. I related what had happened at the pub; that the police wouldn't come and I'd had to go looking for help. They glanced at each other, through the sides of their eyes, but made no comment.

During hours of questioning, my formal statement was taken. Then a doctor arrived. His dark hair and bushy black eyebrows gave him a sinister appearance. He held a torch as he examined the inside of my throat.

'I have never seen anything like it before,' he said, clearly shocked.

My throat was so sore.

Is he going to help me?

'Can I take anything to soothe it?' I whispered.

'Get some mouthwash from the chemist's and take some painkillers.'

Where am I going to find a chemist's at this time of the night? I wondered. As for the painkillers, I couldn't have swallowed any tablets because of the pain.

'We should have taken a photo of the damage but it's too late now. It's one o'clock in the morning, we won't get a photographer now,' one of the policemen remarked.

I felt let down. *Why didn't they think of that before? They already knew my throat was damaged.*

The detectives seemed so self-important, dressed in their suits, smiling and joking with each other; so pleased with themselves. Everything was in their control; they had it all tied up – or so they surmised. But I thought otherwise. My life was in their hands, and it was not quite so simple, and depended on how they dealt with this. They didn't grasp the seriousness of the matter, even though I had already told the police what John had said he'd done to Melissa.

'We will take you home now,' they finally announced.

'No, I need to find something to eat. I'm so weak.'

It was unlikely I would find anything at that time of night, they laughed – 'So you want a takeaway?'

I looked at them, my face straight. What did they take me for? I did not eat junk food, I ate *fresh* food.

Downstairs, a policeman sat at the reception desk. I needed reassurance.

'Is John Sweeney still inside?'

'Yes, don't worry.' He smiled. 'He's in his cell, sleeping.'

In the end, I made my own way home; not so far.

Once I was inside, I placed the chain on the door. Though weak from lack of food, I was too exhausted and in pain to care. I crawled into bed and pulled the covers over me.

John was in jail, so I knew that I was safe – but for how long?

33

On Monday 14 November, the phone rang.

'Is John there? Hello, this is Tony. Is John, there? He was supposed to meet me . . .'

His tone conveyed a sense of pressure and he sounded uneasy.

'No, he's not here.'

'Where is he?'

'I don't know.'

The phone rang again.

'Where is John?'

'I don't know.'

What if he finds out what's happened and he comes here and threatens me?

The phone rang again, and again, and again . . .

Mid-morning, two detectives from the Domestic Violence Team, in charge of my case, came to the flat to introduce themselves. I thought of how much more complicated my case was than pure 'domestic violence' but was so overwrought, I let myself be framed within this category.

They grimaced, screwing up their faces, when they entered the front room. The reek of rolling tobacco smoke and the geranium essential oil hit them like an invisible, poisonous force, lingering heavily. There had been neither the time nor the energy to rid the room of the bad aura.

The phone rang again.

'Just ignore it,' the detectives advised me.

One detective had blonde hair, was more solidly built, wore a suit, and was perhaps early middle-aged. The other, Kirk Davis, was younger, late twenties maybe: good-looking, fair hair, quite tall, also smartly dressed in a suit, and brimming over with confidence. He looked like he was going places.

'John Sweeney was held in a cell in Kentish Town police station overnight, and went to court this morning,' he informed me. 'He was put in Pentonville Prison until he attends court again.'

'What happens when he goes to court again? Will they let him out?' I wanted to know.

'Oh no, they won't let him out,' Kirk Davis reassured me.

'Look, if they let him out, I'm not safe. He will *do* something.'

'Oh, don't worry. We can do things to protect you. We can give you an alarm to carry, and we can put alarms on your door and the windows,' the older one said.

'But that's not enough. He will do something. *He will cut me to bits.*'

Just like he had Melissa . . .

I repeated the exact words John had used, to tell me about Melissa and the two Germans. I told them how he had disposed of their bodies.

'I'm in danger,' I insisted. 'He is a psychopath.'

The detectives took an interest when I described John's bizarre artwork that would tell them so much. *Now* they were interested – but it was no longer there to see.

The next day, Sarah Hill came over to go through my statement with me. She had transcribed my police interviews to create it and told me I had said of John and me: 'We had sex.'

'No,' I corrected her, *'we* did not have sex, *he* had sex.'

'You mean he raped you. Why didn't you say that?'
I *wouldn't* say that.
'Dunno . . . Just said it the way it was.'

I was reading nothing into it that the system could use against me. Let them figure it out for themselves; let *them* put into words what best describes the facts, I decided.

After the attack, I was off sick from work for three weeks; the pain prevented me from moving my tongue from side to side. A fluttering of nerves ran through me, programmed to react to minute stimuli.

The policeman Jim Anderson visited and advised me: 'Although John will spend time in prison, maybe a few months, he will be let out. So you should think about leaving here altogether while you have the chance; going somewhere he can't find you.'

My plan to escape to Australia . . . Perhaps it was time to start putting it in place.

I had given my rent book to Martine, along with the rent money, because, although John was in jail, I was terrified he would get out and I would not be able to go back to the flat for anything. I was late with the month's payment. At the council office, I explained my situation to the council worker; she was understanding.

'Would you like us to rehouse you?' she enquired.

My mind wavered. *Should I let them or not?*

I thought it over quickly. *I have to leave London for good, anyway, before John gets out. I only want to make one move, and that is to leave altogether when I know he cannot find me.*

At the same time, I concluded: *The police and the system are supposed to be protecting me. I should be able and need to believe they are doing so.*

'I will stay where I am,' I told her.

Still, I worried. *Am I doing the right thing?* But I told myself: *I've got to believe I really am being protected. I pay*

197

taxes for police service, after all. One of their duties is to keep me safe.

And, for one week, I was safe. But *only* for one week: on 22 November, John Sweeney was released from Pentonville Prison – on bail.

His bail conditions were he must stay at his parents' home in Skelmersdale, a curfew allowed him to go outside only between 8am and 6pm, and he had to report to the police station daily. He should only come to London to attend court; and should come no closer than one mile from my flat.

I was sceptical. What did that mean anyway? Should I venture no further than a mile from my flat?

Only much, much later would I discover that he was released despite a very serious development. For when the police had searched my flat after they'd arrested John, they'd found in his green canvas bag masking tape, Marigold gloves, surgical gloves, a large plastic ground sheet, rope, a saw, and a waterproof hat and cape.

A body disposal kit meant for me.

Yet it meant nothing to the courts.

The moment I discovered he was out, I was on edge. I *knew* he would be coming for me, it was obvious. Yet the police seemed unconcerned. All their talk of alarms led to nothing and I was not issued with one. I couldn't see what good it would do anyway; if John came to cut me into bits an alarm wouldn't stop him from doing it before the police responded – *if* they responded at all.

During the three weeks that I remained off sick, I lived in fear. Well aware I was being denied the protection I so desperately needed, I left only during daylight to buy food. At night, I left the light off in the front room, for fear that John might see it and know I was inside. I knew this action was futile, however, because I still switched on the bedroom light. He would be able to see that from the lot behind the back garden.

Sarah Hill visited with Jim Anderson. 'We came here one night, during the week, to check up and see if you were all right,' she told me, 'but you weren't in.'

'But I *was* in,' I said. 'I don't go out in the dark, I'm too scared. I only go out during the day when it's light. I leave the light off in the front room. I'm too scared to leave it on, in case he is outside, not that it would do much good anyway.'

Later, I thought: *How do they know that he might not be in here already, and have me hostage again? He might keep the lights out to pretend I was not in. Can't they* see *that?*

I told them that I would be going back to work soon, and how scared I was of returning in the dark. For I remembered all too well what John had told me when he'd broken in through the bathroom window; the plan he'd had if he'd been unable to gain access to the flat.

'Look,' I said, 'he knows it takes me an hour to cycle back from work. He knows that I get back between half past six and seven at night. He will be *hiding*, he'll be waiting for me, and he will *do* something.'

Sarah was nonchalant, and purred: 'Oh, just call Kentish Town police station. They know all about it, and they will be here as soon as they get your call.'

I pictured the scene of John appearing, suddenly, on the doorstep behind me. I imagined saying: 'Oh, just a minute, John, while I go inside to phone the police, to say that you are here,' gesturing with my finger for him to wait a minute.

'But it's no good. He'll *do* something!'

'Oh well, just scream; someone will hear you, and come and help you.'

'But there won't be time, he'll *do* something.'

I thought: *I* can't *scream, that would send him more berserk; and more will happen sooner.* Yet it seemed pointless saying anything; I gave up in despair.

They are crazy, these police. I can't get through to them.

What is the point of saying anything? They don't help, they don't do anything; they are giving me no protection. I feel hopeless, and I'm lost, completely vulnerable.

I'm living in fear.

One evening that November, I stared solemnly at my reflection in the mirror hanging on the side of the wardrobe. It was large enough for me to see my face. My little fingers were placed at each outside corner of my eyes; my palms rested on my cheeks, so that I could also see my forearms.

Gazing at my face, the backs of my hands, all my fingers, my forearms . . . I liked what I saw. I appreciated the shape of my arms, and the petite hands with delicate slender fingers, and the nicely formed nails.

'I don't want anything to change,' I whispered, 'Please don't let anything happen. I want myself as I am.

'Don't let anything change. I'm so scared.'

34

On 30 November, I met my victim support worker, Rebecca: a tall, brown-haired lady who listened and gave explanations and advice. It was Kirk Davis who suggested I visited the Victim Support Office. I was bewildered and shocked to find myself going to such a place – a service I knew existed, but had never imagined needing myself. Yet no one could truly advise me how to stay safe from John Sweeney. In that regard, I was as alone as ever.

In December, I returned to work: I wanted life to be normal, to *feel* normal. Somehow, I felt guilty, as if it were my entire fault I stayed off work; and that people would look down on me. I was embarrassed. I informed Sue that I would be back on Monday 5 December, but she had bad news.

'I'm sorry, Delia, but I have already booked someone else because I wasn't sure if you would be ready. But I will book you for next week.'

The agency only had one week's work on the children's ward to offer – I would have preferred to work with adults, as that was my speciality. The staff on the ward knew nothing of my situation. My state of mind was so fragile I worked inefficiently, was reprimanded, and reported to the office. I was devastated at my shortcomings, and felt worthless. I had attempted to keep my mind centred. It was as though I had been walking on a tight-rope, with forever the risk of falling.

On Monday 12 December, I was relieved to return to familiar work and surroundings, to people who knew me, and were aware of my circumstances; my colleagues were supportive. Though there were only ten days left on this job before it would come to an end, each day there was valuable. I felt safer when I was at work.

Going home, however, was another matter entirely. Each day, after finishing work in outpatients, I cycled through Hyde Park towards Oxford Street, where I turned off. Each time I left the park, I waited at the red lights to cross through Marble Arch, a busy traffic crossing. I had a constant thought: *If anything is going to kill me, it should be this – but I know it won't be this.*

I know what it will be.

On Saturday 17 December, an acquaintance, Tessa, turned up at my flat. I told her what John had done to me.

'I have a friend whose boyfriend was violent,' she told me. 'I want to take you there to speak to her; she might be able to give you some advice.'

She took me on her motorcycle. As we climbed and roared towards what may have been Highgate, the roads became hillier, the surroundings greener. The cold winter wind snapped against my face. We entered the drive of an imposing house that had seen grander days. Tessa led me to the back door, where a girl with long brown hair invited us in. The large room, as far as I can remember, was being used both as a kitchen and a living room. But as my mind was swirling around with so many thoughts, everything was too much to take in.

The girl was pleasant and calm. I explained my situation; the police had recently given me an update on my case.

'John is going to court on Tuesday,' I told her. 'I am afraid they will let him out on bail again. I have told the police I am not safe, but they are not doing anything to protect me.'

Unlike the authorities, she took me seriously: 'You have only Monday; you can't go to work. You *have* to go to the council office and get them to house you somewhere else. You are not safe; he will get you, he won't wait. You have to get out as soon as possible.'

Listening to her gave me the impetus to take action. Feeling slightly calmer and more in control, I decided I would go to the council office on Monday.

'The atmosphere in my flat is awful right now,' I added. 'I feel very uncomfortable in it.'

The girl poured some more tea.

'What you need to do,' she replied wisely, 'is sprinkle sea salt all over the floors of the flat, and on the window-sills, and leave it overnight, before cleaning.'

'What does that do?' I sipped my tea.

'It's an old remedy,' Tessa said, 'to cleanse a place from evil; it absorbs bad vibes.'

'OK, I'll do that.'

I liked the sound of it; it couldn't do any harm. And anything to make me feel a bit better . . . as if I was in control, even just a little bit. The upcoming court case made me nervous. John had been out on bail for several weeks now, and nothing had happened, but perhaps that was all part of his clever plan.

'If you want to do something,' he had once said, 'you keep quiet, don't cause any trouble, then when the police relax – you pounce.'

He had obeyed his bail conditions up till now; the police *were* relaxed. But, if they let him out again, I feared what he would do.

I spent the rest of the weekend exhausted. What had seemed like a strange dream had developed into a nightmare, and was all too real. Despite this, on Sunday evening I fetched a box of sea salt. I sprinkled the whole floor, and every corner, with salt, just as the girl had said. It felt good, as though I was doing something, having a hand in my fate.

On Monday morning, my intention had been to go to the council office to request rehousing but as the day dawned, it found me wiped out, weary.

There is nothing left in me; I am worn out.

It was enough, only, for me to struggle to work and carry on as usual – on automatic pilot.

On Tuesday 20 December, John travelled down from Liverpool to attend court. He was on curfew, and had been staying with his parents in Skelmersdale. The hearing happened while I was at work; Sue knew I was waiting to hear the outcome. In a way, we all were.

'The police are on the phone for you now, Delia, in my office,' she said.

I gripped the phone. *What would Kirk Davis say?*

'Hello, Delia.' He cleared his throat. 'I'm sorry, but I'm afraid I have to tell you that John Sweeney has been let out on bail again, until the 11th of January.'

'*What?* But I'm not safe. What am I going to do?'

I felt as though the answer to my own question was left entirely in my own hands. *No one is going to help me.* I knew it as a fact.

'Don't worry, Delia,' he said, in what was intended to be a reassuring way. 'No one ever breaks their bail.'

'But he *will*, I *know* he will.' As I spoke, I had a vision: 'I see someone with an axe held over his head ready to come down, just like in the movie *Psycho*.'

To me, it seemed akin to a psychic revelation. Yet I sensed in his response how apparently absurd Kirk found it. He laughed lightly.

'Oh, come on now, Delia, that's an old movie! Things like that don't happen here, they only happen in big cities like New York.'

But . . . What is he talking about? I thought. *London is a big city – and so what? It doesn't have to be a big city, it could happen* anywhere.

He seemed amused, and I felt rather foolish when he failed to take me seriously. Yet I knew deep down that I was vulnerable, and could be in the utmost danger.

Sue and the others were anxious to hear the outcome. As soon as I exited the office they gathered round; they thought the outcome unbelievable. Apparently, the fact Christmas was approaching had played a part: John was released to enjoy the festivities.

After the call, I returned to work and completed the rest of my shift. As always at that time of year, it was dark by the time I reached the Co-operative store on Kentish Town High Street, needing to buy some milk after work.

As I wheeled my bicycle out of the shop entrance, I noticed in a shadowed doorway, next to the Iceland store opposite, a tall man wearing a brimmed hat and a long raincoat. John once told me he used to wear such a hat.

Shivers ran through me. *Is he watching me? Could it be John?*

I fled back to the flat on my bicycle.

Every night when I returned from work, I asked anyone I could find nearby on the street if they could see me safely into my flat, and they were obliging. I was worried that John might be lurking, but I had not seen him, as had happened at the Stag in the summer.

One evening as I came home, my next-door neighbour, Mrs Allen, who lived in the house next door, happened to be on the street outside our houses. She had dark-brown hair, and was nicely dressed – I think she was a teacher. Nervous in case John attacked me while I carried my bike up the concrete steps – just as he had once threatened to do – I asked if she would see me safely into the flat, and she obliged. As she did so, she chatted to a friend about her mobile phone, still something of a novelty, while I unlocked my flat door. I opened it, entered, and told her I was OK.

Sarah Hill visited me that evening.

I knew I was vulnerable, and could be in the utmost danger. I thought it best to depart before John had the opportunity to pounce.

'Do you think I should leave here now while I've got the chance?' I asked her. 'I'm thinking about leaving the country, maybe to go for a while to Australia, where I could stay with a friend.'

'Oh no, you can't go right now,' she said. 'John will be going to court on the 11th January, and you might have to be there then, too.'

I was perplexed.

What might I have to go to court for? I'm not the one who is guilty. I didn't do anything.

My chance, it seemed, had gone.

On Wednesday evening, 21 December, just before I left work, Sue presented me with a bottle of red wine.

'This is from Mr Thomas, the consultant – he has given us all a bottle for Christmas.'

I cycled home with it in my bicycle bag; carried it cautiously up the steps. That evening, my gaze kept drifting towards it: I'd left it standing on the kitchen counter.

I would like to open it and have a drink. But should I? Or is that tempting fate?

I stood beside the bottle and fingered its neck, and then withdrew my hand. *No, I'd better not. That might be asking for it. If I open it, something might happen, and I might never get to finish it.*

Nevertheless, I lingered, despite myself. I whispered, as though fate might be listening, 'Why shouldn't I open it? I want everything to feel normal. I should be allowed to have a glass tonight; and again, when I want it.'

In trepidation, I squeezed the bottle's neck with my hand, held it steady between my thighs, and pulled the twisted wooden handle of the corkscrew. The wine poured; I felt uneasy, guilty, as though I were taking liberties.

Am I committing a taboo? Is this a bad omen?

I replaced the cork, and drank the sacrificial drink.

35

Thursday 22 December 1994: the shortest, darkest day of the year. As usual I rose before work and, as always, performed my dance exercises. I held my arms arched over my head, fingertips pointing towards each other. I stretched them to the sides while doing a plié, and bent forwards with a straight back while straightening my legs. My arms reached behind me and upwards, then swung forwards and upwards over my head.

My joints moved so smoothly; they were so supple. Dance had kept my body in good condition, despite all.

Wearing my rainbow-coloured coat, with several layers underneath to protect me from the cold, I lowered my gold bicycle down the concrete steps and set off for the hospital. The last time; the last journey to the department; the last time I would be working with these nurses. For today was my final day on the job.

I won't see them to work with again.

I would miss the comfort and company they provided. The Christmas holiday loomed large before me: empty and alone. I'd arranged to work on Boxing Day, through the agency, and was not looking forward to the festivities. There did not seem much to celebrate in any case. My family were unaware of my situation.

The day was uneventful. Soon, we started closing up

for Christmas; the department would not be open over the break. There was the sense of an ending for us all.

Sometime between 5.30 and 6pm, I swung my leg over my bicycle and began my commute. *Through the park towards Oxford Street; navigate the busy crossing at Marble Arch ...* While cycling, I noticed the clearness of the night and the dry freshness of the air. It was a cold that was bearable; in normal circumstances, I would have enjoyed the ride, yet, thanks to John, these were not normal circumstances.

I felt on edge and tense the whole way back.

Sometime between 6.30 and 7pm, I finally cycled up Leighton Grove. It was dark. That night, there was no one on the street whom I could ask to see me safely into my flat.

As usual, I placed my bicycle against the brick garden wall, in front of the house. I ascended the seven concrete steps. Using a brick from just inside the house, I jammed the door open and went back for my bicycle. The entire time I was alert to my surroundings.

I saw no one.

As I pushed my bicycle upwards over the steps, I looked from side to side, to try to reassure myself that I was still safe.

On the first step: nothing.

On the second step: nothing.

I was on the middle steps when I turned my head to the left; to the right ... and there was John's face behind me, so intimidating, *looking for revenge.*

'You didn't expect to see *me* here, did you?' he leered, a caustic grin upon his face.

I did not scream; I knew it would only make things worse. Yet it was torment to see him there. The answer ran through my mind, unspoken: 'You say this to me, trying to make *me* look the fool, when it is the police you should be saying this to – and we both know that.'

He won't break his bail, the police had reassured me. I had warned them, I had *told* them, and they did not listen once.

John placed his left hand on top of mine, on the bicycle handle; his right on the seat. He pushed.

'Come on, let's go in. I want to speak to you.'

'*No!*'

I pulled my hands back, still gripping the handles, and he let go. With a clatter, my bicycle fell against the hip-level stone wall that divided the house steps from those of the Allens' property next door.

Here it is, I immediately thought. *It's starting now. Just what I said would happen.*

My simultaneous thoughts, and actions, happened in less than split-seconds. *My only hope is if someone is on the street and sees*, I realised grimly; *only then might I have a chance of being saved. If he gets inside with me, I have no chance. He'll cut me to bits. I have no choice but to face him here.*

In one fluid movement, I kicked the brick and slammed the door shut. I confronted him from the top step, and noticed that he now had a hint of a moustache. He was wearing his green Barbour and, underneath, his Mexican top, hood down; then his denim shirt and T-shirt.

He is wearing most of the clothes he owns. He is ready for anything, ready to run.

Escape was impossible. I was filled with fear. *Just as I have told the police, everything is happening as I said it would . . . and I am left to deal with it.*

Moving swiftly, surely, John's right hand reached over the low wall. He retrieved what he had hidden on the steps of the neighbours.

He struck, with a deep thud, the right side of my skull, using the large wooden handle of an axe. I was aware I was still conscious despite the heavy blow. The top of my ear was nipped, and stung. My body swayed to the left with the impact. I sank to the ground, the blow having somewhat dazed me.

I was sitting on the top step with my arms outstretched to the sides. John swung again. *Bash!* The axe handle hit my left forearm. Still the pain had not kicked in. I was in 'flight or fight' mode, the adrenaline coursing through me, necessary for survival – no time to be aware of any sensations of pain.

I shouted throughout the ordeal. *If I'm loud enough, someone might hear.* I chose my words carefully, despite all. To scream or swear would provoke him even further, to cause untold increased harm. I was under no illusion: this was a fight to the death. I had to try to keep my wits about me to stand any chance of survival.

'Go away!' I shouted clearly, my words carrying in the clear night air. 'Leave me alone!'

The axe swung again, the blow hitting my right arm this time. I pleaded inwardly: *Someone come, please. Someone come, before he completely destroys my body. I don't want my body ruined.*

My eyes sent a darting look as every so often I scanned the street, *wishing* someone would appear. But the street remained dark and empty: as dark and empty as John Sweeney's soul.

He dropped the axe, and pulled out a dirty old rusty knife hidden beneath his coat.

I've got to do something.

I kicked, but missed hitting him where I intended. Nevertheless, he lost balance and staggered down a step, cutting himself on the palm.

'You fucking bitch!'

He lunged towards me.

Time was as messed up as my body. It felt as though aeons passed while I hoped for someone to appear before he could harm me any more than he already had. At the same time, his every strike seemed to occur in a matter of seconds. With every blow, I was becoming less and less physically the person I had known myself as.

My brain raced, searching for solutions; for a way out of this horror. My bicycle was still leaning against the stone wall, the only defence available. With my two broken, bloodied arms, I reached over and pulled it on top of me as I sat upon the step. I thought better than to use my arms, given the damage from the axe – but I had no choice, even if it did worsen the injuries.

The warm, wet blood poured and trickled down my face and onto my neck from the gash on my head. I could feel it becoming sticky, clotting, and then feeling cold on my skin.

John picked up the axe once more and went for me: this time with its thick sharp blade at the end of every strike. Rather than my body, he began smashing the metal frame. He destroyed the bicycle totally.

Clang! Clang! Clang! The noise rang out in the still night air.

No more cycling from London to Dover, then Ostend to Amsterdam, like I once did.

Thwarted, John dropped the axe. He returned to the knife and struck, finding his target despite the metal bars of the bike.

The wide, twelve-inch-long blade was thrust through my right breast and into my lung. I knew what had happened; I experienced a hot, burning feeling, with the sound of the penetration in and out. *Sshuh . . . sshuh . . .* as it entered and left my body . . . sucking, slurping.

If he'd got me on the left side, he would have hit my heart – a death blow. I think, now, that in his frenzy he had mistaken the side he had aimed for. But, still, I kept on living. *And he kept coming.* With a firm stabbing motion, he now plunged the filthy knife into the side of my right thigh.

As I held my hands above my head I focused entirely

on John as he dropped the knife, and picked up the axe, waiting for his next move.

He swung the axe again, bringing it level with the fingers of my left hand. And, as I watched in horror, the top of my little finger flew through the air towards the house next door.

That's it, I've had enough.

I was sure of one thing.

I want to die. I don't want to live in this body anymore; I don't want to live in this pain. And I don't want to live in the anger I know I will have, the intense anger at the police and the courts for letting him out and letting me down. They could have stopped this; they could have saved me. And I know I can never, ever forgive them for failing in their duty.

I don't want to live in that anger, I thought. *I want to die.*

The knuckles on the two fingers nearest to my missing digit had also been shaved by the axe's blow; blood poured from my hand. I glanced once at the bleeding, raw mess where my little finger had been. It was beyond my endurance to dwell on it; I shut it from my mind.

John held the axe over his head, ready to come down on me. I turned to face the neighbour's house, and curled myself into a squatting position. Placing my hands and my bleeding, broken arms over my head, I closed my eyes.

Wait now, for the last awful pains. I'm going to die now.

I thought of my mum ... and my dad ... and my brothers. I thought of them each, and how they were so far away, and that I would never see them again, or they me. I clung to the memory of them, their faces; that was the closest I would ever get to them now. I wanted my last thoughts to be of them only.

Then: a noise. I heard a noise in front of me. I parted my bleeding, broken forearms, opened my eyes and peeked through. The twenty-one-year-old son of the Allens, Giles, had appeared at his door: the noise of the axe destroying my bicycle had alerted him to the murder happening outside his home.

I looked to the right; John still held the axe over his head.

So little time is left, he is sure to strike.

I curled up again, eyes closed, and waited for the final blow.

36

Thump! An agonised groan broke the night air.

It belonged to John Sweeney.

I peered sideways to see John holding the axe high – in only one hand. His mouth was open. He was holding his left hand against the small of his back, bending backwards in pain.

Giles had armed himself with a baseball bat. When he saw John poised with the axe, he'd struck him on the back. In that moment, Giles's parents, too, came to their door. In the same instant, John ran, carrying the axe, and crossed Leighton Road to reach Bartholomew Road. He disappeared from view.

Aghast, my neighbours viewed my blood-covered body, and the blood-splattered steps around me.

I flexed my left elbow to see what would happen. Gravity caused my forearm to bend at right angles, displaying muscle, tendons, and a broken end of bone sticking through my skin.

A sacrilege, it feels, to see the insides of my body.

Immediately, I extended my left elbow again, for gravity to take the broken bone of my forearm, along with everything else, back into an aligned position. Horrified, I avoided looking at it again.

I spoke with difficulty to my neighbours, my pierced lung beginning to make my breath bubble with blood:

'He bashed me on the right side of my head with the axe handle. I have two broken arms, and I have a haemo-pneumothorax, from where he stabbed me in the lung, and a stab wound to my right thigh.'

Giles's sister, a medical student, had joined her family at their door; I knew she would understand the medical term I used. Her father turned to her.

'Call an ambulance – quickly!'

He approached me, and glanced down at the bloodied knife lying on the step below me. His wife exclaimed: 'Leave it, don't pick it up!'

I felt so alone, in need of comfort, desperate for someone to hold me, at least to touch me. I needed the warmth of physical contact but I knew this was not possible. Glancing over my body, I looked for somewhere blood-free, and saw a small area on my right shoulder. With my eyes focused on this area, I looked up, and then back at my shoulder, and asked him timidly: 'Would you touch me here, please?'

He placed his fingertips on that small area, and it gave me a sense of the comfort and physical warmth I so yearned for. *I might never feel these sensations again.* I knew, from my injuries, that I was most likely to die.

Suddenly, a police van screeched to a halt and two policemen charged towards us. I was dismayed and angry. *I want an ambulance, I want out of pain; not them, they are no good to me.*

The first one growled: 'What's this all about? What's going on here?'

I feel like they're treating me as though I am guilty.

How dare he ask such a question? I thought angrily. *Is it not obvious I am mutilated and dying, covered in blood?*

Filled with bitterness, I remembered Sarah Hill's words. I sputtered through a bubbly, breathless weak voice laced with sarcasm: 'Ask Kentish Town police station. "They know all about it."'

The blood oozed from my lung. I felt wet inside my mouth. *Blood?*

My answer was not enough; he growled the same question twice more at me.

I was impatient. The second time, I sputtered the same answer. Logic told me that he should know I should avoid talking – all my effort should be concentrated on breathing – but still he barked his questions at me.

The third time I ignored him. I felt like spitting at these police, and hitting them: they were so insensitive, so inconsiderate. Even as my body weakened, the life ebbing away, my anger and contempt for the police escalated as I recalled my previous encounters with them. The precarious way they had dealt with my case had led directly to the circumstances in which I now found myself.

Mrs Allen explained: 'Kentish Town police have been seeing her because of problems she has been having with her boyfriend.'

'Who did this?'

'My ex-boyfriend, John Sweeney.'

I was relieved when they left to search for John, the neighbours indicating the direction he had taken; I wanted nothing to do with them.

Sarah Hill, the policewoman supposedly involved in protecting me, arrived.

'Oh, she's lost the top of her finger,' she commented tactlessly, standing at the top of the neighbours' steps, avoiding the bloodbath before her.

The neighbours made no reply; later, I learned they took her to task for the way she had responded.

Since it had flown through the air, I had blocked out every thought of my absent finger. The horror of everything was too much to endure; I dared not look. Now Sarah reminded me: *I was not whole anymore.*

I seethed at her. I had *told* her, and the rest of them,

what he would do; even *when* he would do it. They had ignored me. Now, I ignored her.

The wailing of the ambulance and its flashing lights only bore into me what I had become. Two female paramedics rushed towards me.

I mumbled the site and condition of each injury, as they dealt with them.

'My right lung has a haemopneumothorax.'

The paramedic laughed. 'I'm afraid we don't understand those terms as we aren't doctors.'

Mrs Allen explained: 'She is a nurse.'

It was obvious what had happened to my fingers; I need not remember or say.

My bright rainbow-coloured jacket, with its thin blue-and-white striped inner cotton lining, was being cut off. I remembered buying it that summer in Camden Lock Market. It was so good for cycling; I had liked it so much. Now, covered in blood, it had become a part of my mutilation; something nice being destroyed along with me. Underneath I wore a quilted Indian jacket in purples and blues. Then a T-shirt top, and a vest.

All cut off.

They splinted and bandaged my broken, bloodied arms. As they did so, I felt the cold hardness of the edge of the concrete step on my back, when they laid me flatter. My right breast was bared to the night, exhibiting the stab wound directly next to the nipple. A sudden, random thought flashed into my mind: *I picture myself as the victim in an illustration for a romance/crime tragedy.*

While cycling, earlier, I had been less aware of the cold, but now I started shivering, my whole body trembling with shock, covered in blood, dying.

I felt the urge to open my bowels. 'My bowels are going to open. My bowels are going to open,' I cried repeatedly, horrified at my lack of control.

'It's all right, just do it.'

The thought was unbearable. If I did such a thing, I was unaware, but it added to my humiliation.

One paramedic carried me by the arms, and the other by my legs, down the steps. There was no time for stretchers; I was bleeding to death: from my breast, my head, my arms, my fingers, my thigh ... So many wounds, so many holes that John Sweeney had riddled me with.

The pain started to grip in as they moved me. A deep, heavy, unbearable pain bore down in my chest.

Something made me turn my head to the right. I slanted my eyes to the corners to look towards the basement flat. The neighbours, from below, had come out to satisfy their curiosity. They must have heard something, earlier, but I knew they had no interest in me. The girl lingered, but her boyfriend turned around and went back inside, indifferent.

Mrs Allen carried the intravenous fluid bag while I was being carried to the ambulance. 'I will visit you in hospital,' she said.

I wished so much that she would stay with me; I needed a familiar face.

Every bump as they moved me aggravated the pain even more.

'The pain, the pain ... God help me, the pain!' I cried out, the words gurgling through the blood.

I made a conscious effort to leave out the 'God' as I cried. God – I had no feeling for it, *what* God? The pain was so terrible. No one should think I was praying to a God that never helped me; it was merely an expression.

I had it in mind to tell the medical staff that I was a Jehovah's Witness, so they might give me no blood: I wanted to die, I wanted them to do nothing to save me. But I was unable to concentrate on anything but the pain. It was beyond my effort to declare it.

Inside the ambulance, one paramedic removed the

patterned brown leather belt I had bought in a market in Mexico; I never saw it again. My pink jeans, from a mall in the States, were cut off to access the stab wound to my thigh. The small odd earrings, one from Mexico and one from India, were removed.

I feel like I'm being stripped of everything I have been as a person, and will never see myself again.

The journey to hospital was filled with agonising pain. As we arrived, I saw, outside the entrance, a man stood watching me as I was rushed in. I found it a humiliation, to find myself being seen in this predicament, which should never have been *allowed* to happen. I had become a part of an 'act' I was unwilling to play in life's theatre, and my audience was this bystander.

The stretcher was wheeled over the shallowest of grooves on matting at the entrance, before we reached A&E. Even these small irregularities of the surface caused me intense pain, each one another earthquake of agony.

The hospital staff gathered round me. I held up my hand to show a female doctor; my mutilated, bloodied hand where a stump sat squatly where something else should have been.

I opened my blood-filled mouth and whispered: 'I can feel my finger.'

So strong was my desire that my finger should still be there that any sensation I had was there only to convince me so.

Then . . .

I remember nothing.

37

Startled, consumed with apprehension, I became aware of whispering, echoing voices surrounding me. I felt somehow ashamed . . .

I opened my eyes. There was a dim light; beeping noises and flashing illuminations. It appeared rather like outer space, but I knew where I was.

Oh no . . . I'm alive.

Now, what hell?

My head was tilted to one side; an endotracheal tube twisted in my mouth, attached to a respirator. I looked down at my beleaguered body to survey the damage. Both arms were bandaged into a plaster back slab to support them; they had not yet been fully encased in plaster, but that would soon come. Later, I discovered that, in theatre, they'd inserted a steel plate and six pins in my left forearm; the bone so broken it could not heal alone. I hated the plate and pins, the feeling I was made of false parts.

I held my left arm up to see what was left at the end of it – I needed to examine the damage. My third and fourth fingers had sutures at each knuckle. *I must have had both fingers bent, so that he only reached the surface of my knuckles with the blade*, I realised. *If I had not, I might have lost them too.* A grave thought.

At the far end of my hand, a swollen, red, blunt ending:

no fingernail, the skin held tightly together by three sutures, was where the top of my little finger should have been. As my medical notes described it, I had suffered a 'complete amputation of the terminal phalanx of the left little finger'. John had chopped it off with his axe.

I tried to convince myself it was not so bad. *Most of my finger is still there; it is only the tip.* But later, when I held my finger in the air and this time moved it around, the blunt ending wiggled aimlessly. I was horrified; it had become a monster to me. No longer a slender, tapered finger but an ugly stump that I would never choose to look at again.

My first thought when the shock of it struck me was: *How am I going to make pastry? I need all my fingers to make pastry.* The fear of making it with less dexterity, of being aware that something was missing, that perhaps I might look at the loss, meant I never made pastry again.

Inserted into the right side of my neck was a central line, with its three intravenous extensions for giving medication and fluids; I was also aware of an arterial line entering my right groin. I looked down towards my foot. On a drip stand, a bag of blood was hanging; I would later learn I had received nineteen units to replace the blood that had poured from my wounds. There was no access for the blood line in my shattered arms, so the transfusion line was placed in a vein at the top of my left foot. My whole body was swollen with fluid, due to all the blood and protein I had lost. Once naturally slim, I now looked fat; my pale skin was tight and shiny.

I have never felt so wretched. I am in a body that is not my own – like death itself.

In fact, I had been close to death, many times. My heart had seemingly failed in theatre: I was given drugs to act as a cardiac stimulant; I was resuscitated. I also had a fractured skull. I had a deeply lacerated lung too.

As far as I was concerned, I had died. This was not

me; this was something else: John Sweeney killed Delia on the concrete steps.

I glumly watched the activity in the Intensive Care unit. Nurses wearing their blue scrubs diligently attended to patients. A doctor, wearing a red Santa Claus hat, passed by with other members of staff, all in the spirit of festivity.

Christmas Day . . .

I was empty.

The policewoman, Sarah Hill, soon turned up.

'Hello, Delia.'

Her voice was subdued, her expression remorseful.

I needed to tell her. Unable to speak owing to the tube inserted down my throat, I wrote with my finger, making several frustrated attempts, until she understood.

'Fucking bastard?'

I struggled to nod my head, waving my plastered arms up and down. Mortified at what had become of me, I began to cry. Throughout the whole experience with Sweeney, I had been numb to any feelings, surviving on adrenaline. Only when it was over, when there was no immediate danger and I had time to think, did all the feelings explode through to my consciousness.

Sarah started crying too. She and the others had a few things to answer for.

I have proven myself right to them, and this is what it has cost me.

Two unfamiliar detectives introduced themselves. I wondered where Kirk Davis and his colleague were, only to realise, much later, that the Serious Crime Team had replaced the Domestic Violence crew.

'It's not a very nice Christmas for you.'

'I wanted an exciting life, but this was not what I had in mind,' I whispered through a strained voice, my throat dry and sore from the tube, which had been removed.

'Did John Sweeney do anything to you down below?'

'No.'

'Do you hurt down there?'

'I hurt all over.'

My body was consumed with pain, inside and out.

The detective, Adrian Farron, told me John had escaped: 'We cordoned off the surroundings near your flat, and along Bartholomew Road, and made a search. Have you any idea where he might be?'

'He could have gone to Liverpool or Germany.'

'Why there?'

'Because he comes from Liverpool; and because he goes to Germany a lot, to work as a carpenter.'

In fact, as I would only learn much later, John had fled to his family: to his ex-wife and kids. He stayed one night with a friend beforehand, during which time he confessed his crime: he said he had 'done' me with an axe and a knife. To his ex-wife, he remarked he had 'done something really bad which would make her hair stand on end'. He'd left her home just before anyone had seen the news appeals that he was wanted for my attempted murder. Now, he was on the run.

Adrian Farron asked: 'Would you like us to tell your parents about you?'

I was shocked: another sudden blow. *What – they haven't told them?* Though it is the first thing hospital staff are supposed to do, they hadn't done it; apparently, because it was Christmas.

And now they expect me to make that decision. How can they do this to me? As if I haven't enough to carry, they want me to bear this burden, as well . . . and I don't want to feel like a nuisance to my parents by telling them.

'No,' I replied.

I knew that no one would come anyway. And that was too much to take, on top of everything else. It would destroy me even more. Mum was sick, and Dad had to look after her, so they could not come.

No one that matters to me is here to see my pain and suffering, and the state I'm in.

The detectives glanced at each other, their expressions uneasy.

Sarah Hill visited often. 'We have two armed policemen guarding the entrance to ICU, giving you twenty-four-hour protection.'

She sounded so impressive, but I was not impressed.

What's the use of that? Only now are they treating it as such a serious case. Suddenly I'm so important, when before it seemed no big deal.

But it's too late now. It doesn't matter anymore. I don't care.

On Boxing Day, Farron returned to inform me that John had got through Customs at the border, and had escaped by boat to somewhere in continental Europe. It was not a surprise. His watchful vigilance, now, would stand him in good stead.

While John was free, I was not: I would never be free from my prison, from this body that was no longer me. A consultant and his team came by, to brief me on my condition; on what had been done to me while I lay dead.

'When we performed the thoracotomy, a surgical incision into the chest wall,' he said, describing the procedure, 'we had to cut two ribs to gain access to your lung to repair it.'

I was horrified; *another* part of me that would never be the same.

'Because of the position of the stab wound, we had to choose to cut in the most painful place to perform a thoracotomy.'

I felt myself deflate further.

Sure, it would have to be.

I was to be spared nothing.

Gauze swabs, saturated in an iodine solution, had been packed into my breast wound. They remained for several days, to clear any infection from the rusty knife, but it soon came time to remove them; a suture was also to be applied to the wound entrance near my nipple.

I panicked as the doctor removed the pack. My heartbeat was so loud, it was racing. I had the irrational idea that everything inside me was exposed and close to the surface of my skin, including my heart. I felt it pounding; my shallow breathing becoming even more rapid. I was terrified of being sutured.

I want to tell them, but I'm too weak to do so. I want to run.

They did the same with my head wound, where John had bashed me with the axe. Like everything else done to me, I was terrified by it and thought: *Why can't they just let me die?*

Every day was a new hell; brought a new procedure that prompted panic attacks. The two thick intercostal drains inserted into my side and lung had to be removed and what is called a purse-string suture applied to the holes.

I whimpered in terror. I thought of how, as a student nurse, I was given instructions to pull those purse-string sutures tight, as soon as the doctor had removed the tube. I'd never dreamt that the same procedure would be done to me – there was no reason why *I* should ever have lung problems.

But I had reckoned without John Sweeney.

I developed surgical emphysema; something else to add to my agony. The abnormal presence of air had entered the subcutaneous tissues under my skin, introduced through the drain sites. There was no treatment; it had to resolve spontaneously, over time. I developed a cough: a loud, dry, rasping cough that rocked me, deep in my lungs, as though they were the remnants of a building shattered in battle, a fierce wind blowing through. Each cough exacerbated the pain. Pain persisted throughout my *whole* body.

'I need something for the pain,' I told the nurse. 'I still hurt all over. Something stronger.'

'We can't give you more morphine, it will depress your respiration.'

I was annoyed, frustrated by her words.

I don't care about my breathing; I don't care if I stop breathing – I just want to be out of pain.

After several days in ICU, I was transferred to the ortho-paedic ward on 28 December 1994. I woke up during the night; I heard men laughing and talking. A staff nurse, with greying hair and a blue uniform, entered my room.

'The two policemen who are guarding you overnight were making too much noise,' she informed me. 'We had to ask them to be quieter. They are sitting outside your door drinking cups of coffee.'

Another policeman, dressed in a suit, visited. So many policemen now; now, when it was far too late.

'We would like to transfer you to another hospital, on the outskirts of London, for your safety,' he said. 'Would you agree to that?'

Why are you thinking about safety now? It's too late. Now they want to save the remnants of what used *to be me. I wanted 'me' as I was – not as I am. I don't care now.*

I sank into myself – I was unwilling to go, but I had given up. There was no fight left in me.

'OK.'

Much later, I was to discover that this unwanted move was also for 'legal reasons'. Had I known, I would have refused the transfer.

Solemnly, I gazed out the window at the view; not Hampstead Heath itself but a pleasant view nonetheless, of the tiled roofs of houses on hilly slopes and tree-lined winding streets. Leafless branches, evergreens, and roofs sparkling with frost. I'd have to leave it, for whatever future the police now had in mind.

I have a hazy recollection from this time: I may have been told that John had turned up at the hospital, with a gun, and said he would 'finish the job'. It was perhaps another reason that prompted the move – and it prompted something else, too.

'We have removed your name from your hospital records in case Sweeney gains access to a computer,' the authorities revealed.

I said nothing, but I scoffed inside: *John has no knowledge of how to use a computer. So much fuss now, when it's too late.*

They asked me, too, to change my name.

'We want you to use another name, as your name is in the papers,' the policeman said. 'Can you choose a name that has no connection to you?'

A surge of resentment ran through me: I was being stripped of anything that was *me*. Nonetheless, I concentrated, my mind heavy with the effort, and dug out a name: 'Elizabeth.'

'Good. And a last name?'

Nothing came.

'What about Drake?' he said cheerily. 'That's it – Elizabeth Drake.'

Everything is being stolen from me. Not only have I been metamorphosed into a decrepit old wreck, but I'm losing my whole identity as well. Myself, as I was, has entered oblivion.

Delia Balmer, RIP.

38

I was transferred to Northwick Park Hospital on 29 December 1994. I'd been there less than a day when a nurse entered my side room to inform me that I had tested positive for MRSA in the wounds to my skull and breast, in the vicious slash left by the thoracotomy, and in my nose. I was transferred to a single room on the Infectious Disease Unit.

Hospital is my prison, Intensive Care my torture chamber, and now I'm in solitary confinement. But the torture did not end there.

Sarah Hill and the policeman visited, both wearing apron and gloves, as a precaution against spreading infection. Although I understood the reasoning behind this procedure, it still made me feel like an untouchable.

'The nursing staff and the doctors have not been told the cause of your injuries in case your identity leaks out,' they informed me. 'We would like you not to tell them anything.'

Is this really only for my protection? I wondered, aghast. *Or is this a big cover-up for the mistakes that were made? How can there be continuity of care if nurses and doctors know nothing about me and what really went on?*

Most pressing of all, I knew I *needed* to tell people what had happened to me: I *wanted* to talk about it. I knew that I'd been messed up by the trauma and needed, for my own sanity, to have that option. Yet it was denied me.

'We are telling them that we are friends,' revealed Sarah's colleague. He smiled. 'Pretend I'm your uncle.'

At first, Sarah and 'Uncle' were my only visitors. The police discouraged anyone else from coming, supposedly for my protection. The enforcement of my silence was allegedly for the same. Nonetheless, at the new hospital I did request to see a counsellor. The on-call psychiatric registrar turned up.

'Can you tell me about the attack, and what your real name is?' he enquired.

'The police don't want me to talk,' I explained. 'I'm not supposed to tell anyone, not even the doctors.'

He tried to persuade me. I wanted so much to, but I obeyed the police request and fought my need to tell him. My spirits sank as I did so. *Here is someone who would listen, why am I bothering about the police?*

I thought it over. *I'm desperate to tell; that someone should know; and he seems very approachable.* I cannot remember exactly what I told him – not the full extent of it, my tongue still tied by some misplaced obedience – but I believe I spoke about the many things that led up to the attack, and how I continued to work all through it.

'It is surprising that you were able to continue with life and work and that you have not had a breakdown,' he observed, 'after going through all that.'

But I had been numb through 'all that'. Now, though, I felt everything, both physical and emotional. Alone in my room, stripped of identity and friends, I felt impossibly isolated. The nurses seemed aware that I had been attacked, but were under the impression that I was unwilling to discuss it. There was no comfort for me – not even in sleep. I began to have strange nightmares that left me wondering about their meaning.

I find myself submerged in murky water inside a car; the doors and windows closed, hearing a bubbling sound as of the escape of air, where air no longer is. Dirty, barely visible, indescribable objects float around me – I feel their fatty, slithery parts wiping against my skin. Body parts? Human tissue? The water is viscid. Floating precariously amongst the debris, my arms and legs flail.

How is it I can breathe in this putrid mess?

The nurses provided me with a portable television. The first programme I watched was a documentary, which engrossed me, about the psychological traits of a psychopath. The next day, I told Sarah Hill.

'Do you really think you should be watching things like that? Doesn't it disturb you?'

'Why?' I asked matter-of-factly. 'The damage is done, what does it matter now? It was interesting to see I was right. Everything about it fits him, and I knew that before this was allowed to happen.'

She was hesitant. 'By the way, I should let you know,' she said, 'after the attack, the police searched your flat.'

What did they do that for? I thought crossly. They had searched it in November after John held me hostage, and there had been nothing there. *I don't like them prying into my things.* It was another invasion, as if I had not been invaded enough already. It was all too much to make any comment.

Alone, as usual, I lay in my room, trying to block out whatever I could by watching the flickering television. A reggae song on a commercial appealed to me – it was very apt, in an ironic sort of way, to my circumstances. 'No, no, no . . .' the singer sang mournfully. 'You don't love me . . .' Its haunting melody became a sort of mantra to me: a confirmation of the obvious, an assertion of what I had long known.

John Sweeney, meanwhile, took the opportunity to assert the same in writing. I did not find out until later, but he now wrote to the police about me. He called me an 'evil witch'; that hurt. He still had the power to get at me.

He sent several postcards to the police, in fact. He sent one from South Kensington, though perhaps that was a decoy; another from Berlin, although the recollection is hazy.

'We received a letter from John at the police station,' Sarah Hill announced.

'What did it say?'

I tried to avoid appearing overly interested.

'Every other word is a swear word, and many aimed at the police: "You cunts, you bastards. I've been framed. I didn't do it." Things like that.'

One, in a play on words, claimed the attack was 'an AXEident'.

'So what do you think of that?' I asked her.

'Just let him keep sending them, we like things like that.'

I had not been at Northwick Park long when Sarah Hill pulled out a pen and paper to take a formal statement from me; she did not only ask about the attack in December.

'Tell me about what happened when he had you hostage in November, Delia.'

I recounted the story I had told before, wondering why I had to: '. . . And they *failed* to look upstairs . . .' I said of the police who'd accompanied me home. I chose the word deliberately, wanting to highlight how they'd let me down.

'Could we say, "The police *did not look* upstairs," Delia?'

How underhand can you lot get? I seethed. *You know you've screwed up, and now you're trying to cover it up.*

'OK.'

Let them play their game – as if I don't notice – but I won't forget.

She continued writing, as if nothing was out of the ordinary.

I'm so fragile. How can she do this to me? I've barely come out of Intensive Care.

Question followed question. I wanted to collapse, even though I was already in the bed. *I feel like I'm being put through hard labour.* I was unwilling and would never have been ready for this, but it mattered not.

'What do you know about his friends?' Sarah then asked. 'Do any of them deal with drugs?'

How dare *they? It's not enough for them to let this happen to me, now they want to use me. They are trying to make me into a grass as well.*

Anger welled up inside me. 'I don't know,' I said indignantly.

When she left, I felt as if the non-existent strength I'd had beforehand had been sucked out of me. I lay alone, listless, disturbed.

Every second of every minute of every day, I endured the pain of what had happened to me. A moment's blow from Sweeney caused a never-ending agony. At Northwick Park, I developed a haematoma, a build-up of blood under the skin around the thoracotomy wound. My lower back felt swollen, as though it was going to burst; my right side was bruised purple. At first, I held the gown away from my swollen, stabbed breast, which was too painful to allow anything to touch it. But after a while I gave up and let the gown drop to bare my front.

What do I care if someone sees me? I'm in pain.

Weeks later, my breast and side were still swollen. I felt something wet; the gown was damp. Underneath it, I discovered my right nipple to be oozing haemoserous fluid (serum and blood). For five days it oozed, until the haematoma and inflammation resolved.

Another part of my punishment.

One day two staff nurses carrying clean sheets, a gown, and a towel to wash me opened the door, smiling, as if the morning was full of promise. One said to her colleague, using my fake name, 'Elizabeth used to be a nurse.'

I frowned. '"*Used* to be"?' I echoed. 'So it's already "used to be". A week or so ago I was working as a nurse, now I'm already a "has-been".'

I may have not been much of a nurse, but I was a nurse.

I felt further deflated.

I am a thing of the past.

Old *now.*

Each night in the hospital, two plump middle-aged nurses came into the room to change my position; given my injuries, I was bedbound, and they needed to turn me. I cringed as they approached and tensed as they started handling me; there was no gentleness in their touch. *I may as well be the rubber doll all over again*, I thought. Every grasp and movement hurt my sensitive body. They talked over me, enjoying each other's chat.

Sarah Hill kept me up to date regarding the actions the police were taking: 'We have continuous surveillance at your flat, and the surrounding area. Alarms have been placed on the windows and door, and will alert the police station if he returns.'

Oh how she is trying to impress me about the lengths they are going to.

Big deal!

Ever since the attack, my rage about the police had simmered inside me. *They let him out, they let him do this. I told them, and they did not listen.* Now, on hearing her empty words, annoyance reared up inside me and I finally snapped: 'When I wanted protection, you did *nothing*! Now, when it's too late, you are giving me all this protection. What's the point? You might as well let him come and finish me off now. *I don't want to live in this body anymore.*'

She was unable to hide the guilt I sensed she felt, but I spared her yet again. She was alone – with me. There were others involved, after all. I was still too weak anyway.

I meant what I said, about John finishing me off. Let him come, I didn't give a damn. I was not scared of him; I was scared of this new body, and of the new, angry life I would now have to lead. If he came, with his axe and his saw, he would spare me that agony. I knew I could *never* accept what had happened.

Yet when had John ever given me what I wanted? Though I exclaimed he should do it, I knew he wouldn't be back; another fact that made the police's belated efforts so preposterous. Sweeney was on the run, and unlikely to show his face anytime soon. He knew the police were on to him, after all: he wasn't going to risk looking for me, he was far too cunning to take the chance of being caught.

Maybe his natural inclinations would do for him eventually, though.

Lying in my bed, I pointed an accusatory finger at the police standing in my hospital room.

'You let him out of prison to do this to me,' I said plainly, *'and he's going to do it again!'*

39

It was obvious; to me, at least. I knew that John was a psychopath: a psychopathic serial killer. If he was capable of what he'd done to me – and to Melissa and the Germans – what was to stop him doing something so extreme to someone else? Nothing! Certainly not the court . . . In letting him out to kill me, and with the police failing to apprehend him now, the authorities had ensured that John Sweeney would be free to do it all again.

Let that be on their consciences.

'Don't worry, he won't get away with it,' a new policeman, Alan, told me.

I stared at him blankly. 'But he *did*. He did this to me.'

He turned his back, and gazed out of the window.

Over time, Alan and I seemed to develop a rapport. We talked about travel, and various other things. Perhaps I minded him less because he'd had no direct involvement in what had happened – he was certainly better than 'Uncle', who proceeded to infuriate me. On his visits, 'Uncle' brought me my post.

'Would you like me to open the envelope for you?'

I glanced down at my plastered arms. *Might as well let him.* 'Yeah.'

He pulled out a card, opened it, and began reading.

I didn't tell him he could read it. I glared at him as he

held it out to me afterwards, and snatched it from his hand. *Nothing is my own anymore.* I'd had to suffer under John's control, and the indignity of him snooping through my stuff; now, he had gone, but in his place were the police, exerting their authority.

As I remember, 'Uncle' had an explanation for his rude actions: 'I thought I should read it first, in case John is trying to make contact with you.'

So what if he does? My eyes fixed a stare on him. *There is no need for you to read my post. I could tell right away who sent it, just by looking at the envelope. Even if it were John, what difference would it make? It is no bother to me anyway.*

As the weeks passed, the authorities started turning their attention to what to do with me when I eventually came out of hospital. A social worker visited.

'We need to start making arrangements for your discharge, where we can place you.'

'I don't want to go anywhere, I just want to die. I hate this body now, I don't want to be in it. I wish they hadn't made me live,' I told her bluntly.

I held up the leftover bit of finger and, as I would now forever do, turned my head to avoid seeing it. 'I *hate* this thing, I can't bear looking at it.' I scowled, my nostrils flaring, mouth downturned.

'But you are a nurse,' she said. 'You must have seen patients with amputations. How did you feel when you saw them?'

A sickening feeling swept through me. I felt as though a brick had been dropped inside my chest, the emotional pain of it was so awful. *Amputation* – the very word made me cringe. *I have an amputation.* Something I had no need for. I visualised, yet again, my finger flying through the air. *Amputation.*

The word, when I see it written, or hear it, bothers me to this day. The same sickening feeling makes me want to scream. It is a symbol of something I never wanted to be. A Christmas present – from the court that let him out; from the police who failed to stop him – along with the rest I received.

'I thought: I hope that never happens to me, I couldn't handle it.'

My eyes dampened with tears, my brows knitted and my mouth pouted, ready to cry. I stared out the window, fixed at the horror dizzy inside my head.

Such crying outbursts were continuous, relentless; my moods always erratic – upset, angry, bitter. Consistently, I said over and over: 'I want to die, I wish I were dead. Why do I have to live in this body?'

The social worker considered me to be at risk of self-harm, and to have suicidal ideations. But I knew I could never go through with such a thing; I couldn't bear the thought of any more pain, I simply wanted my suffering to be over.

But more was still to come.

One day in January 1995, a nurse entered the room holding a small blue-and-white foil packet. 'I have come to remove the sutures from your finger.'

Terrified, I looked down at the red swollen 'thing'. The raw nerve endings were exposed; the lightest touch was agony. Now, she wanted to dig into it with a metal blade to remove the sutures.

'No, it hurts too much!' I protested vehemently. 'Don't *do* it!'

My eyes wide with fear, I shrank back from her and held my hand away. I desperately hoped she would take pity on me. But she had no mercy.

'Hold your hand out,' she said firmly. 'It has to be done. The sutures have been in long enough.'

She took the sharp, small blade from the packet.

'No, *no*! I can't do it.'

She held the base of the leftover bit of finger, and touched the tip of what was left with the blade. I screamed out in agony, and pulled away. She had missed reaching a suture; only touching raw nerve endings that fired exaggerated pain impulses.

I cried in fear; she took hold again. She was determined – no show of empathy – and proceeded.

For one hour I screamed, howled through excruciating pain, as she insisted, and forced me – she would not leave off – to hold my hand still. The sutures were buried deep in the red, swollen 'thing', difficult to reach. She dug with the blade to cut under each stitch, then plucked it free with forceps.

My screams echoed throughout the room. If it were not for the windows letting light in, I fancied myself in a dungeon, being tortured.

'They are out now.'

Hard work for her; it must have been. She left the room.

I slumped forwards in the chair, exhausted, holding the left palm upward so that the hideous 'thing' could touch nothing. Alone, I sobbed. There was no one to console me, no one to hold me in their arms.

It was part of my punishment . . . for having to exist.

'I hate what has happened to my finger,' I told the doctor on his round.

'You won't miss it,' he responded breezily. 'You don't really need it anyway. You can still do things without it.'

Well, if I don't need it, why was it there in the first place?

He was wrong, anyway. I *did* miss it; I was so in tune with my body that I noticed the slightest changes in its abilities. Later, I found an imbalance in the grip, when I held the handle of a plastic bag full of groceries. The lost finger itself I missed for intricate uses. I could not twirl my fingers and hands like a dancer anymore; that elongated elegance was gone. When I swam, there was a difference in the web of my hands as I pushed through the water.

Everything was different. The first time I saw the long thoracotomy scar in the mirror, I gasped.

'Oh no, *no* . . . I hate this ugly thing.'

The contour of my side looked deformed; not the smooth line it had been. Under my arm was a lump of flesh, hanging slightly loose above the scar; below it, the rest of the skin on my side was pulled taut so that I still felt stitched up. The scar ran around my body, from the lateral edge of my breast and almost reaching the spine: some thirty centimetres long, at least. There were two more scars on my side, where the two drains had been. One resembled the letter 'H'.

'H' for hell.

The thoracotomy wound had been closed with thirty-three clips; each one painful to remove as I continued my unwanted recuperation. There were occasions when the thoracotomy scar felt as if it was going to split open: a smarting, pulling sensation that made me panic. The first time, I dared look in the mirror to see if it was really happening. It repulsed me. Only a furtive touch, with my fingers, reassured me thereafter.

The sutures in my breast wound and thigh were removed; and three stitches each, in my third and fourth knuckles. I cringed at the sensation, resembling slivers of ice being drawn through my skin. Those on my fractured head, above my right ear, were removed two days later. The plaster technician removed my arm plasters, then the stitches from both arms. Photographs were taken of the injuries to observe the progress of healing, before he once again reapplied the plaster casts.

At a much later date, photographs of all injuries were taken, to be used in the event of any court case.

Why were photographs not taken when I lay mutilated and covered in blood on the doorstep – like they do with victims of war, and after accidents? I wondered angrily. *Why did they not show me while I was bloated, and covered in tubes in ICU?*

No one will see the true impact of damage, and the full extent of my suffering. I feel like a fraud. What will this photographer think?

As January dragged on, Sarah Hill once again brought up the subject of my discharge.

'I don't want to go anywhere, I just wish I was dead.'

'It's depressing for you here, and watching this TV with its bad reception. It would be better for you somewhere else.'

I looked at the screen, its programme interrupted by unclear vision; scratchy noise.

'I don't want to go anywhere,' I said again, dejectedly. 'I don't care about anything now. It's all too late for me.'

Sarah offered to comb my hair. As she began, she hesitated, a look of uncertainty on her face. It seemed as though she was afraid.

'Your hair seems very fine . . .'

Is she holding something back?

I fingered strands of my hair – only to become aware that clumps of it came out as I picked. When I patted my scalp, I felt a patch of hairless skin at the back of my head.

So I'm going to be bald into the bargain. My body, having endured so much trauma, having been so close to death, had used all its energy and had none left to save my hair.

'I want my head shaved,' I told the nurses.

They thought my request too severe, but arranged a hairdresser nonetheless, who came onto the ward. I still insisted on having my head shaved, but she convinced me to leave about one inch. *The style doesn't suit me, and I never liked short hair, but who cares? I feel more like the convict that I am.*

It was all part of the punishment – yet again, for having to exist.

During one of her visits, Sarah gave me a pep talk.

'And look, you have your aromatherapy . . .'

By that time, I was gaining enough strength to be able to vent my anger. At her words, all the rage festering inside me was triggered. 'Aromatherapy? *What* aromatherapy? How can I do massage like *this*?' I gestured with my two plastered arms. 'These arms are *useless* now! They've lost all their strength.' My voice was shrill.

Nonetheless, as the weeks passed I did gain strength in other ways. I became able to feed myself, though my arms remained redundant for most things. I was at first assisted to sit in a chair, gradually increasing the length of time doing so, rather than lying in bed. In time I became able to put myself back to bed when needed; I had to arrange the pillow at the foot of it myself, to elevate my heels, both black with pressure sores, because I was receiving no assistance. Eventually, I walked independently.

Yet my plastered arms were clumsy, and I had always to be careful with the 'thing', lest it touch something and cause excruciating pain. The nurses offered little help, even though I was struggling. I suppose they were trying to make me independent, but I didn't need that treatment. Thanks to the police, of course, they had no idea what I'd been through.

I need a break, but they won't give me one. I'm still struggling . . . when I struggled so much when he was with me.

On one of Alan's last visits, I made a request of him: this policeman who I was sort of able to talk to.

'Would you let me show you the thoracotomy wound?'

Was it an unspoken statement, as to the severity of my suffering that urged me to make him witness?

Perhaps I wanted him to see: he was *police*, and I wanted at least one of them to have some knowledge of what they had allowed to happen. I wanted to demand it of him: LOOK AT THIS. FEEL MY PAIN. LOOK AT MY MESS. I wanted to shock him into an understanding of their failings, to make him bear witness to what they had allowed to happen.

Perhaps he felt like he must say 'yes'. I walked into the en suite bathroom while he remained standing near my bed. In the shadows of the unlit room, I untied the neck strings at the back of the yellow flannel gown with NHS printed in blue all over it. I pulled it over my right shoulder to reveal my back: to show him the gruesome scar running across it, and the purple swelling.

Our eyes met as I turned; he had no words.

But I think he got the message.

Although my other injuries seemed to be healing, the thoracotomy pain did not subside. A crushing sensation, like a clamp fixed over my breast and around my back along the scar, persisted. It felt like a raw wound that would never heal; no analgesics offered eased it.

Then the doctors told me the pain was due to nerve damage. It might lessen, they said, but I would now have pain *for the rest of my life*.

I gasped when I heard.

'I hear of people like this – now I'm one of them. I don't want to exist.'

This will never be over. What he has done to me is a life sentence, I can never escape.

Towards the end of January, I was finally allowed some visitors; the police at last relaxing their rule, as I no longer contained my anger. A few friends came, and told me that the police had asked them all kinds of questions before they were permitted to visit.

Why don't they mind their own business? I thought. *This is a friend, who has nothing to do with John Sweeney. I'm sick of them meddling in my affairs.*

My aromatherapy teacher and one of the other students visited. I was supposed to have finished the course by now, but thanks to John I had missed the exam: another thing he had ruined.

'I have brought you the herbal essence rock rose for trauma, and other essences too,' my tutor said. 'Also, this cream to apply to your wounds.'

I asked my fellow student: 'Would you put some on for me . . . if you don't mind?'

I bared my wound.

She recoiled in horror. 'Oh – I don't think I can do it.' A look of alarm spread over her face and she stepped back, involuntarily. I understood her shock.

'Don't worry, if it's too awful and you can't bear to touch it, you don't have to.'

'No, I will try.'

The cream was soothing and cooling to the red swollen skin. Her touch was gentle – not like the nurses; and something I had not felt for a very long time.

In February 1995, the day of my discharge arrived. The police wanted to place me in a refuge far, far away, but I insisted on staying in Camden, near the centre of town.

On our way to the refuge, we would return to the scene of the crime.

40

Sarah Hill and, I think, Detective Farron accompanied me. Outside the hospital, I took a deep breath of the fresh, crisp winter air. After some five weeks inside, it was like a new experience. The sun was brilliant, as though there should be a future, but I felt none. Only that I was being released from prison – and what then?

We returned to Leighton Grove so that I could gather some belongings. Seeing it again – walking up those concrete steps on which I'd died – did not bother me. The damage had been done. I didn't feel weak and traumatised; I wasn't that kind of female. Instead, I felt angry – and even more so when I saw what the police had done inside my flat.

'Why are my sheet and blanket thrown off the bed?' I exclaimed. 'I made my bed before I left for work that morning.'

'I warned you the police searched your flat,' said Sarah.

'Well, they didn't need to. They had already done it, and there was nothing. And they didn't need to do *that*.'

I pointed to the crumpled sheets and blanket, thrown in a pile at the bottom of the bed. The disarray made me roar with tears, and I looked for further tampering. I noticed my Japanese mug was on the small table in the living room.

'They have been helping themselves to my tea or coffee. They didn't even finish drinking it. They left it without washing it, and now it has green mould.'

I smelled the mug's stench while I raged into the kitchen with it. Sarah dismissed my suspicions – they had not drunk from the bottle of wine I had opened the night before my 'death'. By now, the wine was rancid, like everything else.

From the bathroom wafted a putrid odour. I banged open the door that partitioned the toilet. Sarah and Farron's heavy footsteps followed my shriek.

The police had splattered urine all over the clean floor and previously unsoiled toilet seat. Stagnant congealed brown urine floated in the toilet basin. The odour of ammonia stung my nostrils. Enraged, I flushed the toilet before they could see the full extent of the mess.

I have been attacked again, made to hurt. I am worthless in the eyes of the police; they have no respect for my things or me; despite all, they insult me.

As we drove to the refuge, I worried about what conditions would be like there, but upon arrival the refuge worker, Joan, welcomed me with a warm smile. She had fair skin, short blonde hair, and was plump. She was so cheerful and easy to talk to, I felt less alone. Joan's office door opened into my flat; she was there on weekdays during the day, if I needed her.

The old Victorian house had been modernised, so was warm and comfortable. A clean, spacious living room had a comfortable couch and chairs. On the wall hung a Peruvian or Bolivian cloth picture, of four Indians sitting cross-legged, wearing shawls, their long black hair hanging under their sombreros. The bedroom's French window opened onto a garden.

I have been fortunate to be placed here, at least.

Joan had experienced domestic violence, and understood why I believed my case had been mishandled. She had acquired copies of John's mugshot photograph from the police, in case he turned up; she gave me copies too.

I stared him down. His familiar expression of false innocence – a falsehood that no one else might discern – struck me at first glance. His eyes were wide open, his look bewildered, as if to say: 'Why are you picking on me? I haven't done anything wrong.' Such a boyish look: *how could he have possibly . . . ?* But my body told a different story.

As I settled into the refuge, I still needed so much care. With my arms still in plaster, Joan had to slice my whole-wheat bread for me at breakfast; a district nurse came to help me shower. Even such assumed refreshment left me reeling: I couldn't let water splash onto my breast as the soft touch of the drops caused discomfort.

Now out of the hospital, I found my experience in Intensive Care was churning through my mind. It gave me an urge to write about it, and its effect upon me, as my memories were vivid – but I was unable to write, with the plaster casts encasing me.

Despite them, in the bedroom of the refuge I attempted to resume my daily dance exercises I had been so accustomed to doing. I struggled, for the first time in my life; unable to perform a full range of movement. I could not even put each hand behind my lower back. The blows of the axe on my arms had injured the shoulder joint muscles; the smooth movements I'd been used to were no more. I could feel and hear them crunching every time I exercised; I still do. Unusual aches and pains now became a regular occurrence.

I don't trust this body anymore, I'm afraid of it.

I cried and I cried, but no relief came. *Before, if I cried, I felt some relief. What is wrong?* Then I realised. *What I'm crying about will never go away – the altered body image. There is no relief to be obtained, there is no way out.*

*

One day, not long after I'd arrived at the refuge, I opened the metal gate protecting the entrance with tears in my eyes. My victim support worker, Rebecca, had come to call. It was the first time I had seen her since before the attack; a world I no longer belonged to.

'You look like you need a big hug,' she said.

'Yes,' I whimpered.

Her warm hold felt extra-firm. My body was so fragile, my shoulder joints felt like they could dislocate. But I kept quiet, and let her crush me – just to have someone hold me in their arms.

Rebecca visited once a week. She dealt with my income support, outstanding bills and cancellations. She drove me to the Bumblebee Natural Foods shop, on Brecknock Road, to buy wholewheat bread. She confided in me; I believe she, too, thought mistakes had been made.

'One policeman told me that he would not have wanted to be left alone in the same room with John,' Rebecca said. 'Did he ever tell you if he had been a mercenary?'

'No, why?'

'Because he had a tent, and a camping stove that suggested he was prepared for anything, and might go out into hiding if need be.'

Perhaps he had done it. Even after all these weeks, John had not been found.

I came upon a police report; one of my original statements from before that December day. 'He will cut me to bits,' I had warned them, written prior to the event. I was walking proof of the truth of my prediction. Now I burned in rage at the clear evidence that they had left me to my fate.

The only companion to that rage was dread. It encompassed me: for months, even years, it remained. I wanted to scream in terror. I was not afraid of John, but I had become afraid of life; afraid of the future.

I am in a blind nowhere.

Every morning, I sobbed. I sobbed all the time and frequently stayed in bed. I felt lost; I was in a black hole. For the first few months I seldom went out, afraid of the cold and of life itself. From the inner depths of my very being, as though from my soul, emanated a deep mournful pain: a moan left unanswered. Sarah Hill visited with another policewoman to see how I was, but my miserable wails were my only response. If her few words were meant to comfort, I gained none.

'We better go, Delia. We're not helping.'

They come to see me, but she avoids witnessing my misery.

As I heard the door shut behind them, I roared louder.

As time went by, I began to venture out. My first trip was to the supermarket, a short distance away on the main road. If anyone brushed passed me, his or her contact was overwhelming. My body was so delicate, the slightest touch felt like I was being knocked over. I avoided being near people.

A supermarket worker placed food items in the basket he carried as we went around the shelves. I gave him my purse to find the money to pay. He hung a bag over each plaster cast on my arms and I walked back with them hanging, rested them on the table, and removed my arms from the bag handles, carefully avoiding the 'thing' from touching.

As the winter receded, I gained the courage to venture further, and found a real-ale pub: picnic tables outside the front, plants, and later, in summer, hanging baskets filled with flowers. Every Sunday, I dressed in something nice, to make it more of an occasion. The bar staff carried my pint of real ale and my roast chicken dinner to the table, and cut it for me.

The worker in the supermarket, and two Italian ladies from a nearby delicatessen, where I bought marinated olives I enjoyed, were the only people I had to talk to. They listened to my story.

A friend from work surprised me with a visit, and a bouquet of fuchsias, on behalf of the others. We had spent our morning breaks speaking about our travel wishes. She had come a long way to see me, but somehow I faded into myself; I seemed to lose touch. Disappointed, I knew I would never see her again.

Martine, however, came a few times, having been blocked from doing so earlier by the police. On her first visit, she studied my body until her gaze rested on the 'thing'. Something I would have expected her to do anyway. She saw the damage; she saw I existed no longer: this was someone else.

The two of us sat with the red wine she had brought, talking through events. We talked about the judge who had released John on bail.

'What a berk,' I said.

Detective Farron accompanied me back to Leighton Grove to retrieve a few more belongings. His behaviour interested me: with his right arm outstretched, he opened the front door and quickly placed his back flat against the corridor wall. With his head facing sideways, he peered around the entrance, a gun held at shoulder level.

Just like in the movies.

Of course, John was not there.

During the visit, Farron and I discussed my case. 'If I had been in charge,' he said, 'this might not have happened.'

I could see why he might think that. Because, as he told me more about what the police had recorded of John's history (some of which I may have learned later), I realised that what happened to me was just the latest in a long, long line of violent acts. *That* was not a surprise.

The surprise should be that the courts still let him out, *despite knowing of it all.*

For John had convictions dating back to the early 1980s for attacking his partners. When, in 1985, his then wife Anne had thrown him out for beating her up, his violence turned even darker. Fortuitously, the police were tipped off that he had secretly returned to her home. When the policemen walked into Anne's bedroom, John suddenly jumped out of the wardrobe, where he'd been hiding – with a hammer in one hand and an axe in the other.

He said he'd only wanted to surprise her.

It seemed those drawings he had made of her – 'RIP Anne' – were indeed a confession of a kind.

By 1987, John was with Melissa. I learned he had gained two convictions that year for violence against her, including hitting her in the face with a stool, and kicking her legs to cause bruising, plus was bound over to keep the peace following a third row. A neighbour reportedly heard him yelling at Melissa: 'Who do you think you are? I'm the one who says what you can and can't do!'

On 4 November 1988, John and Melissa were in Austria. John broke into the apartment of her friend, Ingrid, with whom she was staying (without him), and tied her to the kitchen stove. When Melissa returned, she fought him using her kung-fu skills, persuaded him to leave, and bought him a train ticket to Amsterdam. But he returned, and as she took him upstairs to the apartment, he fractured her skull with a hammer. Along with other injuries, she required emergency surgery.

This was the incident John had hinted at: the crime for which he'd been imprisoned in Austria – and for which Melissa, seemingly blindly, had engineered his release.

From there, they'd gone to Amsterdam, and Melissa had ultimately met her fate. But it was not known what had happened to her. Later, her family declared her missing. Despite investigation, there was still no body to be found.

As I learned the full extent of his offending – that the police had known about, from their files, all along – my blood boiled. Had anyone even *looked* at what he had done before and been convicted of? Given his history, *how* did he get bail in order to come and do me too? It was evident he was a danger yet the courts had let him free.

In time, I made a formal complaint against the police about what had happened. I wanted answers and I wanted to sue. But nothing came of it. The police investigated the police and they got away with what they'd done. It made me so angry. In due course, I was prescribed antidepressants intended to help the continuing nerve pain from my chest. They eased the pain a little, besides improving my mood, but I soon stopped taking them. I resented any possibility of them dampening my fury, and did not want to be dependent on tablets long term.

I don't want them making me pretend everything is all right, when it's not. I can't let myself forget my anger at the court and the police for letting this happen. If I'm not angry, it means I've accepted my situation; that I've accepted their mistakes. They will have crushed me.

About six weeks after the attack, a friend finally contacted my parents to let them know what had occurred. Mum and Dad rang me at the refuge; I listened to their trembling voices and heard their audible worry that provoked a possible feeling of guilt, although I was unsure how I felt.

Yet they weren't the only ones who were worried. My brother Stewart, of course, was told too. Having heard from me what John was really like, he had an awareness of the man who was now on the run. How prescient, now, seemed his question to John on that first visit to the States: a sixth sense had told him there was more to him than we knew.

Stewart regularly called my parents, to check they

were OK. They were often home, bound by my mother's wheelchair.

Until one day when they were not.

Stewart listened on the line, his anxiety increasing as the phone rang in the empty house in Texas.

Was his fear substantiated? Had John Sweeney come to call?

41

So concerned was Stewart that he received permission
from his boss to rush over to our parents' house. What
would he see when he arrived – a madman with an axe,
such as the vision that had once greeted me?

Thankfully, they were fine. It was a false alarm: they
had just gone out to the store. It showcased, however,
how concerned Stewart was. For John was out there,
even now. But where, nobody knew.

Three months after the attack, my plaster casts were
eventually removed. X-ray showed that the bone in the
left arm had failed to unite; it never would. My forearms
had lost their shape and resembled sticks. I rubbed the
long scar extending halfway up the left forearm and felt
the bumps of the pins that held the steel plate. The scar
on the right arm was tethered, with a small depression
over it. Even the palms of my hands had lost shape, now
being almost flat. I noticed every slight detail: these arms
I did not recognise that belonged to a lady I did not know.

When I glanced at myself in the mirror – if I dared –
the female gazing back looked nothing like me. Her
blonde hair was shaved to a single inch depth, her body
mutilated and forever scarred. Her eyes, allegedly blue,
now had a darkness to them that, in certain photographs,
looked black.

It was from the experience she'd had – the weight of

it was visible. The Delia I'd been had always wanted to be free and light, to travel. The Delia staring back was pinned in place, weighed down; light and free no more. I could even see it in her face.

One afternoon, I turned to Rebecca, having a question, and showed her the 'thing'. The pain from it had diminished over time. Now, all I felt was a numb, annoying sensation if anything brushed it lightly. But, lately, I'd noticed something was coming out of the tip.

'Look, Rebecca, what do you think that is?'

'It looks like your nail is growing back,' she replied, 'the nail bed must still have been there.'

I was unsure if I was happy, so I ignored it. But, as the nail continued growing, it curled inwards and dug in, like an ingrown toenail. I was afraid to try to cut it, but eventually I had to. I gagged when I looked at the nail's white colour and its dead yellow tinge. The numbing sensation of the scissors touching it made me come out in a sweat, and cringe. I cried in pain, and retched when I cut too deeply. *It looks like a claw*, I thought. A devil's claw . . . where he had marked me.

That May of 1995, four and a half months after the attack, I began twenty cognitive behavioural treatment sessions with a clinical psychologist. She was in her thirties and of Italian origin. During each hourly session I seethed, unable and unwilling to adjust to the lifestyle changes and physical injuries John had inflicted on me. I imagined, and almost sensed and saw, daggers shooting from my eyes towards her, piercing into her. I stepped into the room crazy, and departed even crazier.

The sessions did not help me. Much later, after my treatment had finished, I saw her clinical opinion written up in my medical notes:

I believe the assault has given rise to significant psychological problems. This event has had a significant impact upon Miss Balmer. Considering that she has had a comprehensive course of psychological treatment to little effect, a complete recovery is unlikely.

Much later, I would ask myself: *can I believe this opinion? Is it true that I will never completely recover?* At the time, however, it didn't make me feel sad, when I saw her letter. Although I did not understand it, contained within my anger was grief, which was expressed and released through anger. I was always angry now – it was how I'd reacted to what had happened. After all that blood had poured out of me on the concrete steps, something else had taken its place: rage. It filled me up, a constant companion that ran steadily and surely through my veins.

It was a symptom of my Post-Traumatic Stress Disorder (PTSD), but when I interacted with people, I had no sign to say that so all they saw was what the psychologist called my 'inappropriate' anger. I simply could not control my rage. Even when intending to speak normally, my voice sounded agitated; people assumed my irritation was directed at them. Always a loner, I became even more alone. I could not reach out beyond the bars of my cage, this body I had become trapped in. But still, I now wonder if, at present, I'm only making excuses for my sudden outbursts triggered by the slightest thing. Is it a result of the trauma, or partly something inside me anyway, due to former frustrations?

The months passed. Autumn, winter . . . One year on from my death. Shortly after the 'anniversary', I found myself close to Leighton Grove. The police wanted me to avoid the area altogether, but I was curious and had wanted to visit the market anyway. Once nearby, I found myself unable to resist the draw of the flat. I strolled along Leighton Grove. I stood outside the house. I looked up at the steps where I had crouched, covered in blood; and then stood on the same spot. I gazed towards the neighbours' steps and garden, searching for my lost finger.

Turning towards the street, I pictured what had happened that night.

Simply being there was in defiance of the law, of the system that had let me down; the system that had still not caught John – though I didn't give a damn whether they did or not. He was their problem now; let them deal with him, as I'd had to without their help.

As I stood on those steps, at the site of my murder, I found I wanted to make my contempt more obvious. I stuck two fingers in the air.

'Fuck you.'

Only four months later, I returned once more. This time: to pack. In April 1996, I left the refuge; I had a new place to live. I would, of course, be living alone.

I returned to Leighton Grove to gather my things. It felt like a funeral, packing away a dead person's belongings. I washed everything, not just to clean, but to wash away the experience. It gave me some satisfaction, as though I were wiping something away.

John's furniture came with me to the new place. The wooden wardrobe, where the mirror once hung in which I'd seen my reflection, a gun against my head. The low futon; the mismatched stools; the fold-up massage bed. People often asked if it bothered me, keeping the furniture, but I did not give a damn. I'd paid for these things with my body; and at some time I hoped to leave London, anyway. Though in a way they reminded me of him, I did not get hysterical about some pieces of wood that he had sawn and chopped and moulded: what did they matter? What mattered was the *body* he had wrecked. *That* was the constant reminder; the prison I could never escape. A stool was just a stool.

The council rehoused me in a desirable part of London;

I had asked for an area with a lot of trees. It would be difficult to keep warm in the old Victorian house with high ceilings, but I had to satisfy myself with the pleasant surroundings. I began the process of unpacking, to help myself settle into the new flat.

Yet what next step could I take? As far as I was concerned, I had died in December 1994 – but I was now expected to exist as I now found myself. Through his actions, John Sweeney, like Dracula himself, had turned me into one of the undead, siring me into a strange new world. I didn't want this secondary existence, but this was my fate.

I began arranging my belongings. Apart from that, there was nothing else I could do but wonder: *Now what?*

42

In February 2001, more than six years after the attack, I was reading the local paper, the *Camden New Journal*, when I saw a news story that caught my eye.

Two boys fishing in Regent's Canal, Camden had pulled up a holdall which had been dumped in the water. When they opened it, the boys found human parts inside. The police were called, and divers subsequently discovered five more bags. The unidentified, dismembered victim had been chopped into ten bits, her spine severed. Her head, hands and feet were missing.

Huh, sounds like something John would do.

I thought no more about it. It was interesting, but it escaped my mind.

By the spring of 2001, life had become more bearable again. I continued to suffer crushing pain around my chest and side; my thoracotomy scar felt like a sharp razor blade at times; and the 'thing' was a constant reminder of the attack. However, there were times now when I was able to find a momentary sense of enjoyment and rise above my depression. Two counsellors along the way had been much help, including a chaplain called David Mason, who listened, gave advice, and put up with my anger; though he unexpectedly died following a cerebral aneurysm, which was another loss. I saw many different counsellors, but only one other, a man who was based at MIND, was of real help to me. Other counsellors sporadically 'supported' me as I went through the motions of living.

During my time with Sweeney and immediately after the attack, I barely functioned. In time, I managed to complete the aromatherapy course. Later, as the years passed, I thought I might as well do something, seeing as the doctors had made me exist, so, as I was interested in the subject anyway, I studied for a degree in Health Studies and Complementary Therapies. I also volunteered as a massage therapist and aromatherapist on the AIDS ward at Middlesex Hospital from January 1996 until December 1999, once I gained some strength in my arms. I was disillusioned with nursing, thought I would never continue, but it became necessary to do so. Yet as my confidence was eroded and I was full of self-doubt, I took a job as a care assistant: an unqualified nurse at the bottom of the pay scale. I continued in that role after the completion of my degree. Recently, I had been considering taking a three-month Return to Practice course, which I had to complete successfully before I could resume the role I'd held before I was 'done'. It had taken me a long time even to consider doing it, but I would soon begin the course, in June 2001.

In short, I had managed to overcome my nerves and anxiety, somewhat, to be able to function normally. Throughout much of the preceding years, I had felt empty. Although still prone to depression, and bouts of anger, I was able to gain some relief from my insecurities, and no longer only act the part on the surface, as I had done in the past.

Then, I met Steve.

We met in The Sir Robert Steele's, a local pub, which had live bands on a Sunday. I went regularly because I enjoyed the music. I remember my first time there: the band had been playing rhythm and blues. The floor space had been empty in front of me, and the beat of the music had finally drawn me into the pub. I began to dance my mix of ballet and modern, feeling part of the entertainment. The lead guitarist and singer finished the number and smiled; the crowd applauded.

'Looks like we have a dancer here today,' he had said.

From then on, I had danced and drunk my pints of real ale there every Saturday and Sunday. A few of the regulars became acquaintances, to have a chat and a joke with. Steve was one of them; I think we met around 1999.

Older than me by about five years, he was a tall, slim man with a hint of a beer belly. He always wore a long-sleeved shirt, suit jacket and jeans, and had sandy brown hair and blue eyes.

'In the sixties I was a part-time hippie,' he told me. Steve liked a good time and a joke, and, along with the other drinkers, we had a few laughs.

For about a year, we spoke to each other just as friends, before he started to invite me out for meals. He took me to his flat to cook for me, drink a bottle of wine, and watch television. He had a varied music collection that was to my taste.

It wasn't hard for me to trust a guy again; John Sweeney, after all, was a psychopath, and I wasn't hysterical like some females, so as to believe all guys fit the same category. When, during one of our meals out, Steve took my hand under the table, I let it be. He took to cuddling me while we sat on his green couch. He satisfied my craving for affection and comfort.

Naturally, I told him all about John – it was my habit to tell anybody and everybody, so outraged was I by what he and the police had done. Following my lead, Steve did not seem fearful that John would come back for me. Though Sweeney had been on the run for over six years now, I still didn't look over my shoulder for him. I didn't think he'd hunt me down, intent on revenge or on finishing me off. Although the police had left me alone at last, and the so-called protection had stopped, I knew he wouldn't run the risk of returning. I did not give him much thought.

Being with Steve, I felt some security for the first time. A certain harmony existed between us. I somewhat found in him the opportunity to move on from the past. He gave me the comfort and knowledge that someone was there for me, which I needed after all I'd been through – I had companionship, and felt safe. When I returned at night from my work as a care assistant, Steve waited for me at the bus stop, and had food and drink ready at home.

In May 2001, things were going really well between us. It was in that month that Steve phoned me at work.

He told me the police were coming to see me at his flat that afternoon.

'I don't want *anything* to do with the police!' I shouted, not caring that I was standing at the nurses' station. My intense anger at the authorities had never gone away; it had only been kept at bay. It could flare up at any time, like a volcano, and this information acted as a catalyst to make me explode.

'You are supposed to be working this afternoon,' I insisted – Steve worked as a bus driver for Dial-a-Ride, transporting elderly people. 'Don't let *them* get in the way.'

But he ignored me. Despite my objections, Steve appeared that afternoon at the hospital and took me back to his flat in a black cab. I shouted and swore the whole way; he *knew* how I felt about the police. He thought he was being supportive, even though I told him outright he was *not* helping me. But he acted as if it was an important matter that we had to deal with.

The detectives came to call that afternoon; new faces again. One of them was called Alice Edwards. She and her colleague sat opposite us at the table and both pulled out their large, shiny, silver-coloured police badges, and displayed them. It was a gesture too close to reality; something I would have rather seen on television. Screwing up my eyes, I held my hands in front of my face and turned away, leaning backwards on the chair – like Dracula trying to hide from the cross.

'Do you know what this is about?' Alice asked.

It can only be one thing. 'Yeah, it's about that creep.'

'We found Paula Fields' body parts in Camden Lock Canal,' she began (the anonymous victim had since been identified through family DNA). 'We traced them back to John Sweeney, who is now being held for her murder.'

An empty grin brightened my face. I laughed a stale laugh.

Had I not told them, after all, he would do it again?

They let him out to do it to me – and now he's done it to Paula.

'I don't think it's funny,' Steve remarked.

Still grinning, I glanced at him.

'I know what she's laughing about . . .'

My raw amusement focused towards Alice; I was laughing at the ineptitude of the law.

'He changed his name,' she added, 'and when we found out his real name, we traced him back to you.'

His existence still stalks me; there is no release.

He'd been on the run for six long years, but time – for both of us – had now run out.

Much later, I learned how Sweeney had been caught. For six years he'd travelled on a fake passport, going back and forth, hitching around Europe, always changing his appearance to resemble someone else. But in 2000 he'd moved to Finsbury Park in north London, calling himself Joe Carroll; living under the noses of those police who were supposedly so keen to trace him. He also went by the names Joe Johnson, Michael Fawcett and Scouse Joe.

He and Paula Fields, a mother-of-three from Liverpool, had begun a friendship; she'd come to London to find a new start. Addicted to crack cocaine, she had begun working as a prostitute. John had paid her for sex and shared her around; he became angry when her dealers started knocking on his window, asking him to pay for her drugs.

In December 2000, a neighbour woke one night to hear a man shouting, 'No, no, *no!*' Later, police would theorise that was the moment Paula discovered John's true identity. She was last seen alive at 9.30am on 13 December 2000, visiting John's address; her body parts were found (dumped with Christmas wrapping paper) on 19 February 2001. They were likely discovered only because the water level in the canal happened to be lowered for work.

Given the known relationship between Paula and 'Joe', it did not take the police long to connect the dots once the headless, handless victim's identity was discovered, and soon they had their prime suspect in their sights. They tracked him to a building site in Shoe Lane, off Fleet Street, and at the end of a working day in March 2001, an Armed Response Unit had surrounded him – before he could reach for the knife concealed in his waistband. At the building site, in his locker tool chest, was a loaded 9mm Luger pistol.

Afterwards, the police searched his room in Finsbury Park, where they found: two loaded sawn-off shotguns; a Webley & Scott .410; a Savage Arms Corporation 16-gauge; and a huge stash of bullets and cartridges. Plus: a brown wig; a machete; an axe; a rounders bat; bin liners; cable ties; a garrotte made of bamboo; and a wood carving of a pair of buttocks shaped into a bench.

They also 'discovered' his macabre drawings. Only

now was his art seen as a key element by the police. Though they had failed to take me seriously when I'd tried to show them long ago, now it became a crucial piece of evidence – but I would only find that out much later on.

During Alice's visit in May 2001, I was not interested in what they had to say – I didn't give a damn what had happened, I just wanted them to stop bothering me. Ultimately, what had happened was this: having discovered John's true identity, the police had found out on their computer that he was wanted for my attempted murder in 1994. They pressed charges, and the case was now to proceed to court that autumn; John would also be prosecuted for firearms offences. He pleaded not guilty to my attempted murder, knowing that in doing so he could punish me more, as it would mean I would be made to go to court.

He would not stand trial for Paula Fields' murder, however. He denied responsibility; and because John was as cunning as he was, he had ensured there was nothing to tie him to the crime forensically. Though it was obvious he had done it, there was insufficient evidence and the charges had to be dropped. For the police and the courts to keep him locked up – this man they knew to be a murderer – they now had to succeed in prosecuting him for his other crimes . . . for what he did to me.

Throughout the months that followed, Alice and her companion came again and again to Steve's flat to see me; usually on my days off, which ruined them. They would question me, tape me, talk at me for hours. Once they'd finished with me, I was drained for the rest of my free time. Though I should have finished my Return to Practice course that summer, their interference in my life meant my attempt at completing it was lost.

Over and over, I told them: 'I don't want to do it.' Yet

they persevered, not taking no for an answer, trying to talk me into agreeing to go to court.

I wanted nothing whatsoever to do with it. It was the court that had let him out to kill me! I didn't want to get involved with the very thing that had caused my death. I had no time for the police and the courts; given my vitriol against them, to be asked to give evidence felt like they were really rubbing it in.

Personally, I didn't give a damn whether John Sweeney went down or not; I just wanted to be left alone. The time I cared about whether he was locked up or not was in December 1994: the police didn't care then; I didn't care now.

'No, no, *no* – I don't want to do it!' I protested again and again.

They tried all manner of persuasion. 'It's your opportunity to have your side of the story heard,' they said.

But it was unnecessary to send me to court to tell 'my story'. I had been telling 'my story' all along: to the police, who failed to listen; and then, after they screwed up, to everyone I could. My side of the story *was* the story – there was no story worth listening to on the other side.

They told me I'd feel better after John was put in prison. They told me another victim, once as reluctant as I to give evidence in court, had felt that way.

'Did the law let her down, only to use her in the end, to tell them what they *failed* to listen to in the first place; the way I did, when I was trying to save myself?'

I did not want to go to court, to have them interrogating me and treating me like dirt – as I knew would happen. John would use any method he could to punish me. I was not fearful of facing *him* in court; it was the experience itself I did not want. I sensed it would change me, in some awful way that I could not quite anticipate. John had already given me enough experiences that ordinary people don't go through, which had robbed me of what innocence I had left, and I had no intention of granting him the opportunity to do it all again.

Steve, to my outrage and dismay, insisted on assisting the police with their campaign. He welcomed them, made fresh coffee, and went out of his way to help. He missed days from work, unpaid. He ran up huge phone bills calling them. He liked to feel important; this aspect of his personality was useful for them.

The rows between us started, and escalated the more he helped them. Instead of giving me the support I wanted, he was in collusion with them. We started drinking more – a bottle of wine each night after working, and two or so on days off, besides beer. Although previously Steve had cut down on his eighty-a-day cigarette habit with my encouragement, he now returned to his former level of consumption.

I warned him – just as I had once warned the police – what would happen.

'No good can come of this,' I said to Steve. 'I don't know what it will be – but nothing good can come of this.'

Like them, he did not listen.

43

'Why don't you stop helping that damn Alice? Listen to *me*, instead! You know I don't want to go to court,' I shouted and cried in frustration.

Yet another argument.

Steve strode towards the wall, made a fist, and punched it with all his force. He worked in Dial-a-Ride's office arranging transport now. His hand bruised and swollen, he was unable to use a computer for a week.

One pleasant evening, perhaps in late September 2001, he prepared us fish, mashed potatoes and vegetables for dinner, presenting it on his favourite plates. He placed one in front of me: it smelled and looked so appetising. He sat down with his plate.

The phone rang, before we had even picked up our forks and knives: it was Alice. I *knew* he would put her before us.

'Yes, I have time to talk.'

I seethed with anger, glared at him, and watched our lovely dinners dying. For fifteen minutes she spoke, about the impending court case in two weeks' time. By the time she had finished interrupting our lives, the lovely meal was ruined.

'Our dinner is cold. Why didn't you tell her we were eating? I don't care about the damn court. I keep telling you: *I don't want to go!*'

Steve's chair suddenly scraped the floor behind him as he bolted up, swearing. He grabbed his plate, strode to the kitchen, and threw his untouched food into the waste; the plate shattered with it. He would never normally have behaved in such a way: it was the police and the courts who were creating all this tension, and causing the splinters between us too.

I cried, in anger and in disappointment: for our wasted meals; for the nice evening we could have had *but for the police*. I followed Steve with my plate, and smashed it into the waste bin too.

October, 2001. I had been granted the week off work, should I need to attend court. The police had spoken to my ward manager; I'd been unwilling to discuss it with him. They were trying to control me again – yet I remained determined not to go.

By this time, I had been recorded by the police for more than three hours on tape. My words had been put in writing. I'd been dragged to the police offices in Kew; I'd had to read and sign all these papers about what had happened to me.

Little did I know that printed on the bottom was: *I agree to attend court*.

The police acted as though it was a done deal. They offered me the chance to look round the Old Bailey, where the trial would take place, before the appointed day.

'I don't *want* to go there!' I protested.

I was *never* going; I said it again and again. They wanted me to go to court to prove what we all already knew. Of course John was guilty! In proceeding, they were making what had happened into a lie. As though the scar across my side was not there; as though my finger had never been chopped. *It didn't really happen, it's not there; you have to give evidence for it to be real.* My mutilated body was telling an incontrovertible truth, yet the fact of what had happened was not enough for these people.

Steve, too, took a week off work, without pay. He was involved now, up to his neck in it. His presence was to support me – but it wasn't strictly support because he was helping the police.

All week we waited, due to some last-minute details. Unless John pleaded guilty, they told me I would have to attend. Steve and I were sitting outside in the sun, at a café on Regent's Park Road, in the minutes before we heard the news.

'I feel like I'm in limbo this week, while we wait for something to happen,' Steve said.

He had spoken my thoughts.

'Yeah, I feel like everything is standing still.'

We drank our coffee, and waited, feeling nowhere. Eventually, Steve looked at his watch.

'It's time for me to phone Alice now. Just wait for me here.'

I felt doomed already, even as he walked away; I knew this potential last-minute reprieve would hardly be in my favour. John knew I was against attending as the detective Alice Edwards had mentioned it, so could use this to punish me even more. I could never see him giving up that chance, no matter the overwhelming evidence against him for what he'd done.

My gaze was focused on Steve as he returned, trying to guess the verdict from his expression.

He spoke as my executioner: 'He pleads not guilty.'

The evening before the court, I remained determined to fight it all the way. I bought two fifty-millilitre bottles of brandy from the off-licence to use the next day and hid them from Steve in the drawer at his flat where I kept some of my clothes. I also prepared a special concoction of essential oils, in an oil base, for a perfume I would wear. They included helichrysum, for deeply held anger and resentment; tagette, for frustration and anger; and orange, for suppression of anger and build-up of tension. I resented going to court with every atom of my being; I wanted them to smell my antipathy coming from my very pores.

On the morning itself, there was an unexpected treat.

'I'll let you have one cup of coffee with Kahlua and cream,' said Steve.

I was delighted he was giving me the Mexican liqueur.

'Would you like me to make you some breakfast?' he added.

Food would dampen the alcohol's effects.

'No, I don't want any breakfast.'

This was hardly a time to eat anyway. As I swallowed the coffee, I savoured its flavour, imbued with the sweetened taste of Kahlua and the smooth texture of fresh cream.

'I'll let you have one more, and then you'll have to get ready.'

This is luck.

Neither of us spoke; we remained quiet. All I could think about was the impending execution swirling around in my head. At least, with Steve beside me, I would not be entirely on my own in what lay ahead.

Still, I had to continue with the few arrangements I had made for myself.

'I don't want you to come into the room while I'm getting dressed,' I announced. 'I'm shutting the door.'

Steve had suggested I wear a purple suit to court. Its straight velvet skirt fell just above the knees; I looked dressed up in it. I scoffed at his suggestion. *I'm going somewhere I'm unwilling to go, why would I dress up for* that? He still seemed to fail to grasp that I was serious about not going.

Instead of the purple suit, I donned my tight,

long-sleeved, black cotton cardigan – no bra. I dabbed
my homemade perfume on my neck, chest and wrists.
My tight black Lycra skirt clung to my hips and thighs,
the hem three inches above my knees. It was the same
skirt I'd worn to visit Martine on that long-ago bank
holiday weekend when everything had changed, but the
parallel was simply a coincidence. I liked these clothes,
but never wore them together. Therefore this combin-
ation, worn with black tights and my black nursing shoes,
would avoid their later association with the court.

I placed a small, dark-blue, triangular nylon scarf,
with small gold coins dangling from the edges, around
my neck; a present from a friend who'd visited Syria.
Discreet, round, dark-blue earrings, which sparkled,
completed the outfit. A small, black plastic bag contained
my comb and keys.

In the top drawer, I fumbled amongst my clothes for
the small bottles of brandy. Before Steve could find me,
I swigged them down at the last minute for maximum
effect. It was a deliberate act of defiance; I would have
had more if I could have got away with it.

Alice came to collect us in her car; to ensure my attendance, no doubt. Reluctantly, I got inside the vehicle. No
one spoke. I imagined myself being led to my death
sentence, without any chance of release. All the way to
court I sat fidgeting in the car, awaiting the slaughter.

The Old Bailey's central entrance was large – but I was
ushered through a side door; perhaps because I was
slated to appear as a witness. Something gave a great
thud as I entered and I turned in shock: a thick, trans-
parent plastic screen had been dropped behind me, sep-
arating me from Steve and Alice, who remained on the
outside.

I felt humiliated; trapped, tricked. A uniformed
policewoman approached, her arms outstretched.

'Get away from me!' I cried out in disgust, flinging my arms at her.

Alice soon requested the plastic screen be pulled up again. I fled towards Steve; we entered the front together.

The interior of the building, with its high painted ceiling, sculptured columns and art covering the walls, resembled a museum or the inside of a palace, but I was too delirious with apprehension to appreciate it. Likewise, I refrained from associating this grandeur with the purpose of the place.

Alice wanted to lead us to an elevator; I refused. We climbed the wide winding staircase, while the protests I broadcast echoed everywhere. Lawyers with their white wigs and black cloaks, carrying paper folders, wandered throughout, appearing unsympathetic to my denunciations. I felt invisible, and as though an unseen force was pushing me on.

'Let me out of this place! I don't want to be here!'

We reached the top floor. I was so noisy that Alice tried to get me into a waiting room, but I refused to be shut inside. A second one was for children.

'I'm not sitting in this poky place either.'

I was told a lawyer was coming to speak to me; in hindsight, it was probably the prosecuting barrister.

'She is looking forward to meeting you,' Alice told me.

'Well, I'm not looking forward to meeting *her*.'

The lady was introduced; I continued shouting. She informed me what I would be allowed to say: nothing about Melissa. Her tone of voice was low and calculating, and had a quality about it that suggested its words could seep into my mind to brainwash me. I took an instant dislike. She was unable to sway me, no matter who she was.

By now, it was 10am. I resisted entering the courtroom, ever vocal and insistent. They continued to badger me.

There seemed no way out. They simply would not

leave me alone. I'd fought and I'd fought – for months I had fought, expressing my opinion in no uncertain terms – but what *I* wanted was seemingly irrelevant. In their eyes, I was going to give evidence whether I liked it or not.

'OK, I'll *do* it,' I spat out unhappily.

I withered inside myself as I said the words. I had let myself down; I *knew* I would leave the courtroom altered. It would do something to me – something detrimental.

Perhaps even more detrimental than what John Sweeney had already done.

We entered the stuffy, stale-aired, wood-panelled courtroom – a complete contrast to all the grandeur outside. Alice escorted me to a wooden platform, with a few steps leading up to a chair. A microphone was attached to the wooden enclosure surrounding it, placed in front of the seat, but I deliberately remained standing, ensuring I was several paces away from its reach. I wanted to do everything I could against them: another form of protest.

The room was full of people sat on wooden benches; those wearing wigs and gowns shuffled around in the front rows. Their voices were subdued. The judge's large desk, currently vacant, was to my left. Steve was allowed to sit on a chair to my right, below the platform but near to me. Behind me, I looked upwards to see a balcony full of *more* people. I was an object being studied under a microscope. They were just sat there: all these people, for whom none of this was any of their business.

John was escorted into the courtroom for the beginning of the proceedings. They offered to screen him off from me, but I refused. *I'm not going to be treated like some hysterical female, screaming at the sight of him. The damage is done. A screen is not going to make me feel better about being here. They are not pulling that one on me. What is bothering me now is the fact I am in this court, about to be interrogated.*

It was all the same to me seeing him again; it was far too late to bother with protective screens now.

I glanced at him from across the courtroom. He looked pretty much the same as he had the last time I'd seen him; not even any older, really. Then again, why would he, other than from the natural passing of the years? He'd been free all this time – working and travelling and doing his art. *I* was the one who was messed up, who worried seeing her face in the mirror, wondering how much he might have aged me, my eyes black with the darkness he'd inflicted. I'll bet he enjoyed that part of seeing me again, given he knew how much it would hurt me.

I was very matter-of-fact about seeing him again, simply accepting it would happen. *Oh well, there he is. He's done this to me and they've made me come here – and there he is. He is going to punish me now, and they are going to allow it; no, to* facilitate *it.*

The judge's entrance broke the minimal activity. Everyone stood up. In contrast, I deliberately bent over and fiddled with my shoelace, just to be opposite to the norm. I didn't care who he was; I wasn't putting on any airs and graces for him.

It was someone like him who had let John Sweeney out to kill me.

Once everyone had settled down, the judge discussed with the robed court people whether everyone would be able to hear me, as I refused to sit down. I remained standing throughout the whole procedure, away from the microphone.

Yet, despite the discussion, they certainly *could* hear me. For I held nothing back. I let rip with my reproach for the system. I stopped at nothing to go against their demands, to show my absolute disgust in them and what they were making me do. My spontaneous outbursts issued forth at each moment.

'The law is a load of fucking crap! I am going to work

twelve-and-a-half-hour shifts, and I will be made to pay taxes to keep *him* warm, and feed *him* well. While *I* am going to be poor and cold when I am old.'

The judge gave a hint of a nod.

A Bible was suddenly produced for me to swear on.

'I don't believe in God,' I told them.

They insisted that I swear to some other words.

And so I chose my own.

'I swear that this is my broken arm . . .' I held my arm up to display the scar. Had they run their fingers over it, they would have felt the unnatural presence of those false-part pins.

'. . . I swear that these are my two torn tendons . . . my lost finger . . .' I continued, my voice shrill with rage. I turned my head away as I held up the 'thing': the best evidence there could possibly be of John's violence towards me. I still refused to look at it directly; incensed at the very sight of it.

Finally, I pulled up my black top to bare the thoracotomy scar and twisted my back on the court to display the indelible mark that visibly cut my torso in two. '. . . I swear that this is because of the stab wound to my breast and into my lung.'

44

After my words, the judge postponed the trial until 2pm, and everyone filed out of the courtroom. I gained some satisfaction knowing that my outburst had caused obstruction and had brought proceedings to a halt, but I still wasn't free. A stay of execution was all that had been achieved.

The air was fresh and the sun bright and warm, this day at the end of October 2001. I strode across the road to avoid Alice; she followed, however, allowing me no leeway, nor a moment out of her sight.

'Delia, you have just made a fool of yourself. No one has ever done that before.'

A flutter of embarrassment waved through me – but no, I had *told* them I was against doing this, so what did they expect?

'Well, there is always a first time,' I said.

'If you don't do this, you won't get your compensation, you know.'

'What?'

That's blackmail, flashed into my mind. I was stunned. *This is the* legal *system, but they will go this low to get what they want.*

We sat at a café around the corner on the Strand; Alice bought us frothy cups of cappuccino. The aroma of fresh coffee was inviting. As much as I wanted it, I let it grow cold, sitting on the table in front of me, out of spite. I noticed a bar across the street.

'I want a drink.'

'You can't drink before you go to court.'

I frowned. *I'm sick of being controlled, and told what to do against my will.* I knew she would prevent me, but I demanded it anyway; anything to be awkward.

If I was doing this, having been forced into submission, I wasn't going to make it easy for them.

That afternoon, the court reconvened as per the judge's direction. I was standing on the platform, in the witness box, when I touched Steve on the shoulder and pointed to the back of the room.

'Look, that's the psychopath . . . over there.'

A uniformed policeman flanked each side of him. John seemed in fine form as we viewed each other across the courtroom. He gave a sarcastic smile and drawled, in a patronising tone: 'Hello, how are you?'

I ignored him. 'See – that's him,' I said to Steve.

But although I was angry at John, I was far angrier at the court and the police, because they were the ones who had allowed the axe attack *and* this second assault in court to happen. Anger was wasted on John now; no amount of it could subdue that wild beast anyway. Therefore my fury was directed towards the court and the police: those who should have protected me, but failed to keep me safe – and not only me, for that matter, but poor murdered Paula Fields too; though I did not think of her then. My mind was overwhelmed as my latest torture at the hands of John Sweeney was about to begin.

John's barrister stood in front of the judge, some distance from me. He had thick black eyebrows, dark hair, was tall and slim, and wore a black suit. He was a man I had no quarrel with, a stranger – but he was going to pull me apart. I stood, too; my back pressed against the wooden panels in the box, as far from the microphone as I could get.

A woman, wearing a white wig and a black cloak, placed a jug of water and a glass on the pedestal table, near the front of my box where the microphone was.

'Would you like a glass of water?'

'No, I want wine.'

All day, my mouth had become drier and my voice hoarser, but I had resisted quenching my thirst.

John's barrister took my response and twisted it: 'I am told you drink excessively. Is that true?'

'I don't think two pints of beer at the weekend is a lot. I couldn't drink during the week anyway, because I have to work.'

My answer was smug. *How* dare *he insinuate such a thing? He is wasting my time and energy. This is all the rubbish John has told him.*

'He's crazy, he's a psychopath.' I glared at John.

'Aren't you a bit crazy yourself, Miss Balmer?'

'I can't be that crazy. I studied for a Bachelor of Science.'

(Forever in my mind runs the thought that I should have said: 'You would have been crazy too, if you had gone through what I did.')

'You refused the screen that was offered to hide Mr Sweeney from your view. Can you tell me why?'

I'm not being treated like some hysterical female, screaming at the sight of him. The damage is done. A screen is not going to make me feel better about being here. They are not pulling that one on me. What is bothering me now is the fact I am in this court being interrogated.

'What's the point of that? I know what he looks like.'

(I wish I had added: 'When I stood on the doorstep, and turned and saw his face before he attacked me – just as I had predicted – the time when it mattered was *then*. When I knew I needed protection, and got none.')

'You allowed Mr Sweeney to move into your flat with you. Can you tell me why?'

'Because I am soft and stupid, and couldn't see through him.'

In the back of my mind lurked other reasons, but pride prevented me uttering such weaknesses, in front of all these people whose business it was not. *Because I was so alone . . . so alone and insecure. And my age was turning against me. It might have been the last chance for me. I wanted to believe I was still young; and that someone young still wanted me.*

'I believe you have a refrigerator that belongs to Mr Sweeney.'

This is crazy. He is using such stupid things to protect John when they know damn well he is guilty.

'I didn't want a fridge, I didn't ask for a fridge. He bought the fridge.'

How dare *he bother about a refrigerator, after the hell I have been through with John?* I was livid.

'*What?!* Does he want his fridge back? He can have it, I don't want it. It doesn't work properly anyway.'

(I should have thought to fill it full of cockroaches, as well: 'Dedicated to John'.)

I screwed up my mouth in irritation. Through this man, John was stirring the muck for me. I was at his mercy . . .

He had none.

'You went with John Sweeney to Mexico, didn't you?'

'No. He went with *me* – I was going anyway. And he spoiled that trip too.'

'You travel because you like to take drugs, isn't that right?'

I was fuming. 'I travel because I like hot countries.'

(There are many more reasons I could have given:

culture, food, history, scenery, beaches – but I was so overwhelmed with his accusations, I felt like my brain was going to explode. Why should I have to defend myself, anyway?)

'You take LSD, don't you?'

I was alarmed. *John is really trying to get me into trouble. Not only has he destroyed me, now, through this man, he is destroying everything about me. I am a victim, and the system is allowed to do this?*

'I had it twice, when he spiked my coffee with it.'

'Twice a week,' he replied with conviction.

Who the hell does he think he is, telling me what I do?

'No . . . twice.'

He changed tactics suddenly.

'You have herpes, don't you?'

I was livid with rage. *He is making me look like filth in front of all these people. How dare they do such things? What has that got to do with this, anyway?*

'So? I get cold sores. Lots of people get them.'

I was so embarrassed. All those eyes in the courtroom centred on me.

'Mind your own business,' I snapped, the shock and shame of it searing me.

'Answer the question,' he insisted.

Pain was pulling me apart. I felt like my body was disintegrating, and should crumble to a heap on the floor.

'Why won't you answer the question?'

'Because your question is not relevant.'

Why should a roomful of strangers know my personal details? It is of no consequence to them; there is no need for them to know. I have been exposed.

My mouth pouted, as I held back the deep crying roar inside me. I resisted giving him full satisfaction, but John knew he had won again. I didn't look at him – I didn't want him to see how I felt – but he was no doubt sitting there listening to it all, and *enjoying* it, as he punished me through them. He couldn't have hurt me more if he'd plunged another rusty knife straight into my heart.

I wanted to lash out; I wanted to wound my assailant just as he had wounded me. I fixed his barrister with an icy glare: 'It was someone like *you* who got him out on bail to do this to me.'

The man's gaze darted in the opposite direction but I think the barb hit home. Perhaps no one else noticed – but *I* did.

Throughout the whole afternoon, I cried, yelled and swore. Once, in the grip of my pain and humiliation, I reached out my hand to Steve – but the judge disapproved, and my only support and comfort was denied me. Later, I learned that behind my back Steve had been told even to avoid eye contact with me. We were merely puppets; they treated us as they liked.

As I ranted and raved, swore and screeched, the judge intervened: 'The proceedings must be held in an orderly way.'

Disinterested, I retorted: 'The law let him out to do what he wanted to. He mutilated me, and I died.'

I directed my next remark at Sweeney: 'You can feel happy with yourself now, you got to do exactly what you wanted to do.'

'You were given compensation, weren't you, Miss Balmer?' his barrister enquired.

'Yes, and I used it to buy a new bicycle – and *that* was stolen.' I glared at John. 'So you can be pleased about that, too.'

Over and over, I reminded them of what they were doing to me, lest they should forget their own part in this travesty: 'They punish the victim ... They punish the victim ...'

Eventually, in the face of it, the judge allowed a short break. Steve was the last to leave. I followed him, needing comfort, but a black-cloaked woman blocked my advance.

I howled and screamed around the room, trying to dodge her and the few others still present.

'Let me out of here! Get away from me!'

But I was truly a prisoner, amongst strangers who barred me. I felt like a caged animal. My space was invaded; I kept being touched, by people I wished not to be touched by: complete strangers. Strangers in their white wigs, strangers in their stuffy black clothes, molesting me with their wishes or accusations, preventing me from escaping. I swiped at them when they tried to stop me reaching the door. My hand shook, and I spilled a plastic cup of coffee all over one woman's black gown. *Good!*

There was no controlling me; I was a wild beast trapped in an abattoir. Not until it was known to them that my screaming, shouting and crying would persist did anything change.

Only then did they allow Steve, my only source of comfort, to return to hold me.

45

Fifteen minutes later, the strangers filed back into the room. I sobbed in Steve's arms as each passed. Some avoided looking at me; some had their heads bent, and looked at the floor. Others looked up at me through the corners of their eyes. A few gave me a furtive glance, while others studied me.

I felt ashamed; I was nothing better than a spectacle. *What are they thinking?*

Then the barrister resumed his torture and degradation of me, twisting my words and making me out to be a liar. He spoke to me always as though *I* were the one who was guilty, and I had to defend *myself*. I was punished for being punished, and put to shame; spoken to and treated like dirt.

'Now, Miss Balmer, you say that you ducked and dived to avoid being seen by Mr Sweeney, on the night you went to get help from the police in November 1994. So you knew where he was, did you?'

'How was I supposed to know where he was? I don't have extrasensory perception, do I?'

'You weren't really lying on the kitchen floor, were you?'

Words of fury jumped from my mouth. My right arm shot above my head, my index finger pointing in circles. My voice filled with sarcasm, I snapped: 'No – I was flying in the air.'

I wanted to hit him.

I glanced at the female lawyer, sitting in a front row nearby, who had instructed me on what I could and could not say. I was saying it anyway, somehow.

'. . . And then, there are the other things he did, that I'm not supposed to talk about.'

Why did John get to keep his secrets, when mine were all exposed?

The barrister continued to ridicule me. When I said John had 'done' my throat, he tauntingly repeated my words in such a way as to make me look stupid and a fool. In fact, I'd purposefully phrased my words in that way, although not necessarily consciously. To me, it was as if John was just 'doing' another job, a quite matter-of-fact thing, as I see it, in his eyes – because that was how he treated females, always: trying to pull out a girl's tongue to silence her *was* matter-of-fact to him. Yet I was afforded no opportunity to explain my reasoning, there was only more manipulation.

The barrister suggested that after John 'did' my throat we both went to bed to sleep. I retorted that we did not *both* go to bed, but that *he* went to bed, and that *I* went to bed. (Actually, that was not the case. After he 'did' my throat, and while he had me hostage, he held me by the wrist and dragged me through to the bedroom. Then *he* had sex. But the barrister had me so wrung out, and so distraught, that I had no energy left to think, or the ability to repeat what I had already told them in statements so many times before.)

He questioned me on the night I lay awake next to John, as he lay sleeping. He suggested I was free to escape. I was *not*! I was in extreme fear and could not possibly know how deeply asleep John was. Had I tried to escape, John would have woken up, and my lot would have been worse. But no matter how I tried to explain, the barrister changed things so that nothing made sense. The law was farcical: it treated the people it was meant to give justice to as fools, as toys to be played with, in whichever way it suited them.

I disliked repeating over and over the same thing I'd said a hundred times before. My words had already been put in writing, and I'd been recorded for hours on tape. Yet they had forced me to come here and submit to their punishment and degradation of me. It might as well have been John Sweeney tearing me apart again. For just as he had hacked off my finger, his barrister now hacked away at me too, chopping off my honour, my integrity, my dignity . . . until nothing was left but rage.

'It was all a big *drama*, wasn't it, Miss Balmer? It didn't *really* happen, did it?' He held his head high from across the room, his eyes fixed on me, his voice arrogantly suggesting I was either lying or imagining things.

I wanted to tear him apart. Without realising, I found myself in front of the chair rather than at the back of the box. I slammed the side of my fist, hard enough to bruise it, on the top of the wooden partition.

'It was *no* drama! I was living a psychological thriller.'

Words flew from my mouth, as I recounted John's final attack; and the noise of the knife as it pierced in, and out, of my chest. Any drama came from my words and actions – my audience engrossed – not a movement, any sound, only their gazes fixed on me. I didn't look at John as I described how he had killed me; I paid no attention to him. My energy was directed entirely into my account, my rage visceral as I told the truth, shouted it from the witness box for all to hear.

It was only when I heard my voice booming from the court speakers that it occurred to me where I was standing, right next to the microphone. I retreated to my corner in front of the wooden wall – the posterior panels of my cage.

The man was driving me crazy. I collapsed against the wooden panels, screeching.

And something happened, then. Had the barrister finally had enough of me; could he see how much he was tormenting me? Did he realise he was destroying me and had the humanity to find he could not take it anymore?

'Can I get out of here now?' I asked.

The black-cloaked woman answered: 'Yes.'

I stepped forward, fists clenched at my temples, my mouth wide open, roaring anger, pain and humiliation. My eyes were wild as I saw them all staring at me: I was the trapped animal, now free to escape, but stunned.

Steve held me, then led me out.

'They punish the victim!' I shouted behind me to remind them.

While Steve went to the Gents', I took flight, flying down the winding staircase. My shouting and crying echoed throughout the chambers of the courthouse.

'They punish the victim . . .'

Alice tried – and failed – to catch me.

A uniformed policeman, standing inside the entrance, smirked when he saw me approach, enjoying my torment. *I hate him; I hate the system. I want to punch some truth into him* . . . But I had to run.

Outside, a bright light flashed in my face. Alice told the photographer he could not use the image. It was dark outside; I had lost a whole sunny day. She grabbed me around the shoulders and chest, and locked my arms; then handed me to a policeman to do the same.

'Get off me!'

I swore and struggled, until Steve released me to himself. He held onto me while I sobbed. Then he began to cry, too. 'Delia, it's my fault. I helped this to happen.'

My knees gave way, and my body collapsed, as I sank

further into his grip. It was too much to bear, hearing his truth. *Finally*, he had seen he had been doing the wrong thing – but only now, when it was too late! I could not bear it.

Alice drove us back. I sobbed. Back home Steve and I drank a bottle of wine. No food that day; I had no interest in eating.

Eventually, we retired to bed – but there was no peace even in sleep. During the night, I woke up crying, after a nightmare spent back in court, while that man made his pointless accusations that served no purpose and tore me apart, just as John Sweeney had.

I clung to Steve, anxious.

'Something awful is going to happen,' I warned. 'I don't know what it is. But something awful is going to happen.'

46

The following day, the London headline news interviewed me. It gave me a flutter of excitement, being filmed by their TV cameras, but I felt embarrassed to be in that situation. People who had known me in the past might recognise me on the programme. What would they think?

Look what I have come to. This.

Was this my 'fifteen minutes of fame', the one we all have just once in our lives, which Andy Warhol spoke of? If it was, I felt let down. An anti-climax. If I wanted any fame, it was to be as a ballet dancer – not this.

I have become everything I never wanted to be.

During the interview, the journalist took me by surprise with an unexpected question: 'Do you have any advice to give anyone else in a similar situation to yours?'

I shrugged my shoulders: 'Oh well . . . They could try going to a refuge . . . it *might* work.'

No sentiment, no conviction, no hope. Only something to fill the silence with empty words.

'Cut.'

Why should I care? I thought. *It was someone else's problem. It was all over for me – too late.*

I was now in a position I resented: able to inform others, to help them. But no one had helped me. I had been unable to help myself, so how was I to help anyone else now?

Those first days after the Old Bailey, I gripped Steve: 'I'm scared, I'm *so* scared! I want to hold on – I'm so scared.'

What was it I feared, apart from what had already happened, surrounding that court? Was I holding on to the last remnants of what had been between us? To be lost forever, never the same again?

Steve held me and, at first, I took comfort from his arms, as I had since I had met him, when he'd made life bearable again. However, that comfort dissolved as my bitterness increased towards him for having helped the court.

For three days after the court, I was hoarse. My lungs felt as if they were full of bricks and I had a deep, dry cough. The constant pain I always had around my chest – the nerve damage John Sweeney had inflicted, which would never, ever heal – was much worse. It had a similarity to my suffering in Intensive Care, in fact – it was rather like being put through it all again (physically, never mind mentally). All thanks to the incompetence of the law the first time round, and at the hands of the law itself this time.

It turned out the nightmare I'd had on the evening of my ordeal was only the start of things to come. Vivid dreams disturbed my sleep now, as again and again I was gutted in that court. My mind kept replaying the scene in court, forcing me to relive it. I was so traumatised I was required to take six weeks off work; I was on edge for all those days and weeks, and well beyond that too. Everything bothered me, no matter how trivial: all unbearable. People bothered me, even their very presence. Actions, words and noise bothered me. I snapped at everything, my nerves taut and tight. I was unable to bear my own presence even – having to exist was a penance.

I had first hated myself after the law had allowed me to be mutilated but, now, I hated myself again – for how the law had used me in that court; for what they had done to me. Something had been taken away from me, and left a sense of bad taste. One night, several weeks later, it revealed itself: *If I had any honour left in me before, it was taken away from me in that court. I have no honour now.*

I sank into a deep depression, tangible, that lasted for months; that never went away. Having gone through the court experience I had lost a certain innocence. No person, living a 'normal' everyday life, could count such a blemish as part of his or her own experience. It set me apart where I wished not to be. I was cut off from the world, as I had been when that thick Perspex screen had suddenly descended at the courthouse. But the divide, now, would never lift again.

On 6 November 2001, John Sweeney was found guilty of my attempted murder. Apparently, he shouted abuse at the jury when he was convicted and had to be forcibly removed. I wasn't there to see it happen. What should I care? What good was it to me? I wasn't interested; I never had been. The only thing that whole court process had meant to me was more punishment – there was no such thing as justice.

His sentencing was adjourned for reports, so the papers said. I read the coverage of the case; the guys at Steele's pub gave me the clippings. The press got so many things wrong it made my blood boil: once again any control over my own story was denied me, and what had happened to me was manipulated by others. I was merely a puppet, blowing in the wind.

It was in the papers that I learned John hadn't forgotten me in those six years on the run. Instead, gory memories of causing my death had been added to his art collection. The papers reprinted the image: he had called the drawing 'The Scalp Hunter'.

The colourful sketch, drenched in red and brown, showed my bloodied scalp, my previously long blonde hair dangling from it, clutched triumphantly in his hand. A bloodied axe was tucked into his belt; scrawled on the axe head was his date of birth, surrounded by 'MADE IN LIVERPOOL'. On the blade edge, he had used Tippex to cover his name.

On the bottom right-hand corner, he'd written: 'December 94. Came to [sic] late, stayed to [sic] long'. On the back he had inscribed: 'May you die in pain! Inspired by and dedicated especially too [sic] Delia!' Tippex covered my name.

On the left-hand bottom corner, meanwhile, he'd written: 'I will live and die as I choose! I don't believe religion! Or the fucking law! There are no rules. My lifes [sic] an open door!' His lawlessness writ plain for all to see.

I also read about another drawing he'd done of me, the 'Cornered Cockroach', which showed my face on the creature John most despised, about to be crushed under his foot. That bothered me: it was another insult. With Melissa, he'd drawn nice pictures of her alongside the macabre ones, but with me he had created only ugliness.

But, then, he had *loved* Melissa. I knew that. He didn't love me. Even if he did kill her and chop her to bits, he loved her in his own warped way.

I was just being used.

The papers talked about Melissa, and Paula, now the trial was over and they were free to do so. They said John was suspected of butchering two former girlfriends. Of course, there was nothing the law could do about that now. I read every piece on the case that I was handed. I saw my age printed there in black and white for the whole world to see: a private hurt that burned every time I saw the double digits. *More humiliation*. I read that the judge had said, after I'd left the court, 'Let's hope after this she will feel better.' I was enraged when I read that. I thought: *What a cheek! Does he really believe that?*

Left alone one day in Steve's flat, while he was out at work, I stood in front of the mirror, loathing myself for having given in to the court – to the system that had let me down. I scowled.

'You stupid bitch,' I reprimanded myself. 'What's wrong with you? I hate you.'

Then I glared at myself, seething with anger, with nowhere to unleash it ... except towards myself. I smacked my left cheek with my right palm, and did the same to the other side. My cheeks were red and stinging. I clenched my fist, and thumped myself on the head. My skull felt bruised, and was sensitive when I combed my hair. I cried in front of the mirror, and continued my abominations. I had to drag myself away in order to force myself to stop.

After the court case, I found I could no longer rise above that deep depression I'd sunk into. Previously, when Steve and I were happy, I'd been able to do so; to find some momentary sense of enjoyment. Although my dread of life, and of the future, had never faded completely after I died, it had subsided thanks to Steve and the hard work of my counsellors. Now, in the wake of what had happened, it became intense again. I hated a new day and getting up in the morning. There was nothing left of *me* anymore – the court had cleaned it out with verbal blades sharp as John's axe. I had been stripped clean, and all that was left was my anger.

I tried to get help; the hospital where I had been working provided a staff counselling service. The counsellor proved attentive and I warmed to her.

'They exposed me in a roomful of strangers, telling them things that don't matter to them, but matter so much to *me*. Nothing to do with the attack!' I declared.

As I related it, my crying was uncontrollable; I left the room in tears. The counsellor, moved by my distress, cried at the door too, as she watched me leave. I did not see her again.

Nor was Steve a comfort. Not anymore. In the days after the court, he had tried to soothe me, but my bitterness only increased towards him for having helped them.

'Why can't things be like the way they were before?' he pleaded.

'They can *never* be the same,' I said passionately. 'You *helped* them, instead of listening to me. You let them destroy everything between us!'

'I thought I was doing the right thing.'

'Well, you weren't,' I snapped. 'You should have listened to *me*!'

When we set out to enjoy ourselves now, the two of us always rowed. Everything was spoiled. Steve was never any good at handling stress, and the way he dealt with it was always in the wrong way. One cigarette replaced another. He opposed going off sick, or taking a holiday, and his hyperactivity increased my edginess. I had to be careful what I said; he never seemed to understand things, usually took them the wrong way. Then the rows began again.

We drank two or three bottles of wine every night of the six weeks I was on sick leave. When I returned to work, part-time at my manager's direction, we continued during weekends, starting with a Chardonnay in the morning, besides beer at the pub. We drank to escape, to blank it out. I wanted to drink to drown it. I had lost my spirit, and seldom danced anymore. We were both stressed out and it had a terrible effect on us.

A few weeks before Christmas 2001, Steve's daughter visited from Scotland. Earlier in our relationship, I had put aside my feelings of wanting to be the only one for him, as well as my natural dislike of a partner having children, for he had been so good to me. Now, however, with his daughter's arrival the old bitterness snuck up my throat like poison. Apart from being his daughter, she was also a policewoman, which went down very badly with me. I did not want to meet her, but it became inevitable.

She had blonde hair and was slim. Tall, like Steve, with the same body movements as he, the resemblance was too close for comfort. Despite her job, her pastel-blue, Indian cotton shirt gave me the impression she looked laid-back – not like the police. *Can I try to soften my spite towards her?* I wondered. *She is really undeserving of this blow, but can I stop myself from lashing out?*

She held out her hand. My clasp was brief, barely touching; my response to her greeting was curt. Steve let her sit between us at the round dining-room table. All the anger, the hurt, the bitterness and pain surged from me.

She departed only two days later. I left the bedroom, where I'd been waiting, and watched her from the front window as she walked away, her head downcast. I could sense her distress, and I hurt too; I hated myself. Steve had desired so much that I meet his daughter, and I had let him down. I had slashed his tenderness and affection towards me with my bitterness.

I believe he tried to forgive me, but how could he forget? I felt uneasy when he took me out now, or bought me meals. It was all mechanical, empty, no feeling – except anger and pain, bubbling beneath the surface.

It was only a short while after this, on 13 February 2002, that John Sweeney was finally sentenced. In the intervening months, he had also been convicted of fire-arms offences for the stash of guns the police had found when they'd raided his home. He was given four life sentences, to run concurrently.

What a load of crap, I thought when I heard. *Life? It*

didn't mean life. Indeed he was ordered to serve a minimum term of only nine years and one month. He was eligible for release in April 2011. But I would *never* be released from my prison.

As far as I was concerned, John's sentencing was just a big anti-climax. It didn't change anything, and they locked him up far too late to save me. Now, I would have to pay taxes to keep him in prison, while I tried to struggle on with life. It wasn't fair.

It wasn't justice.

47

I began writing letters to those in so-called authority. I was outraged by what had happened; at the inhumanity of the legal system that punished the victims and let murderers get off scot-free. My first correspondence was via Detective Alice Edwards, addressed 'to whom it may concern' at the Serious Crime Group.

I would like you to know what it feels like having been made to go to court. You would say that no one forced me to go, yet I know you have ways of making people do things whether they like it or not [. . .]

I was told I would feel better afterwards; once John Sweeney was put in prison. [. . .] So now I am supposed to feel better. Alice Edwards said she hoped to see me smile after all this. I smile even less. She spoke of the purgatory I remain in since I was mutilated; and that that should end after I had been to court, and seen Sweeney put away.

My purgatory has no end; it is as bad as, and worse, than it was before. I died on Thursday, 22nd December 1994. My funeral was on the day I was forced to go to damning court, to be sent back to hell; and I remain in hell now, tormented by what has been done to me there. The injustice, the unfairness of it all.

Since the law came to bother me, I have lost all control of my life. I was given no choice in what I wished.

It may as well have been John Sweeney all over again. Only this time the law controlled me; and because they are so, they are allowed to get away with it, and have to answer to no one, no matter how horribly they treat me.

Since that day of hell in court, the nightmares, and waking up in the middle of the night, have become more frequent again. In the early hours, my mind churns and churns over. I have spent a whole night reliving the court, being tormented. The caged animal, my space being invaded, and no escape. [. . .]

That day of hell in damn court was a complete waste of my time and energy. Nothing constructive came out of it for me. [. . .]

The law and court treats people in this manner, then takes no responsibility for its own actions. If it is so necessary to degrade someone like me, and to increase my trauma, you should be providing the counselling I need, and pay for it as well, after the injustice you have imposed on me. You expect me to be put through that, then leave it to me to patch myself together again, as best I can; having already had to do this before. You should also provide counselling for the deep distress caused Stephen. [. . .]

I never cared what happened to John Sweeney. I just wanted to be left alone. You have done me no favours, why should I do you any? [. . .]

I remain in deep anger and bitterness,
Yours truly,
Delia Balmer

It was but the first of a litany of letters. I received a reply from an employee at the Serious Crime Group. He thanked me for my 'assistance', clearly missing the point that I had been forced to attend court against my will. 'I do not accept your thanks,' I wrote frankly. 'In fact, to

be blunt, you can all stick your thanks up your ass. I
consider your thanks an insult.' And I continued:

> You write about the 'great ordeal' that I had, as if it was
> quite an acceptable thing for the law and the court to
> put someone through. You might as well torture someone
> against his or her will, and then thank him or her for it.
> Indeed, what you did to me was mental torture, and you
> are thanking me for having done it to me. Apart from
> losing all honour, I was gutted in that court. All that is
> left is anger and bitterness.
>
> The 'great ordeal' you subjected me to has compounded
> the trauma already caused me by Sweeney.
>
> While studying for a BSc (Hons.), I wrote a project
> concerning a disease process, Post-Traumatic Stress
> Disorder. My paper outlines the physical and mental
> effects of trauma. I enclose copies for those involved in
> my punishment in court.

And I would not stop. I next heard from the Victim Liaison
Service and responded promptly.

> I have received your letter dated 7th June 2002. [. . .]
>
> [So] now you want to give me information about
> sentences and structures, and the criminal justice process.
> I need no information about the criminal justice process;
> there is no justice as far as the victim is concerned. The
> victim is made to go to court, to be made a victim once
> again by the law; while the one who is guilty is allowed
> to see them being punished.
>
> As far as sentences are concerned, you have the impu-
> dence to suggest that the guilty person may, at some
> time, be allowed to write, phone me, or actually be allowed
> out, and then to possibly have contact with me. Also he
> may be allowed the right to see any assessment reports.
> He should have no rights at all. I have been given no

rights at all, throughout the whole affair. After what I have been put through in that Old Bailey, this is another slap in the face and humiliation, even to suggest such a thing might happen. All the rights are in his favour; I have no rights, and never did, as far as the law is concerned.

Your pamphlet informs me of the Victim's Charter, regarding standards of service I can expect: from criminal justice agencies, such as the police, and the courts. I have yet to see what standards I can expect from them. The court allowed someone out on bail to mutilate me, previous serious offences were not even taken into account; and the police gave me no protection when I told them the extreme danger I was in.

Then they dragged me into court to punish me more, so they could put John Sweeney in prison. I am unimpressed with these 'standards of service' given me, but livid with rage and find the whole thing farcical, as far as so called 'justice' is concerned. It is certainly not in my favour. As far as I am concerned, the law has no standards, and certainly no ethics. [. . .] The law is on the side of the criminal, and against the innocent person.

If there had truly been any standards in the law's service, and if I had truly been given any rights, I would have been listened to, and taken seriously, and John Sweeney would never have been allowed out of prison on bail to mutilate me. He would have been dealt with there and then, and I would have avoided being made to go through this agony, and punished yet again in that damned Old Bailey court.

The law and court is unethical in the treatment given to the victim. What it does is wrong, and should not be allowed.

I wrote to anyone I could think of; I needed to express my fury to anyone of importance. I typed letters of complaint to the Prime Minister, Tony Blair; the Home Secretary, David Blunkett; and the Metropolitan Police Commissioner, Sir John Stevens – to name but a few. I wanted to expose the injustice, for the authorities to know what they'd done; what the legal system did to victims. In my case, the rights of the perpetrator had been prioritised above all else, and I was sure mine was not the only case where such a thing had occurred.

Glenda Jackson, MP, was the only one who sent me a direct reply. All she could do was provide me with information, received from the House of Commons library. It outlined recommendations regarding the 'Speaking Up for Justice Report: Measures to assist vulnerable or intimidated witnesses in the criminal justice system, June 1998'. She also wrote to the Home Office minister responsible for criminal justice and victims' rights.

The measures suggested, and other information received, did nothing to address my unrelenting agony, however. Nor did I find my letter-writing campaign empowering, for I did not receive the answers I wanted. I wanted them to tell me they knew how they had destroyed me; that the system was all wrong. To at least *acknowledge* the damage done to me.

But there was nothing like that. *At least they would know I was not sitting on my backside saying nothing*, I thought. But as had always been the case with me and the authorities, speaking up and speaking out brought no relief; no acknowledgement.

It had ever thus been the way.

I returned to my own flat; moved out of Steve's. It felt final, but there was no point in persevering, when we forever ruptured into rows. Tension filled the atmosphere between us. We were trying to hold onto something gone, and there was no longer any point in fighting it.

We still saw each other. He would visit from time to

time, but it wasn't always very nice. He was angry too. On the occasions we went out together and tried to enjoy ourselves, rows always developed. Once, we were in my kitchen when the tension rose. I banged my forehead and forearms on the edge of the sink. It was not enough – Steve did not get the message. I was unable to get it into his head what the court had done to me, and to us.

Steve kept shouting. So I lay on the floor and banged the side of my head on the radiator. I was trying to make him see what it had come to, how the court had destroyed us both, but he was in too much of a state himself to see. I was trying to express physically my rage and frustration, but no matter how many times I banged my head against that metal radiator, there was never any relief, nor was he able to offer any comfort anymore.

Life, implacably, went on. In June 2002 I began another attempt at my Return to Practice course, but I took no hope or joy in doing so. I was depressed; I could see no future, not even when I successfully completed it.

That autumn, near the anniversary of my degradation in court, I wrote again to Alice Edwards:

So now it is a year on, a few days here or there, since that fatal day that remains deeply entrenched in my memory, my emotions and my whole physical being. I hurt to the core; the pain inflicted on me then is another raw open wound that never heals.

These last hours I have been here alone in my flat and, yet again, I feel twisted up inside and have chest pain. The memory of what was done to me in court is strong, this so near the anniversary of that awful day. It is always there, though, and I have been in grief ever since.

Tonight seems to signify the fading, and the end of any happiness, peace of mind, and content I had finally been able to find, so long after I had been mutilated and 'died'. Stephen became a big part in this; and with him, for the first time, I felt some security. A certain harmony existed between us until you turned up, then things started to decline, until the Old Bailey finished it off with a big bang.

I was gutted in that court; I have no spirit. I hate myself, and hate what the law has made me into.

Bitterness had escalated in me; I was now rotting in it. The court had destroyed everything ... and I was worthless.

Most nights, I sat alone at the dinner table, picking at my food. I stabbed at it with the fork, sneering as I placed it in my mouth, wanting to throw it across the table; wanting to spit it out. *I like the taste of food, but I don't want to eat it. It is keeping me alive. This body won't let me stop eating. This body won't let me die; all that would happen is that I would just feel worse. So I have no choice, I'm forced to eat.*

I chewed and swallowed, hating myself for it: another penance; another punishment.

48

Steve's health began to deteriorate. By that time, he and I saw each other less. He told me that he'd had a knee operation, but was vague about the details. In January 2003, at a friend's party, he fell and broke his rib. He developed pneumonia, and after release from hospital complained of severe pain. He insisted on taking my painkillers, of all varieties and in excess, to no effect.

'Why don't you go to the hospital?'

'Stop nagging!'

I turned my back, angry and hurt.

I am not a nag.

All afternoon he growled and swore, and rushed around my living room. Later, at the hospital, he was told he had an abscess on the lung, was admitted, and a drain put into his side. A red rash developed over his body, and persisted for a year.

Yet all that was to prove the least of his troubles.

In February 2004, Steve phoned – I had last seen him the previous summer.

'I was on Finchley Road just after New Year,' he told me. 'I bought a bagel. When I tried to swallow it, it wouldn't go down.'

He was diagnosed with cancer of the oesophagus.

Several weeks passed before I saw him again. I was afraid – I wanted someone for me. I still hurt so much;

felt so fragile. We both needed comfort, and I had none to give him.

Steve put his arms around me, and held me close. It had been a while since we had embraced, and I was startled; I could wrap my arms right around him, my forearms overlapping.

At first, I chanced that we could get along again. Rows did spark, but not always as severe, or as frequently. Sometimes we were harmonious. But, over time, I found it increasingly difficult, so I withdrew. Though we both wanted someone, we only gave each other more stress.

As the months passed, Steve became like a coat hanger. He pulled his belt tighter around a once ample waist. He progressed to eating soft food, until he could no longer swallow even water.

It was a warm, sunny day. I was gazing over his small balcony at the trees and plants in the communal garden when I heard Steve, who had been taking a shower, call out: 'Will you put some cream on my back?'

The skeleton stood in the bathroom with his back to me: the first I had seen of his skin hanging from bones. I picked up the bottle of cream through a blur of tears, and howled in a state of mourning.

'Never mind,' he said hurriedly. 'Don't put any cream on.'

'I will, you wanted it.'

A curtain of tears prevented me from seeing, but I felt the dry skin draping over bone. I stroked the shoulder bones, the ribs, hips and leg bones. There was no stomach. I finished my job, my face and neck wet with tears.

Late that summer, perhaps, we sat on either end of his comfortable green couch. By then Steve had been given laser treatment to shrink the tumour, causing more pain; then chemotherapy, which worsened his condition.

We were distant from each other as we sat side by side; he no longer held me. It was rare for him to speak his true feelings, and if he did it would be only once, before evading the subject once again.

'I am on a downward spiral,' he said. 'Ever since that court case my health has been deteriorating.' He cast his eyes down at his battered body. 'Look what it has done to me.'

He was crying while he spoke the truth. I felt close to him, then.

One night in September 2004, Steve offered to make me dinner, as he once used to. I was apprehensive things might end up in disaster, given our tendency to row, but he insisted. I felt uncomfortable he was cooking; uncomfortable about eating in front of someone who was starving. Yet he said benevolently: 'Sit on the couch, and watch the costume drama. I will bring it up to you.'

We somehow seemed to be yearning for times lost, trying to recapture them.

I was nervous, fearful that the harmony wouldn't last, but nevertheless I lost myself in watching the programme. The constant stress I always felt under now slipped away, just a little, as I allowed the show to transport me and my mind far away from there.

Steve duly presented me with a plate. The food upon it appeared dull; it tasted bland and lukewarm. But how could anyone who was denied food, who was dehydrated and starving, do any better?

I placed it on my lap, the way I always did.

'Why did you put it there? Put it on the table!'

Steve's outburst of anger was so unexpected; I had only done what was usual. Sparks of stress bolted through me at his words. My throat tightened; my chest pain returned. I dropped the plate on the small table – I simply couldn't take the stress. In a panic, I rushed up and out, howling, running down the spiral staircase.

Steve struggled downstairs to the dining room, following behind me.

'Delia, Delia,' he said. His voice was urgent, quick.

I looked at him, my eyes full of the shock that had engulfed me.

And, as we stared at each other, he stretched out his arm for me to grasp his hand.

I hesitated, wanting so much to reach out, to hold and to touch it. But I was unable to allow myself to do so; the pain and the anger between us had ripped us apart. I could not attempt to recover what the court had stolen from us. Bewildered, in too much anguish, I turned away, sobbing, ran out the door, down the stairs and then across the street.

On Wednesday 6 October, at 8.15am, they operated, opened and closed him. The cancer had spread. A stent was inserted to widen the narrowed oesophagus to allow him to eat, but it caused more pain. When I visited, his anger was directed towards me. I ran from the ward, twisted up inside; I did not visit again.

When I passed his home the following week, on my way home from work, I looked up towards his flat window from across the street. Against the blackness of the October night a light shone, and the brightness of the television flashed against the walls. Once, he and I would have been watching it together, seated cosily on the couch. But the court had done for all that: it had ripped us apart, inside and out.

I saw his dim figure at the balcony, once, before he descended the interior spiral staircase. As I went about my daily commute, it was reassuring each night to know that he was there, although I was unwanted.

Then five or six weeks passed.

No light seen.

I enquired. Steve was not in hospital, I did not know where he could be.

It was December before there was any more news. On Tuesday 7 December 2004, in that dreadful month I so despised, now ten years on from the attack, another thing happened to sour the season forever. Following three night shifts, and a two-hours-late finish, I made my slow way home. I had almost reached my flat. My eyes smarted with tiredness, and with the brightness of the cold, fresh morning. My only thought was to sleep for a few hours to ease my aching body. It was my day off.

'Hello, Delia.'

I was oblivious to who was approaching.

'Oh, hello.' I recognised Steve's son. 'How is Steve?' I asked.

'Dad died last night around 1am in Edenhall Hospice. He went peacefully.'

I avoided listening, not wanting someone to be there first; to know, and to tell me. Someone closer to him than I could ever be – it had always been my hang-up. One of my insecurities, which Steve could never understand.

He waved a piece of paper in his hand. It seemed it was all that was left of Steve, and his son had that – I did not belong.

I desired to escape, to vanish, to no longer exist. So I turned my head away. I wanted to crumble; I felt weak, tired, rejected. I wanted someone to be with me. But there was no one, now: there was no Steve anymore.

I felt as in another void. The constant pain in my chest became deeper, the tightness in my throat more intense.

I felt bitter, too. 'They did this,' I told his son.

But his son said, 'No one is to blame, Delia.'

In my opinion, that was a lie.

'Yes, they are,' I insisted, before I scurried away and shut the door on the world. 'The police and the court killed him. *They* did this.'

Alone in the flat, I mused: *Forget a desert island, I am*

stranded on an iceberg, forever slipping off into the depths of the cold dark ocean. There is nowhere to turn and no one to turn to.

In my mind, John Sweeney wasn't the only one who got away with murder.

49

In February 2008, I made my way home after a trip to Panama and Costa Rica. Travel, as it had always been, was the only brightness in my life. To return to the gloominess of a London winter was always difficult – but that year a new darkness awaited me on my return.

'The police want to speak to you,' the next-door neighbour said. She also informed me that they would be coming to see me at 11am the next day.

'What do they want?' I asked her without interest, and more out of annoyance. 'I want nothing to do with them.'

It was rare for the neighbours to talk to me. When they met me on the street, they seemed to avoid me, like a leper. Perhaps it was my mad, screeching moments about the injustices done me, which released my pent-up tension, which made them keep their distance. Only one nearby neighbour seemed to appreciate my sorrow: 'Your eyes are so sad,' she once told me.

I still blamed the police and courts for what had happened to Steve, and to me. The whole court thing had had a devastating ripple effect, starting with the flashbacks and nightmares I'd had in the days that followed, but continuing for months after that as every day I had battled against my nerves, anxiety and fear. My mouth had hurt, my gums were red, sore and tender; chest pain radiated out towards my neck and down my left arm. It was the symptom of a heart attack, but I knew it was not that. It was stress – caused by everything leading up to Steve's death. I wanted to run away, from my wilderness of loneliness and despair.

The neighbour gave me the police's phone number. I threw it down on John's massage table and ignored it. Nonetheless, I was so angry at the intrusion that I stayed up late, despite jet lag.

At some point in the past few years I had been assessed by yet another counsellor and he had said: 'All the horror and the terror of what has happened to you are consumed in your anger. It is your anger that gives you strength, and without this anger you would not be able to carry on.'

It seemed to fit, I thought.

And I found, even years after what had happened, that I was unable to move on from that anger – much of it arising from the system which had let me down. People talked to me about finding closure, but there was no such thing. 'Closure' was just a convenient word, dug up to make other people feel that everything was tidied up and taken care of, so they needn't feel uncomfortable about me. But so-called closure couldn't wash away my pain or memories, or remove my scars or replace my finger. Alice Edwards had told me going to court would help me move on, but I was even more stuck.

But it wasn't Alice who had come to call that February of 2008. The doorbell rang promptly at 11am the day after my return. I knew who it was; I crept out of bed, jet-lagged, and ambled towards the door. A policewoman in uniform stood on the doorstep. I had been expecting the visit, so it was no surprise.

'John Sweeney is due for release in April 2011 at the earliest . . .' she began.

I didn't let her get any further. 'That's an insult to me, after all the suffering I've been through, and then after what they did to me in that court.'

The message had been delivered, and there was nothing much else to say. She could see quite clearly I was uninterested when I told her I wanted to be left alone.

But they wouldn't leave me alone. All the stress and chest pain returned in full force, as it had been before, as they continued to keep in contact: they would not let it drop.

They would not let it drop because they were finally going after John for the murders.

The paltry sentence he had been given for attempting to murder me meant he would soon be released: a known murderer was going back on the streets again. Though the authorities had not cared about that when it was my life on the line, they thought they ought to do something about it now.

They were helped by some developments in Holland. All this time, Melissa's body, so they thought, had never been found. There had been no evidence to back up my claim that John had killed her other than the fact she had vanished from the earth. It remained an unsolved cold case. But, in 2008, the Dutch police used new forensic techniques. A previously unidentified body, which had been buried in Rotterdam Municipal Cemetery, was exhumed for a cold case review. The head, hands and feet were missing, so there were no dental records, and at the time it had been discovered, in May 1990, DNA had not been sufficiently advanced to produce an ID. That wasn't the case now. A match was found with blood DNA samples held on file from family members. On 29 January 2008, police confirmed the body found in Rotterdam was that of Melissa Halstead: John's former girlfriend.

John had never mentioned Rotterdam in his confession to me; I would have remembered. But that was where Melissa's body had been found. It is probable he killed and dismembered her in Amsterdam, then travelled with her body in bags the fifty miles to Rotterdam, before dumping her in the Westersingel Canal, a stone's throw from the local police HQ. Police theorised he'd used the saw from his carpenter's kit to chop her to bits.

Though I was unaware of what was happening behind the scenes, the identification of the body sparked a renewed investigation by police. A unique joint investigation between the British and Dutch forces was formed in 2009; the first joint European and British investigation of its kind, not involving drugs. A European budget of 2.6 million Euros was awarded to help them find evidence for the murders of Melissa Halstead and Paula Fields; then, invoking a little-used law from 1861, the authorities plotted to bring both cases to court in the UK. The law allowed a British national to be put on trial for a murder committed anywhere in the world in the British courts. It was important, because, despite the expensive inquiry, there was still very little hard evidence to link John Sweeney to either murder. But, in trying him for both Paula and Melissa's murders simultaneously, the lawyers could say to the jury: 'What are the chances of this happening twice to known girlfriends of this same man and him *not* to be the murderer?'

Yet I didn't know any of that; I didn't *want* to know. All I knew was that the police were hassling me again. And, to my horror, despite the way I had been brought to the brink of destruction last time, despite my constant and emphatic protests, *they wanted me to go to court again.*

They insisted. For the next three years, after that unwanted visit in February 2008, they kept pestering me about it. One day, on my morning break at work, I began to cry – I was adamant I would have nothing to do with it: 'I don't want to go to court and be put through that again.'

My ward colleagues comforted and supported me. But the police were determined I should go.

'And what if he gets out anyway?' I asked. After all, they had not managed to get him for Paula's murder back in 2001 – would anything be different now?

'We will have to relocate you,' they said.

What a joke, I thought. *They know he is dangerous, but they will waste all that money in court again; and then I may need to be relocated. Well then, they can send me to a nice hot country, where I will be comfortable. Maybe that's a good idea – what about Brazil?*

I wanted nothing whatsoever to do with it – there was no such thing as justice, it was the job of the court and the police to keep him locked up, not mine. Why should I do them any favours? They hadn't done me any favours.

Summertime, 2010. I drank three-quarters of a 350-millilitre bottle of brandy – no breakfast – knowing the police were coming for me. They wanted to record me – *again* – this time on video. I was dressed in a sleeveless pink vest, an old grey nylon T-shirt with no bra, and my old blue jeans; my knees were visible through the holes, a flap of jean hanging from one.

They were calling me; I opened the front window. The policeman from Holland was with them: a man with a broad face, broad shoulders and sleek brown hair.

'I'm not going, I'm not doing any video.'

The brunette policewoman, whom I had first met on the doorstep two and a half years before, shouted, 'Delia, let us in!'

A group of neighbours watched my performance, and my arms flailed as I leaned out the window: I was a desperado, flaunting the law.

'If you don't want everyone to know, let us in.'

'I want *everyone* to know how the police and the court let me down!' I shouted.

The next-door neighbour gained my permission to enter and eventually persuaded me to go to the station, accompanied by her.

At Holborn police station, she sat next to me on a comfortable couch in a small room. The Dutch detective and the policewoman sat opposite, a table between.

I refused to answer the detectives' questions regarding Melissa Halstead. When it was crucial to me, the police had not listened. In court, I was told not to mention it.

I am doing them no further reluctant 'favours'.

In my fury, I banged the glass of water on the table, and jumped as it bounced and spilled.

They left the room, and soon returned. The Dutch detective was stern with me. I was unimpressed. 'I thought you were on my side,' I told him; he had seemed reasonable before.

'It seems like the police here [those working on my case prior to the attack on me] have missed some things,' he said.

'*Yes*, that's *right*,' I stated emphatically.

Understatement of the century.

I did not answer any questions while they filmed me, I just shouted and raged. My neighbour answered a question regarding Melissa, knowledge of which I had given her.

Afterwards, there was more devastating news. I had been under the impression that the reason for the video and attending the police station that day was so that I would *avoid* having to go to court. According to the policewoman, however, I had made no formal declaration against going; therefore the judge would demand my presence.

The date was approaching; still nothing could persuade me.

'You wouldn't like if we placed you in handcuffs, and the neighbours saw you being taken from the house by uniformed police, would you?' she warned.

Do I care? I had done nothing wrong.

Alone, I stood in front of the small mirror in which I had once seen myself with a gun against my head, and I bashed my skull with my fist, in anger and frustration. I was crying and swearing.

Neither did I, but I found myself hurtling towards the black hole nonetheless.

What will be left of me afterwards?

'Don't do this to me!' I cried to the police, over and over – but they did not listen.

About two weeks before the case was due to come to court in March 2011, there was another visit from the police-woman, who had come to tell me there was no way out.

'You have to go,' she insisted.

I was standing next to the table in the living room; she was sitting nearby.

'Don't make me do this,' I pleaded. 'Look, I've already started doing this again . . .'

I bashed myself on the head, once, to demonstrate how badly their demands were affecting me. She appeared shocked and dismayed, as if she had not expected such an act.

It seemed I might have got through to her.

Finally, the police took note: they arranged an interview for me with a forensic psychiatrist. He sat and talked to me for an hour. He asked me questions about my family, my upbringing and my job. He wanted to hear about my travelling and I told him which countries I had visited.

Then we started discussing the court. Like a red rag to a bull, the mere mention of it lit a fuse in me. I got angry; I slammed my fist on the table; I ranted and raved.

After he had seen me, he decided attendance would be detrimental to my mental and physical wellbeing. He liaised with the relevant people, and I was finally excused from court.

Tears of relief trickled from my eyes as they drove me back home.

This is the best the police have ever done for me.

Epilogue

In March 2011, John Sweeney stood trial at the Old Bailey for killing Melissa Halstead and Paula Fields. He pleaded not guilty to both murders; he said he'd been set up. My statement, describing how he had confessed to killing Melissa, was read before the jury. John said I had 'invented' the story 'out of jealousy' because our relationship was 'sour'. To explain my knowledge of the details of her murder, he declared I had a 'vivid imagination' and must have 'guessed' what proved to be the facts. He said he had attacked me not for 'grassing', but out of 'spite'. It was unfair he could not cross-examine me, he stated.

To me what *was* unfair was that he should even have the opportunity to try.

I did not go to court, of course; I followed the story in the press. It was there I read that John interrupted proceedings by shouting out: 'It's all lies!' He declared that the prosecutor was a smarmy 'prick' and shouted his insults from the witness box.

His defence was that another killer was to blame; for Paula's murder in particular. Strange as it may be, two men who liked to dismember women had been operating in north London at identical times. John tried to pin his crime on Anthony Hardy, the 'Camden Ripper', who had been jailed for life in 2002 for the murders of three prostitutes. He had sawn up their bodies in his bath, cutting off their heads and hands, and then put them in bin bags for rubbish collection. He'd been free at the time of Paula's death and it was suggested that he was responsible for her murder too. But Hardy's method for disposing of the bodies was very messy, whereas Sweeney's was such that they were not easily found or identified, nor was there quality forensic evidence. The modus operandi of each killer was too different for Hardy to be a serious suspect.

As for Melissa, reference was made to the 'Rhine Rhur Ripper', Frank Gust, a German who had killed four prostitutes in the Netherlands – but he had not been in Holland at the time of Melissa's death. Instead, the evidence stacked up against John for her killing. Melissa's sister, Chance O'Hara, appeared by video-link from California during the second day of the trial. In the summer of 1987, she and her seventeen-year-old daughter had visited Melissa in London. John had been 'possessive' and 'angry', she said. More compellingly, two whole years before her death Melissa had told her sister that, if she ever went missing, John would 'make sure nobody would ever find her body'.

For almost two decades, they hadn't.

Yet the most critical piece of evidence, according to the police and the prosecutors, was John's artwork. The prosecution stated that the 'best evidence' was his drawings, which gave 'a compelling account of his life' and were 'autobiographical' and 'confessional'. They had now become 'vital clues'. In 1994, the local police station in Kentish Town did not take my original warnings about Sweeney seriously, nor did they examine the artwork I presented to them as evidence. Had they done so, Paula Fields – and perhaps others, too – would still be alive. *I* would still be alive – still be *whole*, not mutilated as John had made me. I was so angry when I read what they'd said about those drawings. When it had mattered, they had not paid attention yet now they congratulated themselves on their brilliance in bringing such critical evidence before the court.

And what evidence it was: John had been busy. When the police went to arrest him for the murders in his prison cell in April 2010, they found fresh artwork depicting his crimes. A sketch of a nude female, her breasts dangling, showed her cowering in the foetal position, her feet and hands and head chopped off – her hands would have been shielding her head from her attacker, had either head or hands been present. But, as in the case of both Melissa and Paula, the killer artist had removed both.

Dismembered female body parts littered his work, as did references to the Devil. In one blood-red sketch, clearly in homage to the altercation between John and Melissa in Austria, when he'd fractured her skull with a hammer, a guy held a female by the throat, about to strike her with a weapon held above his head. The artwork read: 'A romantic weekend for two in Austria', and there was a smaller caption too: 'Vienna – the waltz of the world'.

He had scribbled on another drawing, 'RIP Melissa Halstead' – a statement written at a time before anyone knew for sure that she was dead. Though he'd covered the words in Tippex, a forensic lamp revealed them. And his other writings, too, were a source of clues; his poems artistic forms of confession that left no room for misinterpretation – such as one scribbled carelessly on the back of a lottery scratchcard which talked about Melissa and his having 'chopped her up in bits'.

In all, the police recovered 201 drawings, which formed part of the case against John Sweeney. A police criminologist later told a documentary-maker that the artwork 'was a key element – the jury had a clear picture of a man of savage, murderous intent'. John tried to dismiss it, saying his artwork was 'nonsense . . . bullshit . . . drunken tosh' that he had made while 'stoned out of his head' on cannabis and LSD. So would the jury buy it? Would they be as blind as the police in Kentish Town?

During the trial, Brian Altman QC, prosecuting, apparently stated: 'Time had not diminished [Sweeney's] fascination and preoccupation with dismemberment.' I wondered how, given they knew what he had done to me, they could ever envisage that it might do so. Time did not seem a factor, it was irrelevant.

On 4 April 2011, it turned out that it was John's feeble defence that was irrelevant. On this date, the jury found him guilty of the murders of Melissa Halstead and Paula Fields. It had been twenty-one years since Melissa had died and almost two decades since I'd first met John, and invited a serial killer into my flat. According to the press reports, he showed no reaction to the verdict and walked calmly out of court. On Tuesday 5 April, Judge Justice Saunders delayed sentencing, after John refused to leave the cells. I read in the press that he wore earplugs in court, and wears them in prison. These details enrage me. Why was he allowed these 'rights'? Was he not there to be punished?

'These were terrible, wicked crimes,' the judge eventually declared to the court, in John's absence. 'The heads of the victims having been removed, it is impossible to be certain how they were killed.

'The mutilation of the bodies is a serious aggravating feature of the murders. Not only does it reveal the cold-blooded nature of the killer, but it has added greatly to the distress of the families to know that parts of the bodies of their loved ones have never been recovered.

'The method of disposal of the bodies demonstrates there was a substantial amount of planning which went into the killings.

'Why the killings occurred, I cannot be sure, but I am satisfied that this defendant is controlling in his relationships with women and, chillingly, that control extends to deciding whether they should live or die.

'I have no doubt that the seriousness of these offences is exceptionally high.' He therefore concluded: 'A whole life order is the appropriate sentence.'

John would die behind bars; he would never get out of prison.

In that respect, at least, we were alike.

It was a sentence the judge presumably felt forced to give. Some of the media coverage described John as 'one of the most dangerous men in Britain'. He'd told the police he'd had thirty or forty different relationships over the previous twenty years – but in his account said they were mostly non-violent. Yet something didn't add up. Because at least a handful of John's ex-girlfriends seemed to have vanished off the face of the earth – as had Paula Fields, until the canal water level was lowered for work; as had Melissa Halstead, until improved technology came calling. Other former girlfriends and associates cannot be traced: a trainee nurse, Sue, from Derbyshire, who frequented the north London area before she went missing; Irani, a Brazilian, who worked as a cleaner in kitchens in north London and who regularly attended the pubs and clubs there; Maria, a Colombian, whom John knew circa 1997 and who went missing from Highbury in 1998. He drew some of these girls, too. The police stated there was enough evidence in the artwork to suggest harm had come to at least two of them.

The newspapers had a field day writing about it all. I read every article I could find. I did so because I wanted to see what they were saying – and, over and over, what they were saying was *wrong*. They got the details of the axe attack on me wrong. They said I had 'bravely' given evidence in the attempted murder trial in 2001 – when I had been forced against my will to do so. I read that the reason I did not give evidence in 2011 was because the judge allegedly stated I was confused. That really riled me; I was *not* confused, I was traumatised.

Over and over, I read different versions of *my* story. Once again, it seemed I had no power or control over my own life.

It irritated me; it niggled and slipped beneath my skin until it became an itch I simply had to scratch. So I started writing – writing a book. Writing *my* story. One with all the facts as they happened. One with the full truth about the police and the court. Over the years, I had started and then stopped writing my memoir, giving up many times, but now I felt I *had* to do it, no matter what. I had been putting it off for too long – the truth needed to be out there. I wanted to add my own voice to these others who were forever getting things wrong and claiming to speak for me. I wanted to expose the system; I wanted to set the record straight.

And so I really plugged into it. I spent every day off from the hospital writing all day long, from morning till night. I can't say, necessarily, that it was cathartic: what I did find was that it was relatively easy for me to write an account of living with a serial killer. Perhaps surprisingly, I almost enjoyed that aspect, trying to immerse myself in it. What was far harder was to get past those experiences – to get past the final axe attack on my doorstep – and describe the living hell of having survived. I couldn't face getting to the moment when I woke up in hospital with my finger missing and my body destroyed. *That* was what bothered me; what bothers me still.

The police knew I was writing the book. I had one final conversation with them, when they came to the flat – perhaps to tell me personally of John's sentence for his double murders – and we talked frankly about the case. I scribbled down the information they gave me so I could refer to it in my book.

'How do you feel now that John Sweeney has been put in prison for life?' one of the policemen asked me during the visit.

'I feel just the same as before,' I replied frankly. After all it made no difference to me: I'd been done, it was too late. Prison would never take away the emotional and physical scars that John had given me for life.

Nor did I think it was the right sentence. Personally, I think he should have been tortured and put down slowly. For given that he now lives on, in jail, I am actually paying to support him through taxes. That makes me so angry.

The policeman told me something else that made me angry, too. According to him, at that critical court date of 20 December 1994, when John had been bailed until the January of the following year, the Domestic Violence Unit had been unaware of the hearing, and were not at court to challenge his release.

No one had been speaking up for me.

No one had been standing up for me.

No wonder John was set free to come after me with an axe.

There are no surviving court records detailing John's bail application for me to find out anything more. But I know what happened: the whole system seemed to be twisted in his favour.

I researched my book fully, exploring every avenue open to me. And, as I did so, I mused deeply on what I knew of John, and of his murders.

'It has added greatly to the distress of the families,' the latest judge had said, 'to know that parts of the bodies of their loved ones have never been recovered . . .' It was another form of control: only John knew where the missing body parts were.

But I have a theory, at least, for where they might be. For once, on that frightening trip to Germany in the winter of 1993, John had told me that he'd stuck the aquarium containing his dead tarantula in a brick wall at the building site where he'd been working. Could he not have done something similar with the missing body parts of his victims? Perhaps, somewhere across Europe, concealed in the walls of a building constructed in the 1990s, Melissa's head or hands reside, unbeknown to anyone but John.

That is what I believe he did with them.

When I look back on my relationship with John now, it's the sort of thing you read about in a novel or watch in a movie, it doesn't happen for real. But it did, it happened to me. He was a psychopath, and I lived for three years with a serial killer. I was living in a psychological thriller – *and it was all true*. The camera I had looked for, when tied to the bed as he ranted and raved before me, was not there: there was no one, and nothing, there but John.

I still have the *Ich liebe dich* cushion he gave me. It dangles from the knob of the wardrobe door; sunlight over the years has made it go paler on one side. Sometimes it spins to show the blue words stitched upon the plush pink silk, but I always turn it back. I keep it as some sort of symbol, until a day arrives when I am finally ready to let it go.

The messages he wrote on my body, however, still stand the test of time. I had a chest X-ray recently, for an unrelated reason, and the report mentioned the 'healing fractures' of two ribs. They were the ones the doctors had cut when they performed the thoracotomy in 1994. Actually, they are probably the healed scars from the cuts. Even after all these years, the scars and the pain are a constant reminder of my life with a serial killer. I still don't trust this body, and what might go wrong with it; it is still a stranger to me. I am trapped in this prison with no chance of appeal. John wrote in his artwork that he wanted me to die in pain – well, he got his wish: I will do so.

Yet I don't only have a physical legacy. Now and again, I still have nightmares, though I can never recall them when I wake. Once I woke up sobbing, but felt no tears on my face. Another time, I was trying to scream but no sound would come out.

Only certain counselling has helped me, but I'm still not perfect. As I said before, there is no such thing as closure – I don't believe in it. Apart from that, I have never had an acknowledgement from the authorities for how they let me down and then destroyed me twice over in the court. That is just one of many things that make it impossible for me to move on.

I tend to suffer from severe anxiety and depression and anger. Sometimes I don't look forward to waking up in the mornings. I worry about being 'stuck', time passing, and never really being able to move on, and to do what I would like to do.

Nonetheless, there is one day on which I always feel happy when I wake – a day, any day, on which I will begin a new journey, travelling to some distant land. As always, travelling still offers me comfort, escape and excitement; a way of drenching my world in colour, such a contrast to the gloomy greys of London life. I keep exploring, whenever I possibly can.

In January 2017, I took a trip to Costa Rica. I find, when I go away, I can forget about my anger for a time, and feel a bit like a different person. It's the only way I can ever feel close to how I used to be. I love travelling around, seeing new things and meeting new people. I can be the person I would like to be. There is something interesting to see and do every day.

In Costa Rica, I liked to sit on the veranda outside my room, seeing the trees and the sparkling bay below, perhaps a cruise ship drifting by on the distant horizon. I enjoyed watching the monkeys, and the toucans and other colourful birds, come to the tree where food was left for them; and spotting the large iguana, who scrambled up and down that same tree in search of sustenance.

Yet I didn't spend all my time there, relaxing as it was. I also spent time with the local families, eating and drinking at nearby restaurants as Latin music played. And we went to the local *soda*, where the whole family were artistic. They made traditional food, which tasted so good. And their son, who was talented, strummed his guitar and sang.

As I listened to the rhythms, I got to my feet. I felt the music through my body; music that helped me try to forget.

Beneath a Costa Rican sky, I danced.

Acknowledgements

I would like to thank Robert Smith, my literary agent, for making this book possible. Thanks also to Kate Moore for her contribution to the book. Thanks to Alix Kirsta, Merle Gordon and Lizzie Enfield for their support and encouragement; and to Detective Inspector Steve Smith for his assistance. Also, thanks to Natalie for her understanding and support and to Martine S. in recognition of her great sacrifice. In memory of my Dad for having bought me my first laptop, which helped me write my story.